COMPETING FOR
ELVIS

SAVAS JOHN

Copyright © 2013 by Savas John.

Cover Illustration by: Marvin Paracuelles

Library of Congress Control Number:	2013914449
ISBN: Hardcover	978-1-4836-7890-0
Softcover	978-1-4836-7889-4
Ebook	978-1-4836-7891-7

All rights reserved. No part of this book may be reproduced or transmitted in any form or by any means, electronic or mechanical, including photocopying, recording, or by any information storage and retrieval system, without permission in writing from the copyright owner.

This book was printed in the United States of America.

Rev. date: 08/28/2013

To order additional copies of this book, contact:
Xlibris LLC
1-888-795-4274
www.Xlibris.com
Orders@Xlibris.com
137428

CONTENTS

Prologue 9

Chapter 1	Jeremy Shrinks, 5:30 a.m.	11
Chapter 2	Terance Best, 5:00 a.m.	17
Chapter 3	Hank Hunk at Home in LA	24
Chapter 4	Bobby Shrimp	31
Chapter 5	Jeremy Shrinks Gets a Phone Message	42
Chapter 6	Terance Best	46
Chapter 7	Hank Hunk's Birthday Party	48
Chapter 8	Bobby Shrimp	52
Chapter 9	Jeremy Shrinks Receives a Phone Call and Gets Ready to Go	58
Chapter 10	Terance Best Receiving His Phone Call	60
Chapter 11	Hank Hunk Receives a Phone Call and Gets Ready to Go	63
Chapter 12	Bobby Shrimp Getting Ready to Go	65
Chapter 13	Jeremy Shrinks on His Way to Las Vegas and Thinking All the Way	67
Chapter 14	Terance Best on His Way to Las Vegas	70
Chapter 15	Hank Hunk on the Way to Las Vegas	74
Chapter 16	Bobby Shrimp on His Way to Vegas with His New Friend	78
Chapter 17	Jeremy Shrinks Arriving in Las Vegas, What a Trip	86
Chapter 18	Terance Best Arriving in Las Vegas	90
Chapter 19	Hank Hunk Arriving in Las Vegas	93
Chapter 20	Bobby Shrimp Arriving in Las Vegas	99
Chapter 21	Jeremy Shrinks Getting Ready for the Meeting	106

Chapter 22	Terance Best Getting Ready for the Meeting..................108
Chapter 23	Hank Hunk Getting Ready for the Meeting..................110
Chapter 24	Bobby Shrimp Getting Ready for the Meeting..................112
Chapter 25	Jeremy Shrinks Arriving at the Voodoo Lounge..................115
Chapter 26	Terance Best Arrives at the Voodoo Lounge..................118
Chapter 27	Hank Hunk Arriving at the Voodoo Lounge..................120
Chapter 28	Jeremy, Terance, Hank, and Bobby at Graceland..................122
Chapter 29	Back at the Voodoo Lounge..................131
Chapter 30	Jeremy Shrinks Getting Around Town..................137
Chapter 31	Terance Best Looking for an Opportunity..................141
Chapter 32	Hank Hunk's Idle Time with Special People..................145
Chapter 33	Bobby Shrimp Pleasantly Thrown Off Course..................152
Chapter 34	Jeremy Needed Something New in His Life and Found Something Wonderful; It's a New Beginning..................158
Chapter 35	Terance Best's Meeting with the Restaurant Owners..................178
Chapter 36	Hank Hunk, Lunch at Poolside with Shirley and Jackie..................187
Chapter 37	Bobby Shrimp, Supper with Kate and Then a Wonderful Surprise..................193
Chapter 38	Back to the Voodoo Lounge to Plan the Trip to Reno..................205
Chapter 39	Arriving in Reno..................217
Chapter 40	Reno Competition and Elevating Hank..................224
Chapter 41	Reno's Elvis Competition..................229

Chapter 42	Back in Las Vegas	238
Chapter 43	Jeremy Shrinks Back in Las Vegas	250
Chapter 44	Terance Calls Home	258
Chapter 45	Hank and Shirley	261
Chapter 46	Bobby Shrimp, Conceiving Hank's New Look	268
Chapter 47	Jeremy Has Lunch with Kie	273
Chapter 48	Bobby Shrimp Making Arrangements with Terance Best	279
Chapter 49	Hank Hunk Receives Bobby's Phone Call	281
Chapter 50	The Four Men Plan for the Resurrection of Elvis	283
Chapter 51	Jeremy and Hank Find a Tailor	290
Chapter 52	Bobby Finds the Barber	297
Chapter 53	Terance and the Guitar	300
Chapter 54	Terance is Back in His Hotel Suite with the Guys	304
Chapter 55	Thursday Is a Very Busy Day for the Boys	310
Chapter 56	Thursday Night is a Big Night for Jeremy Shrinks	316
Chapter 57	Terance Closes the Deal	321
Chapter 58	Hank Hunk, Tonight Is the Big Night Out for Hank	326
Chapter 59	Bobby Shrimp, It's Time to Fish or Cut Bait	333
Chapter 60	The Guys Spend the Day Together Before the Competition	338
Chapter 61	The Boys' Last Night at the Voodoo Lounge	344
Chapter 62	The Competition, January 9, 2010	347
Epilogue:	The Beginning of a New Life	357

Prologue

THE PHONE RINGS, and the voice at the other end informs the receiver the day and time when the secret meeting will take place. The caller is very precise about what is expected. The receiver is very obliging and ends the call with a confirmation that he will be present and immediately begins to fantasize about the meeting and makes plans to leave town.

The caller makes three phone calls, one to Yukon, Oklahoma; one to Coral Gables, Florida; and one to Los Angeles, California. The message is always the same. The calls all originate from Lynn, Massachusetts. A miracle needs to happen, and if it does, it will change their lives forever.

destitute. To make matters worse, his mother was suffering from chronic depression. She was far from being mentally fit to take care of a very complicated young boy. They lived for most of his adolescence in the poorest section of town where he recalls agonizing nights listening to his mother complain about her lonely and destitute life. To overcome these terrible experiences, he locked himself in his room and immersed in rock-and-roll music sung by his idol on his 45 rpm record player. With all the misfortunes in Jeremy's pitiful life, he had one thing going for him: he was blessed with exceptional intelligence. His God-given gift, however, was not a benefit. Being a very lonely boy, he wanted to fit in with the rest of the kids. Unfortunately, his peers were a long way from being bright; thus, he suppressed his intelligence and purposely underachieved at school so he could remain in the lower-level academic class groups. His tragic adolescent life somehow nurtured an inner spirit that would one day liberate him from the doldrums of his life. For years, Jeremy was able to convince everyone, including his mother, that he was a dunce. No one ever picked up on his act. His ability to be someone other than himself would later become a major advantage for him. With all the external and internal forces pulling him down, it's no wonder he had a hard time mixing with normal people; and being frail, shy, and self-conscious coupled with an awkward appearance certainly didn't help. In the right environment, he could have been a significant achiever, way ahead of all the other people in his life; however, growing up without a father and a sociopath mother, a life as a loner was his only recourse. The fact that he was also somewhat lazy didn't help matters. He did, however, have one other God-given gift that even he didn't realize he had until later on in life.

 Jeremy has become the ultimate underachiever. He's been avoiding life's opportunities for over fifty long and disappointing years and often wonders how he got so old so quickly. Leaving the kitchen, he enters his cramped bedroom, looks at his rotund girlfriend sleeping in his bed, and wonders, *How much better would life be without her around?* He reaches in the drawer of the night table next to his bed, removes his Timex watch and reading glasses, walks back into the kitchen and pours himself a second cup of coffee, grabs his car keys, and makes his way to the front door. Parked outside is his decrepit 1971 Ford Falcon with a brown army blanket covering the tattered front seat. On his way to work, he listens to the local radio station playing all the oldies from the late fifties to the late seventies. The drive to the convenience store takes Jeremy around twenty minutes. As he travels to work, he can't help but notice that there are people looking at him and making uncomplimentary gestures as they drive by. Jeremy is convinced that he and his car are conceived to be a perfect match.

Suddenly, there's a very mesmerizing voice on the radio. It's Elvis singing "I'm All Shook Up." The sound of Elvis's voice enlightens him. He begins to sing along, not caring who sees or hears him even when stopped with the windows open. He sings louder and louder, and his voice is now clearly audible over the radio. Jeremy is singing jubilantly, unaware that he's being eyed by a couple of fiftyish-year-old women looking and laughing at a crazed fool in a shit box car. As his voice elevates above the radio, his singing captivates them. The women are no longer laughing. They're shocked by what they are hearing. The funny-looking little old guy's voice is unmistakably Elvis's. Jeremy pays no attention to two gawking women. He's in a mind-altering trance. He looks in the rearview mirror and sees not the middle-aged balding lonely loser—not at all; what Jeremy sees is a handsome young man singing his heart out. What a delusion.

In a flash, it's all over for Jeremy's fantasy. It's now back to the cold oppressed reality of his distraught life. He arrives at the convenience store at exactly 6:00 a.m. Hani, the Indian girl from New Delhi, is behind the counter waiting on the regulars. The customers all greet Jeremy with a kind word and quickly move on. Jeremy moves in behind the counter to help out Hani. Hani looks up at him and smiles. She explains that more milk is needed in the cooler. He immediately heads to the back room and starts loading the dolly with cases of milk as he's done every day at 6:10 a.m. for the past twenty odd years. As he's stocking the shelves, he stops to gaze out into the store. His eyes fall upon a couple of well-dressed customers involved in an animated conversation about the wonders of Las Vegas. As Jeremy looks on, he contemplates that maybe somehow he could have been one of those energetic, happy-go-lucky, accomplished people rather than the guy packing milk in a cooler.

The day goes by very quickly. The store is bustling with customers buying coffees, sandwiches, cigarettes, milk, lottery tickets, and scratch cards. Jeremy usually operates the lottery machine. It makes him feel important. He becomes unraveled and loses control of himself when the machine malfunctions and always makes a wisecrack remark about the situation. The customers enjoy the entertainment and jokingly offer their condolences. His conversations with them are short and limited to mostly trivial topics.

Having difficulty communicating with people particularly when he was a young child resulted in him isolating himself all through grammar school. Unfortunately, no one detected his problem. If only he could have been inspired to use his genius, there's no telling what his accomplishments could have been. Jeremy never blamed anyone but himself for his disenchanted life. He didn't blame his mother or his father or even his ex-wife, Karla, who wanted to be his mentor. Unfortunately, Karla was not content with his laid-back lifestyle. She wanted more from Jeremy. She knew he suppressed his intelligence and that he had the ability to go places in life. She argued continuously with Jeremy about his lackluster lifestyle. Karla attended a two-year junior college and was now looking forward to spending another four years at an Ivy League university. Their relationship began at a friend's graduation party while she was attending junior college. Jeremy was somewhat better looking then. He had a very likable face, a good disposition, and a bashful personality. It was very appealing to Karla. He was very complimentary and polite, and when engaged in conversation, he could respond very articulately. Karla Collins knew immediately that Jeremy Shrinks wasn't the average everyday Joe you meet at a friend's party. There was something about him that struck her. His mannerisms, his eye movement, his body language, and his humble and genuine disposition were all very captivating. Had she known that overcoming personal tragedies developed his character, she may have acted more compassionately. Karla was a very perceptive person; thus, she immediately recognized Jeremy's good nature and intelligence. It was obvious something good was going to happen. Jeremy was a breath of fresh air. He didn't boast about his accomplishments or his brilliance or his ability to make large sums of money, as did the well-to-do college guys she had dated. Those guys never lasted more than three dates. She spent many nights thinking about how and when the right man would come along. She wanted someone who was easygoing and, above all, smart. Her very successful father possessed all of those characteristics. She saw all of her father's virtues in Jeremy, and before long, their friendship quickly turned into a caring relationship. Karla soon fell head over heels for her newfound love. She knew he was going to be a part of her destiny.

After a year of being together, Karla coerced Jeremy into proposing to her. It would be a marriage made in heaven. She would be the aggressive and attractive young woman. He would be the good-hearted, lovable genius. They would complement each other and bring happiness and good fortune to their family. She would go off to her Ivy League college, and Jeremy would take up her father's offer to attend college.

Karla and Jeremy were married on May 15, 1978. The wedding was spectacular, though somewhat one-sided. All of Karla's college friends, family, and high-school friends were there. They numbered in the hundreds, while only a handful of Jeremy's family and friends attended. He could never quite believe how someone like Karla could fall for a guy who had to bluff his way through life just to be accepted. They were miles apart in many different aspects of their lives. However, it was their love of rock and roll that brought a common delight to their lives. So it was fitting that Karla would have a lively rock band for the wedding.

Toward the end of the reception and after a couple of bottles of wine, the newlyweds were immersed in the celebration. The band was really rocking. Karla thought it would be great fun to see Jeremy do a karaoke to an Elvis song. She tried to coerce him into getting up on the stage. At first, Jeremy refused. But after being encouraged by Karla and all their friends, Jeremy gave in. Karla thought that this was going to be a riot and a memorable way to end the ceremony. Karla never heard Jeremy sing. Jeremy was somewhat light-headed and a bit giddy from the wine and all the festivities. He got up on the stage, got in front of the mic, and listened while the band played "Love Me Tender." Everyone was expecting a fool's performance. As he stood behind the mic, the band picked up the song from the beginning. Jeremy looked out at the wedding guests and then over at his smiling wife, Karla, who was still egging him on. Jeremy took a deep breath and began to sing. His compelling voice filled the air with supernatural splendor beyond expectation. His voice rejuvenated the memories of Elvis. The crowd was suddenly silent. Karla was staring at her lovable husband with a frozen look of amazement. She couldn't believe what she was hearing. Somehow, Jeremy was replicating the beautiful and powerful voice of Elvis. Everyone was shocked. At first, they thought Jeremy was mouthing the words to the song. But as he sang, he was able to transform himself. His voice became so perfect and authentic, it put everyone in awe—particularly Karla. Not a sound could be heard except for Jeremy's captivating voice, or more accurately, Elvis's beautiful voice. It was a miracle. The wedding guests were mesmerized. The rock-and-roll band was left starry eyed. Karla was left with tears on her face. The world will be theirs.

Chapter 2

Terance Best, 5:00 a.m.

IT'S 5:00 A.M., and the sun hasn't risen in Coral Gables, Florida; it's early, and the air is a little warm but dry. Terance Best is shaving in his ultra-chichi master bathroom. Terance is a very nondescript-looking forty-seven-year-old WASP. His appearance is somewhat contradicting to his personality. He exudes an air of confidence that could be easily taken as condescending. In retrospect, his air of confidence motivates people who know him for his accomplishments. People who don't know him that well get the impression that he is somewhat of a snob. His image contradicts his good-hearted nature. The day starts early for Terance. Monday through Saturday, he's up at 5:00 a.m., out of the house by 6:00 a.m., and in the office by 6:30 a.m. Today, however, is different. Today is the long-awaited business trip Terance has been waiting for. His friends, family, and coworkers all know about his trip to the Nevada. Terance needs to check up on the status of a large tract of land that Southern Investment Ventures and Land Equity Corp., SIVLE Corp, has been working on for the past three years. The survey team recently completed the boundary survey and the topographical survey; the land planners have been working diligently finishing up the master plan. When finished, the project will become one of the largest planned urban developments in the USA. Their years of hard work is now ready for presentations to the planning board, board of appeals, Conservation Commission, and the city council. The approvals from the regulatory authorities will ensure the development ability of the project. It will create thousands of jobs for local trades in

Las Vegas and will be a role model for future developments. Every developer, contractor, politician, and lawyer within two hundred miles of the site knows about the project. To date, the SIVLE Corp court has over $125 million of its money invested in the project. When the last condominium, single-family home, office building, and shopping village are completed, the investment will be well over $2.5 billion. This kind of endeavor is what gets Terance Best up in the morning. Big land deals are not the only thing that motivates Terance Best. There's something else that attracts him to Las Vegas, and it's not making large sums of money. Not all of Terance's trips to Las Vegas are for business. There is a very special event that attracts the multimillionaire developer to come and participate in something that would boggle the minds of those who know him. This event is as important to Terance as his multibillion-dollar project.

Terance heads to the kitchen, where he enjoys a cup of coffee, a bowl of cereal, the *Wall Street Journal*, and a large glass of orange juice that's waiting for him, all prepared by his valued cook and confidant, Antonio. Terance's wife, Terri, is not up at this time of the morning, nor are his two young children. Terance enjoys the business of making money but not as much as he enjoys being with his family. They always come first. He believes he's blessed by being able to enjoy the simple things in life while participating in the most difficult.

Terance's father was a wealthy hardworking businessman from Connecticut. He made a small fortune in the transistor business in the sixties. Fortunately, he sold the business just before the bottom fell out of the electronics industry. His father was a good person but not a good father. He wasn't someone Terance could depend upon for fatherly advice or affection. Terance's father expected academic excellence from Terance and was disappointed that he was not ranked number one in high school. He was also disappointed that his son was not an all-star athlete. Trying to please his father was extremely demoralizing because his father never showed any enthusiasm for Terance's accomplishments. He graduated second in his class at the prep school he attended in Andover, Massachusetts, where he was an accomplished musician. He also became an Eagle Scout at age sixteen. All of this went unnoticed by his father. No compliments, no embraces, no father-son talks, nothing. When Terance's family moved to southern Florida in the late sixties, his father somehow got into the banking business, where he managed to become one of the wealthiest businessmen in the Miami area. All Terance's father's wealth and prosperity never did much for Terance's self-confidence. He never received any inspiration or fatherly advice from his extremely strict father. Fortunately, Terance's mother was the exact opposite of her husband. She was somewhat kooky.

The way the story goes, according to his mother, is his parents met in New Haven, Connecticut, where Dad was studying engineering at Yale; however, the story has changed over the years. The more reliable account of their coming together was described by Terance's father. The way the father tells the story is that they were introduced at a friend's home in Londonderry, Connecticut. Terance's mother's junk box car wouldn't start, so Dad offered her a ride home to Hartford. The rest was left to fate. Mom was a very beautiful young woman, and Dad was a geek. She never really had any strong physical attraction to him, but he was certainly attracted to her. Mom knew that Terance's father had something to offer. He could provide her with the good life. So she decided to go along for the ride. They got married, and after fifty-one years, she never regretted her decision.

Terance's mom loved her upscale life, her friends, and most of all, her loving children. She enjoyed giving gifts to everyone in her life. The most valuable of all gifts were her unselfish love and affection for Terance and his two young sisters. Her virtues became the foundation for Terance's success in life. She was a very religious person and lived a life built around her faith in God. Everything and everyone was guided by God's grace. She explained to her loving son, Terance, that if you're a good person, good people will be attracted to you; and if they like you, there will be nothing that will stand in your way. She preached this to Terance all the years of his young life. Terance remembers a time when he was embarrassed about his grades in junior high school. His mother consoled him and said, "It's important that you get good grades, son, but what's more important to me is knowing that you are trying hard and are concerned about your accomplishments. But more importantly, it's knowing that you're a good boy and everyone likes you." His mother's message has been his guiding light throughout his adult life. He has never stopped trying to improve on everything he does; he leads a good life, and lots and lots of people like him. When he looks back at his life and sees his mother's face full of joy and kindness preaching her message to him, he realizes that it was his mother's kooky world and affection and not his millionaire father's money that got him where he is today.

Terance explains to Antonio that he will call him when he reaches Las Vegas and to remind him to tell his secretary, Julie, that he will be calling her at 11:00 a.m. when he arrives at the Las Vegas office.

He heads out to the garage with his briefcase and cup of coffee, gets behind the wheel of his BMW with the license plate number 1 10 35, and drives to the airport, where his company's Learjet is waiting. During the flight to Las Vegas, his thoughts drift between his up-and-coming project and his very special up-and-coming event waiting for him the next time he visits Las Vegas. This next special visit will not be via his private jet, nor will he have the fanfare he's accustomed to awaiting him at the airport. On this visit, Terance will be a very different person, a person that nobody knows about except a small group of misfit companions.

The jet lands at a private airport eight miles outside of Las Vegas. As the plane taxis up to the gate, Terance looks out the window and sees two well-dressed men and one very professional-looking woman waiting on the tarmac with glowing smiles on their faces. They're his junior partners that he handpicked for the company eight years ago. Terance personally groomed them. He wanted to make sure they had business savvy, loyalty, and trust needed to represent his company. Knowing he needed to put a lot of faith in his young partners, he listened emphatically. Eight years later, they earned wealth beyond their wildest dreams. They respected Terance for his business sense and his willingness to take chances, but more importantly, they admired him for his down-to-earth personality, his wholesome values, his love of people, and his generosity to those who were not as fortunate as him. Paul Capalluso, Donald Williams, and Cathy Sanders are Terance's family when he is away from home.

The cabin door opens, and Terance quickly runs down the stairs to the tarmac and immediately embraces his waiting partners. The first question Terance asks is about their well-being and if everything is on schedule. Cathy explains that everything is on schedule and going as planned. They're going to meet at the office this morning to review the presentation, go over the financials in the afternoon, and be at the Bellagio at 7:30 p.m. for supper. Terance rolls his eyes and smiles, and the four of them proceed to Paul's Land Rover and head for SIVLE Corp's offices. When they arrive at the office, Terance looks up at his eight-story reflective glass office building with the SIVLE Corp's logo on the upper floor and thinks to himself that it couldn't get any better than this. As they enter the lobby of the building, a middle-aged woman greets Terance with a warm embrace and a cup of coffee. The woman is Mary Wells, Terance's administrative secretary. Walking together to the large conference room, Mary relates all of the messages for the past two days. He knows the senders of all messages and isn't prepared to respond until he has met with his staff. He, however, gets one message from someone in Massachusetts who Mary said was very pleasant on the phone, but she thought it was odd that he didn't leave his name or a call-back phone number. Terance doesn't respond to Mary's concern. He knows who the caller was and why he had to be so discreet.

Assembling around the large conference table, the four executives begin talking about the progress of the project. Kathy has some very exciting news to announce. She recently received a letter from the Las Vegas Board of Appeals. Terance looks over at Kathy and comments, "So what did the letter say?"

"The news is all good. We have the last of the three permits to extend the development into parcel three."

Terance is well aware that parcel three had some zoning and conservation issues that somehow slipped through the seller's cracks when the parcel of land was being conveyed over to the SIVLE Corp. But all of that is now behind them. Paul informs the group that the architect submitted the final drawings for the buildings and that he is extremely excited about the way everything looked. He added the styles range from Spanish villas to innovative modern architecture all featuring green design. Paul gets up from his chair and begins setting up the presentation boards on the five easels that are at the end of the conference table. When he is done, Kathy, Don, and Terance immediately rush over to look at the boards. Don remarks, "Wait until the brokers get a look at this. This is going to knock everyone off their feet."

Kathy replies, "This is not going to be just a run-of-the-mill planned development—no, not by any stretch of the imagination. Nothing like this has ever been attempted before, at least not in this country. This will raise the bar for all the other projects in the area."

The group is overwhelmed by the sensitivity the design had to the natural and built environment. The design team transformed a delinquent industrial/residential area that abutted a large parcel of desert into an oasis of trees, lakes, and beautiful structures that looked too good to be true. Terance immediately dials up the architect's cell phone and congratulates him on his team's work. Don rolls out the project schedule that ran the whole length of the conference room table. Don is very excited about the good news that Kathy had brought to the meeting, and the wonderful work the designers produced is the finishing touch. Wanting to get down to business, Don explains that the project is on schedule and Terance should give the approval to proceed to the next phase. Don explains that his finance guru had secured all the financing and that he has personally drawn up contracts with listing brokers and interviewed design build contractors and public relations and marketing consultants. Everything is in place for Terance's final review and approval. Terance has only one question and that is how the project looked financially going into the last phase. Paul's answer is right to the point: they might be sitting on some inventory for up to three years because he perceived the real-estate bubble would eventually burst in Nevada. Paul explains, even with the land as a nonperforming asset, they should still be in great shape for the next turnaround if they don't overbuild. Paul explains that a lot of homework was undertaken prior to bringing the project to the approvals stage. The public relations team had touched base with the politicians, the Las Vegas casino businessmen, the local permitting authorities, the building trades, and that they all proved to be a very strategic move on their part. Paul notes that in order for the project to be successful, a lot of public infrastructure had to be in place, and the casino owners had to be peddling their influence to the decision makers in the city. The casino owners knew the value of having more people with disposable income. Thus, they were willing to lend a helping hand with conveying the project's benefits to the politicians and the local permitting authorities. It all came together in a very neat and orderly package. Terance knows he has no one else to thank other than his three hardworking partners who labored night and day to bring this project to fruition. To bring the meeting to closure, Terance gets up from his chair and gives each of them a round of applause and announces that it is time for a relaxing meal at Bellagio to which they all agree wholeheartedly.

Chapter 3

Hank Hunk at Home in LA

"IT'S A WONDERFUL day to be alive," Hank's grandma says to her one and only grandson, Hank, whose real name is actually Henry, but all his friends and family call him Hank with the exception of his grandma and father; they call him Elvis. Grandma comments, "You know, Elvis, you should be outside soaking up some of that beautiful California sun and thanking the Almighty that you are alive and are blessed with looks that no one else except you can match."

Hank answers back, "Grandma, this is a fine day. I'm going to take the car out and drive down to Laguna to pick up some calamari and tuna and bring them back home for the barbecue for my twenty-third birthday party tomorrow afternoon."

Grandma replies, "Elvis, let your daddy go to Laguna. It's your birthday."

"No way, I'm going. I also plan to pick up Kayla on the way back so she can spend the weekend with us."

Grandma replies with glee, "Now that's a great idea, my handsome boy. Bring that pretty friend of yours home so we can all talk about your wedding."

"What wedding? I'm not ready for a wedding. I'm too young."

Grandma raises her voice. "When do you think you're going to be ready, when I'm six feet under?"

"No chance of that, Grandma. You're going to live to be over one hundred."

"Maybe, just maybe."

"I'm going outside to let Mom and Dad know what I'm up to."

Grandma snickers, "The boy's twenty-three years old, and he still has to go ask his mother and father for permission to go buy some fish. What's this world coming to?"

Hank leaves the house and walks into the backyard, where his mother and father are planting vegetables in their raised bed garden. Hank's father looks up at him and says, "What's going on with you today, Elvis, and oh, by the way, what do you think of the garden?"

"It's, perfect, Dad. I only wish you and Mom would let me do some of the planting."

Hank's father answers sarcastically, "We would have two hours ago, but now it's already 11:00 a.m., and we wanted to get everything planted before your party tomorrow. And by the way, big boy, after this birthday, there will be no more parties. You'll be in your midtwenties and ready for your big day."

"What big day are you referring to?"

"You know what big day," Hank's father snaps back.

Hank replies, "No, I don't know what big day you're talking about."

His father responds, "I'll give you a hint—it's the same big day you and your grandma were discussing in the house a few minutes ago."

"Oh, that big day. I'm not ready for that big day, at least not right now, but maybe in the near future. I need to get my career in order before I can even think of getting married, or as you and Grandma put it—'the big day.'"

Hank's father responds jokingly, "You know, Hank, you're so lucky. You have the perfect girlfriend and the wherewithal to design the perfect home. Just think of it, Hank, you can design your dream house with all the goodies you architects know about. You can make your dreams become a reality."

"I have the dreams all right, but there's just one small problem: I don't have the money to do it."

"Oh, come on, Hank, you will get the money someday, mark my words, the time will come."

"You're absolutely right, Dad, that time will come, but that time is not now."

"So what are you going to do right now?"

"I'm going down to Laguna to pick up some fish and other stuff for the barbecue."

"Oh, come on, Hank, it's your birthday. Your father and I can pick up the food."

Hank comments, "No thanks, because on the way back, I plan on picking up Kayla."

Hank's father adds, "Picking up Kayla? Now you're talking. Your mother and I sure like having her around the house."

"I know you do, and so do I."

"You don't say?"

"That's right, I don't say."

"Well, Hank, just remember one thing: don't let the good ones get away. How about you pick up some tuna steaks for the grill and some calamari?"

"That that's exactly what I had in mind, and I'm counting on you to fry up the calamari."

"Now you're really talking, Elvis. What a day this is going to be, son. Your mother and I will pick up the hamburgers, hot dogs, chips, and drinks, and, of course, your birthday cake."

"I'm ready to go. I'll see you later around 7:00 p.m."

"Don't you mind about anything else. Your father and I will take care of the rest of the things for you. You just watch yourself driving down to Kayla's house, and give her mother and father our regards."

"I sure will."

"Do you need any money?"

"Of course not, I have plenty of cash and a credit card."

"We don't want you paying for anything."

"I know, don't worry about it, you can pay me later."

"We don't want our baby boy paying for anything on his birthday."

Hank has no intention of letting his mother and father pay for anything.

Hank's father looks over at his wife and comments, "Sweetie, our baby boy is going to be twenty-three years old.

Where did the time go? It seems like yesterday he was dancing around the floor to our music."

"I know that, but he's still our baby boy."

Hank's father turns to his son. "Hank, before I forget, you got a phone call from some guy from Massachusetts. He seemed very pleasant on the phone, but he wouldn't leave his name or phone number. He just said he would call you back."

Hank knows who the caller was. He says good-bye to his mother and father and heads over to the garage, where his mint 1959 white Thunderbird convertible is parked. The car's license plate number is HND DOG. Hank recalls what his grandma said: "It sure is great to be alive." Hank gets in the car, turns on the radio, and backs out of the garage. As he clears the garage doors, he puts the convertible top down. He glances down at the gas gauge and realizes that he's low on gas. The drive is sixty miles to Laguna via the Coast Road. He'll need to get gas.

As soon as he arrives, he parks at the pump and heads over to the mini-mart, where he's approached by two middle-aged women who stopped dead in their tracks to gawk at him.

Hank enters the mini-mart and greets his Indian friend Shaker, the proprietor. He looks at Hank and says, "You lucky dog, I saw those two women trying to pick you up."

"They were not trying to pick me up. They were just trying to be friendly."

"Oh yeah, sure, they were just trying to be as friendly like two dogs in heat. If I looked like you, I would have been all over them like bees on honey."

"Well, Shaker, you should've tried to be more friendly when they were paying for the gas."

"Yeah, sure, all the women who buy gas here are looking for someone who looks like me."

"Maybe they are. How do you know?"

"Maybe you're full of it. No halfway good-looking lady in LA is looking for an old, short, bald Indian man behind a counter in a mini-mart selling gas and candy."

"Well, Shaker, you never can tell, some women like short bald guys. And the fact that you're from India may be intriguing."

"Intriguing my ass."

"You can never be sure until you give it a shot. However, I wouldn't be buying tickets for two for the theater quite yet. And not to change the subject, but I would like thirty dollars' worth of gas and also let me have a couple of boxes of Good & Plenty and put it all on my credit card."

"You got it, my friend, and if you do decide to call the pretty lady, maybe you can arrange for the double date for the two of us. I'll take the one that's kind of fat and not so good looking, and you have the cute one. What do you say to that?"

"I'll keep that in mind. Now, how much do I owe you for the gas and the candy?"

"Thirty dollars for the gas. The candy is on me, but remember, I'll be looking forward to that double date."

"Forget about putting the gas on the credit card. I'll pay in cash."

"Cash is good. And you, my friend, have a good day."

Hank raises his hand over his shoulder, waves good-bye to Shaker, and walks over to the Thunderbird to pump gas. As he's walking toward the car, two young girls look up at him as he passes by. They both smile and giggle and look back as Hank walks by. Hank doesn't bat an eye. He walks to the T-Bird, pumps his gas, and takes off.

He drives along the Coast Road to Laguna. He loves the hills and the winding roads. He drives by a beach where hundreds of people are swimming, surfing, and enjoying the sun. *What a great way to spend the day,* he thinks. And what a great day it's going to be for him. He passes by a group of small shops across the street from the beach and allows a group of pedestrians to cross the street. As he comes to a stop, two very good-looking mothers with their teenage daughters catch a glimpse of Hank sitting in the convertible. As they pass by the front of his car, they both turn around and offer him a thank-you wave. Not watching where they're going, they nearly trip over one another. One of them shouts over to him. The two teenage daughters look at their mothers in disgust.

Ever since Hank was about seventeen years old, people have been gawking at him. All his friends in school—there were many—called him Elvis, although most of them had no idea who Elvis was. In the beginning, Hank enjoyed all the attention; but soon after, it wore on him. He never liked being the center of attraction. He liked people, all kinds of people, and they all liked him. He was one of the most popular boys in his high school. Right before his high-school prom, Hank received dozens of calls from girls asking him if he had a date. So as not to hurt anyone's feelings, he decided to take his cousin Diane, who was one year behind him in high school. After the prom, he kept some distance between himself and the girls in his class. It wasn't an act of conceit. He didn't want to be romantically involved. He just wanted to have friends. Hank was very wholesome, sincere, and a good-hearted young man. The older he got, the more he realized he wanted to be with a woman who shared his virtues.

When Hank met Kayla, he was attracted to her immediately. Hank was introduced to Kayla at his friend Jack's twenty-second birthday. Kayla immediately caught Hank's attention when she talked about her trips to Yosemite and her interest in boats, gardening, hiking, camping, and most of all, her interest in historic buildings. Hank always knew that someday he would meet someone who shared his interests, but never would he have imagined it would be someone as beautiful as Kayla and, to boot, someone who appreciated buildings. Early on in their dating, they would drive around in Hank's Thunderbird and marvel at all the old buildings. It was a wonderful experience for Hank. No other woman gave Hank that kind of companionship.

Hank is nearing the neighborhood where Kayla lives. The area is populated with charming villa-styled homes. The closer he gets to Kayla's house, the bigger and more beautiful the homes become. He turns onto the long winding driveway that leads to the beautiful Spanish mission-styled home. Her father had it built when Kayla was a child. The house is magnificent. It is set back four hundred feet from the street.

The driveway is lined on both sides with mature royal palm trees. The peastone driveway culminates into a full circle drive that has an eye-catching water fountain centered on the front door. Hank parks the Thunderbird off to one side and heads toward the house. As soon as Hank rings the doorbell, he could hear the family's dog barking. He waits a moment until the door opened. Adriana, the housekeeper, and Carmela, Kayla's Australian terrier, greet him. The moment Adriana sees Hank, she smiles and grabs his hand and says, "Come on in. They're in the backyard having lunch."

Hank walks through the polished marble floor foyer and through the glass doors that opens onto the rear patio overlooking the pool. Sitting under an umbrella-covered table were Kayla, her sister June, her brother John, her mother Marie, and father Joe. June yells over to Hank, "You're just in time for lunch."

They all greet Hank very warmly. Kayla gives him a big hug and a kiss on the cheek.

Kayla's family thought the world of Hank. They know that he is a perfect match. Hank gets along wonderfully with the family and always feels very much at home with them even though they are very wealthy and Hank's family is not. Joe and Marie consider their good fortunes a blessing. They use their money for the good things in life. They have their priorities in order. The family comes first. It is very important to them that their children, particularly Kayla, the oldest one, have their priorities in order; and for that, they immediately took a liking to Hank. From the first time Hank walked through their door, he impressed them with his admiration for their beautiful home, his love of gardening, his family ties, but most importantly, his admiration for Kayla. Hank is the apple in Kayla's eye. Her high standards for choosing friends, particularly men, make it obvious that Hank has to be someone very special. Joe and Marie knows their daughter is very lucky to have him around, and the fact that he looks exactly like Elvis makes it all that more delightful.

Chapter 4

Bobby Shrimp

"TWO DOWN AND one to go," Bobby Shrimp says to himself. "Maybe I'll make the last call tomorrow. California is three time zones away. Yes, I'll call tomorrow. Today, I will spend the rest of the day putting the finishing touches on the exterior restoration of my 1953 pink Cadillac. Just looking at it makes me feel alive. All I will need to do is the interior, and it will be ready to show."

It's been two years to the day that Bobby recalls driving to Oxford, Maine, on Mother's Day with his girlfriend, Lynn. During their drive, Bobby noticed a wrecked car behind a broken-down trailer. The car was covered with junk, and the convertible top was ripped to shreds, and the interior was open to the weather. What caught Bobby's eye was the color, faded pink. The car was rusted, dented, and generally weather beaten, but that didn't matter to Bobby; it was a 1953 pink Caddy, just like the one Elvis drove. He couldn't believe his eyes. He brought his car to a screeching halt and backed up as fast as he could. His girlfriend yelled in his ear, "What the hell are you doing? You're going to cause an accident."

"You'll see," answered Bobby.

As he stopped the car, he pointed to the back of the trailer. When the car came into view, Lynn smiled, looked over at Bobby, and said, "It seems your dreams have come true. It's a pink 1953 Caddy, you lucky dog. Do you think you can get the owner to sell it?"

Bobby quietly said as he was looking at the car, "There's only one way to tell."

A second later, he's out of the car and rushing toward the trailer. As Bobby approached the shabby rusted-out trailer, he tried to imagine who would be living in a dump like this. He visualized an old man coming to answer the door, the old guy who had probably forgotten about the car in the backyard. Bobby knocked on the door and immediately heard a barking dog from inside. It was the only sound he heard. He knocked a bit harder—to no avail. He moved to the right of the door to look in the window to see if anyone was at home. The place looked empty, so Bobby took out one of his Bobby's business cards from his wallet and wrote a note on the back of the card: "Please call my shop or home at your convenience." He placed the card under the door and started walking back to his car. Halfway down the walkway, he heard a voice behind him yell out, "Hey, you, what do you want?"

As he turned around to see who's calling, he's surprised to see a young man about twenty to twenty-three years old standing in the doorway—not the old man he had imagined. The guy was very thin and had light-brown hair, long sideburns, light-blue eyes, and a very light complexion. He's wearing some very scruffy-looking clothes. He looked like he just got out of bed. Bobby walked quickly back to the trailer. He extended his hand out and introduced himself. From the expression on the guy's face, Bobby could see that this guy could care less who was extending his hand to him. He just repeated his question, "What do you want?"

Bobby is a very easygoing guy and was not at all taken back by this guy's attitude. He's been in contact with a hundred guys just like him. Bobby looked at the kid straight in eyes and said with a somewhat demanding tone of voice, "Who owns the Caddy?"

The kid felt Bobby's intensity and realized this guy was no one to screw around with and immediately changed his attitude and answered, "I don't know? It was in the yard when I bought the trailer."

Without blinking an eye, Bobby intensely stared at the young kid, who now was somewhat intimidated by Bobby's presence; he suddenly became very nervous. Bobby said, "I want to buy it."

"I don't know if I can sell it. It may belong to someone else."

"I can take care of that when the time comes. Now let's get down to business. How much you want for the car?"

"I have no idea what it's worth."

"I will give you $1,000 cash today. Now how does that sound?"

"I said I don't know if I can sell you the car."

There was silence for a moment, and then Bobby heard a voice from behind the young guy. Bobby can't see who's talking, but the voice sounded like it's from a very young woman. When she came into view, Bobby saw a very innocent-looking girl in her late teens, early twenties, holding an infant. Bobby noticed the young girl was pregnant. She asked the young kid, "How come you haven't invited your friend in?"

The young guy answered, "He is not my friend. He wants to buy the junk box in the backyard."

"Well, mister, why don't you come in? Would you like a Pepsi?"

"Well, I don't know if I should come in."

Bobby was waiting for the young guy to invite him in. The young girl looked over at the young guy and said, "Oh come, Billy, let's invite the man in and his wife who's been sitting in the car out on the street."

"She's my girlfriend."

With that, the young girl yelled out, "Hey, you, in the car, come on in." Lynn immediately got out of the car and walked to the trailer. When she arrived at the door, the young woman extended her hand and said, "Hello, I'm Kim, and this is Billy, and that over there is little Billy Bob. Come on in."

Bobby hadn't noticed the young toddler sleeping on the sofa. The young girl turned the infant around whom she was holding in her arms.

"And this is Johnny. He's fourteen months old."

Lynn made the introductions. "I'm Lynn, and this is Bobby." She then asked the young girl, "How many months along are you?"

COMPETING FOR ELVIS

"I'm six months."

"What are you hoping for?"

"A baby girl, of course."

And Billy said, "A baby boy."

After Bobby realized the situation he had stumbled upon, he really regret the tough-guy act he put on the young kid. Bobby knew what it's like to be intimidated. He immediately began to lighten up the mood, and with that, the four of them moved into the living room. Bobby and Lynn noticed how sparsely the trailers furnished. Lynn asked Bobby, "What's the deal?"

"Bill doesn't think he can sell the car because he doesn't know who owns it."

"All you need to do is to go down to the Registry of Motor Vehicles and explain that you don't have the title for the car. You will need to bring the vehicle's VIN number, year, make, and model. The registry will run a check back ten years, and if the vehicle was not reported stolen, they'll issue you a new title. The fee is minimal."

At that moment, Bobby joked, "I told you I could take care of that problem."

Billy said giddily, "I guess you can."

"So what's the problem?"

"I don' know what the problem is. I offered Bill a grand, cash, for the rusted-out old car, but I don't think he likes the offer."

"I don't blame him, you cheapskate, one grand, are you kidding?" Lynn then turned to Kim and said, "We will give you $5,000 cash and will have the car off the property immediately."

Billy looked at Lynn and said, "Are you serious—five grand cash?"

"What? That's not enough?"

Kim replied, "I don't think the car is worth $5, let alone $5,000."

"Have you two ever heard the expression 'one man's junk is another man's treasure'? This trashed car is Bobby's treasure. Bobby's hobby is restoring old cars."

Bobby abruptly cut in and said to Lynn, "Are you out of your mind—five grand for this junk car?"

"Do you want the car or not?"

"Of course, I want the car."

Bobby then looked over at the destitute young couple and said, "Well, guys, do we have a deal?"

Kim and Billy looked at each and together said, "Thank you, God, do we ever have a deal."

"Make your call, Bobby, and let's get this done today. It's Mother's Day, and my mother is waiting for us."

Immediately, Bobby took his cell phone and called his brother Jesse. Jesse answered on the first ring with "Hey, Bobby, what's up?"

"Jesse, I want you to go over to the shop and pick up the flatbed and drive it up to this address." Bobby asked Billy what the address was.

Billy answered, "62 Traveler Road, Oxford, Maine."

Bobby instructed Jesse to come to 62 Traveler Road, Oxford, Maine. Bobby then instructed Jesse to go into his office and get $5,000 in cash from the safe in the closet next to his desk. Jesse asked Bobby if he was kidding about driving up to Oxford, Maine, with the flatbed and $5,000 in cash on a Sunday afternoon on Mother's Day. Bobby explained that he was not kidding, and Jesse would understand the urgency of his request when he arrived. Bobby asked, "When do you think you can get here?"

"It's now 11:00 a.m. Give me about a half hour to get the truck and the cash and two and one-half hours to get to Oxford. I should be there by 1:00 p.m., or 1:30 p.m. the latest."

Bobby thanked Jesse and remarked, "Wait until you see what I got."

"I can't wait."

Bobby explained to Billy and Kim that his brother Jesse will be arriving with a tow truck and the cash later at around 1:00 p.m. or 1:30 p.m. At this point, Kim looked at Lynn and said, "This is not a joke, is it?"

"This is no joke. Jesse will be here no later than 1:30 p.m., and at that time, we will be back to personally hand you the money."

"You sure you're not kidding? You guys know what you're doing?"

"You and Billy made Bobby's day. Don't worry, Bobby knows exactly what he's doing."

At that, Kim said emotionally, "If this all happens, it will be a lifesaver for us."

They all shook hands, and Lynn and Bobby headed back to the car.

As soon as they drive off, Bobby looked over at Lynn and said, "Are you nuts? I could have had that car for a grand, now I'm paying five times that."

Lynn looked at Bobby, and with a smile, she said, "Don't be a jerk. Did you see how those two kids were living?"

"What has that got to do with the value of the car?"

"You big phony baloney, you know that car will be worth over $50,000 to $60,000 when you're finished restoring it."

"You're right, I am a jerk, and now you're making me feel bad."

"You should feel bad. Everyone knows you're a good-hearted guy. They were very innocent needy kids. What else should you have done?"

With Lynn's remark, Bobby took out his cell phone and rang up Jesse.

"Jesse, this is Bobby again. Take $7,000 from the box and bring it up to Oxford."

"Seven thousand?"

"Yeah, $7,000."

"I'll do it."

Lynn looked over at Bobby, smiling.

"Now that's more like the Bobby Shrimp I know."

Bobby and Lynn headed off to Stoneham to pick up Lynn's mother. Lynn promised to take her mother out for lunch. Lynn thought they could have an early lunch and make it back to Oxford by 1:00 p.m. with her mother, give Kim and Billy the cash, and help Jessie load the Caddy onto the flatbed. Then Bobby, Lynn, and her mother could celebrate Mother's Day and Bobby's good fortune all at the same time.

The ride to Stoneham went quickly. Bobby and Lynn assumed that they would arrive at Lynn's mother's house at noon. When they arrived at Lynn's mother's house, it was only 11:30 a.m. The drive only took thirty minutes. Bobby could see Lynn's mother, Irene, looking through the window. So they quickly got out of the car and headed to the front door. Lynn's mother opened the door and greeted both of them and said with a half smile, "What the heck took you two so long to get here? You said you were going to leave at 7:30 a.m. That was four hours ago."

"We had to make a stop on the way."

"A stop, what do mean a stop?"

"You'll find out soon enough. Are you ready to go, Mom?"

"You two just got here and already you want to leave."

"We're taking you out to lunch in Oxford."

"Oxford, why are we going to Oxford?"

Lynn looked over at Bobby, smiling, and said, "We need to pick up something."

"What do you mean pick up something?"

"You'll soon see."

"All right, hold on. Let me grab my purse. Why is everything such a big secret with you two? Oh, by the way, I almost forgot, I need Bobby to help me take the riding lawn mower out of the basement and start it up so I can cut the grass this week. I have gas in the yard."

When all was done, the three of them headed off to Oxford. It was now 12:45 p.m., so Bobby drove hastily. All the way down to Oxford, Irene kept commenting how fast Bobby was driving and kept nagging at Bobby and Lynn to tell her why they were going to Oxford. She didn't get a response from either of them.

"You haven't said a word since you arrived. What's going on?"

Irene tried to get Bobby to say something by asking where they were going to have lunch. Before Bobby could answer,

Irene commented, "You know I didn't even have breakfast this morning."

"Mom, I think we're going to Rudy's."

"Rudy's! Isn't Rudy's kind of expensive?"

"Mom, that's OK, it's kind of a double celebration."

"A double celebration! Is this what I think is?" Irene now became very excited.

"No, Mom, it's not that."

"Well, that's too bad. You know I am not getting any younger. As a matter of fact, you're getting older too, and the clock is ticking."

Lynn knew all about the "clock ticking." She and Bobby had recently talked about their relationship. Bobby seemed to be interested in getting married. His business was doing quite well, and he would like to settle down and have children. While on the other hand, Lynn was not so sure about her future with Bobby. She's five years older than him, and things would probably work out OK, but somehow she's just not ready to commit to marriage, or maybe she's just not sure about Bobby.

Bobby, Lynn, and Irene arrived at Traveler Road in Oxford at 1:25 p.m. Irene looked out the window at the shabby trailer and said, "What on earth are we doing at this dump?"

"Mom, you'll see in a second." With that, Irene sees Jesse coming up the road with the flatbed.

"Lynn, is that Bobby's brother, Jesse? What the heck is he doing here?"

"OK, Mom, I'll fill you in. Bobby bought a car this morning, and Jesse's here to bring it back to the shop," Irene said sarcastically.

"A car? Well, isn't that nice. What a wonderful thing to celebrate together—Mother's Day and Bobby's new car—oh, what a lovely day."

"Mom, please relax. This will only take a few minutes, and we'll be off to Rudy's," Irene responded sarcastically.

"Is Jesse going to join us with the flatbed?"

"No, Mom. He is going back home with the car as soon as Bobby and he load it on the flatbed."

"I'm so disappointed he's not coming with the tow truck."

Lynn abruptly replied, "Mom, stop being a pain in the ass."

"OK, I'll keep my mouth shut, but hurry up, I'm starving."

"Thank you, Mother."

At that moment, Billy and Kim came out of the trailer with the two little children. Irene commented, "Oh, look, isn't this nice—it's the Beverly hillbillies. Are they going to join us for lunch at Rudy's?"

"Keep it down, Mom. They own the car, and they are very nice people."

Bobby quickly got out of the car. None of Irene's sarcastic comments affected him in the least. All he could think of was getting his dream car back to the shop. Jesse got out the flatbed and walked over to Bobby, Kim, and Billy.

"Hi, I'm Jesse, Bobby's good-looking brother."

Kim replied, "I'm Kim, and this is my husband, Billy, and we're very glad to meet you."

Jesse looked around and asked Bobby where the car was. Bobby pointed to the back of the trailer. Jesse asked, "Should I try to bring the flatbed to the trailer, or should we try to muscle the car out of the driveway?"

Billy said, "The car won't budge. You'll need to bring the truck right up to it. I will move some of the junk away so you can back in."

"OK, let's do it."

Jesse jumped back into the truck and backed carefully over to the weed-infested lawn in front of the trailer. Bobby and Billy quickly removed the junk blocking access to the car. Since Bobby and Jesse were very experienced with towing disabled vehicles in tight conditions, within a few minutes, they had the car on the flatbed and chained down. Jesse and Bobby just stared at the car sitting on the flatbed. Jessie commented, "You are so right, brother. The car is perfecto."

Kim walked over to Irene, Lynn, Bobby, and Billy to join them as they stood in front of the car. Jesse jumped into the flatbed and drove the car and truck down the driveway and onto the road.

As the flatbed approached the driveway, Irene looked up and said, "What the heck is that hunk of junk?"

"It's Bobby's new toy."

"How much are these people paying him to take this piece of junk away?"

"Keep it down, Mom."

Jesse came over to Bobby and said, "Here's the envelope with the cash."

Bobby handed the envelope to Billy and asked him to count the cash. Billy ignored his request to count the money and put the envelope in his shirt pocket. Lynn asked Billy to count the money.

"Nah, I trust you."

"Billy, please count the money."

"Lynn, we trust you."

"I know you do, but we insist you count the money."

Billy agreed and handed the envelope over to Kim. Kim opened the envelope, removed the cash, and began counting. Meanwhile, Irene's eyes widened in a painfully looking way at the sight of all the one-hundred-dollar bills. As soon as Kim counted beyond the $5,000 they had agreed upon, she looked confused; and when she finally reached $7,000, she asked, "What's the extra $2,000 for?"

Lynn looked at Kim and said, "It's Mother's Day. Go buy yourself something nice."

"But we all agreed to $5,000 and now you're giving us $7,000."

Irene said in amazement, "I can't believe you are giving them $7,000 for junk box. Are you crazy?"

Lynn snapped back at Irene, "Mom, get back in the car!"

"With that kind of money, they can go and buy two more of those beautiful trailers."

"I think it's time we go, Bobby."

Billy looked at Bobby and said, "Bobby, you don't know what this means to Kim and me, you just don't know."

Bobby replied, "I can only guess what it means to you. However, what I do know is what this car means to me."

Kim looked at Bobby and Lynn and said, "You are both very generous. Billy and I were in desperate need of money until you two came by this morning. I just don't know what to say."

Lynn said, holding Kim's shaking hand, "Don't say anything. Just spend the money wisely."

Bobby waited in the car and watched Jesse drive away with the Caddy on the flatbed. Bobby looked over at Lynn said, "This is a very, very good day for me."

Irene said under her breath, "This is a very good day for him. He buys a junk box worth nothing for $7,000, and this is a very good day for him? I would hate to be around him when he has a bad day."

The flatbed drove down the road with the Caddy on top, and Bobby, Lynn, and Irene drove to Rudy's restaurant and had a wonderful afternoon celebrating Mother's Day and Bobby's good fortune.

Chapter 5

Jeremy Shrinks Gets a Phone Message

JEREMY AND KARLA'S wonderful wedding day is long gone, and their marriage lasted only eleven years. Karla had high expectations for Jeremy. There was no telling how far he could have gone with her ambitious endeavors. After a number of attempts at impersonations, singing alone, singing in groups, singing behind the scenes, singing off the set, and so on, it seemed, at this point in his life, nothing good was going to happen, particularly fame or fortune. And as time went on, it became more apparent that along with all of Jeremy's misgivings, his marriage with Karla was coming to an end. There were a number of reasons for their demise. One wonderful blessing was given to them during their marriage, and that was the birth of their daughter, Marie. She was the one that kept them together for eleven years. She was the best thing in Jeremy's dismal life. Fortunately, two years after the divorce, for one reason or another, Karla and Jeremy began spending time together with Karla's new husband, Jack, the contractor, and Jeremy's low-roller girlfriend. The four of them got together on a number of occasions and actually enjoyed one another's company, particularly Jack and Jeremy's girlfriend. Marie was the center of attraction when the group gathered together. Jeremy was always at Marie's beck and call. He spent almost as much with her as Karla did. Jeremy was a good-hearted and loving dad, and Karla knew it. She admired him for that.

In all that has happened to Jeremy, no one to this day has been able to recognize his gifted intelligence. He continues to keep it buried in the closet of his enslaved life. Something that should have been so beneficial somehow turned out to be so destructive. Over the years, Jeremy digressed into a low-life existence. He bounced from job to job until he ended up, lucky for him, as the assistant manager at a convenience store. The job gave him exactly what he wanted in life—just enough money to live on, minimum responsibility, no heavy lifting, and most of all, the opportunity to be completely autonomous from the rest of the world.

Excitement and inspiration have not been a part of Jeremy's life; however, there are two, and only two, very compelling things that keep him going: the first and most important one is his daughter, Marie, whom he watched grow from a baby into a young woman with enormous amounts of energy and ambitions, way beyond what he could have ever envisioned for himself; she is his entire world. The second one is with four very unique friends whom he meets with once a year in Las Vegas, Nevada. These friends are socially miles apart from Jeremy's low-life existence. But they don't know that, and over the years, they have gravitated closer to one another and formed a close relationship based on their obsession in a very diverse event. This event is kept secret from everyone in Jeremy's life, including Karla and Marie. The combination of being with his special friends and participating in the event has given Jeremy a reason to be inspired.

Today is a special day: he and Karla are heading down to Miami to spend a weekend with Marie at the University of Miami. Marie was accepted with a full scholarship. Evidently, God blessed her with Jeremy's genius and Karla's ambition, although everyone, including Marie, claims her intelligence came from her mother. Jeremy knows differently and has never challenged Marie's opinion on where she got her smarts. Somehow, Jeremy is comfortable knowing that Marie feels that she got where she is because of her ambitious mother and not her lazy father. Marie has been on the dean's list since her first semester. She participates in numerous extracurricular activities and has a huge amount of friends. She is a very busy girl but not so busy for her mother and father, whom she adores. The time they spend together is very precious for each of them.

Marie's been in college for nine months. He remembers the emotional experience he had when he had to say good-bye to his little girl at the students' move-in day. Jeremy couldn't keep the tears from clouding his eyes. The emotional experience that came over him came as a complete surprise. He will never forget that moment as long as he lives. He remembers all the other mothers and fathers saying good-bye to their grown-up children and how much of a somber experience it was for everyone. Jeremy was very lucky that Marie got the scholarship because he knew that there was no way that he could've paid the tuition. Jeremy's generation of devoted parents, who spend so much of their lives at swim meets, soccer games, baseball games, hockey games, football games, lacrosse basketball, the Boy Scouts, choir, and so on, are all part of the baby-boomer generation. These are the things that many of the boomers missed but now have been given a second chance to relive them through their children's accomplishments.

Jeremy recalls the 5:00 a.m. wake-ups and rides to the swim practices miles from the home. He enjoyed bringing her to the swim meets, but he could never bring himself to actually watch Marie compete. His fear that just being a spectator could bring disaster to his precious daughter was enough to keep him away. So he waited in the lobby, in the car, or at the vending machines. Karla, on the other hand, was right at poolside watching her daughter swim. She cheered her on; she clocked her time, and she was always there to give her the support she needed. At the end of the year, when the swim team held its awards meeting to hand out the trophies, Jeremy was the proudest father in the room. To see his daughter accept multiple awards was overwhelming for him. When Karla and Jeremy attended Marie's private high school awards night, Marie was sitting up front with all the honor-society students. When principal of the school asked her to stand up so that she could be recognized for her scholastic accomplishments was a very emotional moment for Jeremy and Karla. Marie's recognitions included her acceptances from colleges across the country, scholarships, her grade average, and her subject awards. Jeremy became so consumed with emotion that he could hardly take control of himself. It was difficult to equate what caused his emotional experience. Could it have been his pride in his daughter, his disbelief that someone like him could have fathered a girl with so many accomplishments, or could it be that these acclaims could have been his if he didn't suppress his intelligence? It was a very sobering experience.

So now it's evident that his daughter has achieved all of those accomplishments that he could have if he had applied himself so many years ago. Knowing he's been a failure to the most important people in his life has been a demoralizing experience for him. But that's going to change. Marie will one day be proud of him. To accomplish these things, Jeremy will need to make drastic changes in his life. But now is not the time. Now was the time to be with Karla and Marie and enjoy the moment.

Upon returning home from Miami, he had a message on his answering machine. Although he leaves no name, Jeremy knows who it is. The message excites Jeremy, and now he has something else to look forward to. It's time for Jeremy to head West.

Chapter 6

Terance Best

TERANCE'S VISIT TO Las Vegas is just as exciting as it was ten years ago, when he became interested in developing tracts of land in the outskirts of the city. The fact that the city of Las Vegas is a utopia for development excites Terance the minute he arrives at McCarran International Airport. The mega buildings, the open land areas, the business opportunities, and the millions of people who visit the city each year are enough for Terance to want to be a part of its future. However, above all the excitement, it's the desert that attracts him to Nevada. He sees development opportunities that can change people's lives and feels he needs to be on the ground floor to make it happen. He's involved in the planning and development of all his projects. Being a devout conservationist, his planned developments are environmentally sensitive.

Aside from Terance's business endeavors, there is one other reason why he's attracted to Las Vegas, and it's not what one would expect from someone with such a high-profile life. It's kind of strange, but at the same time, it's very gratifying. This strange attraction is about a competition that he shares with a very unusual group of guys. These guys are complete opposites of Terance. His rendezvous time with them is quickly approaching. He's never hinted to anyone why he goes to Las Vegas when it's not for business. His secret life with his four friends is a contradiction to his status. However, as one gets to know Terance, his involvement with them becomes a confirmation to his character. At times, Terance suffers from paranoia thinking about the consequences that would arise if someone were on to him. Terance is not one who thinks negative; however, he is a bit concerned about being found out.

His participation in the upcoming event is something for him to look forward to; although risky, it's very rewarding in a very different way. Terance's wealth and lifestyle are miles apart from his companions; it's a very well-kept secret, which allows him to be accepted for his generosity, loyalty, but mostly because of his devotion to their cause. Terance recalls the telephone call his Las Vegas office received from the anonymous caller. The call was a confirmation for his secret trip to Las Vegas. Terance knew the caller and knew he would be giving the time, the date, and the meeting location for their rendezvous. The caller was one of the participants in the up-and-coming event. Terance and the mysterious caller are joined by three other companions, all of whom compete against one another in a very unusual event that takes place onstage in front of hundreds of people. For one reason or another, all of them keep what they do together a deep secret. Terance, of course, would face the greater consequences; but strange as it may be, it was the risk of being exposed that intrigued and rejuvenated. There is, however, something greater than the risks and his friends' companionship that take him away from home. It's something more exciting than many of the other challenges in his life. Terance and his friends share a dream, and it's this dream that attracts him to Las Vegas. The time has come, and Terance has to get prepared.

Chapter 7

Hank Hunk's Birthday Party

KAYLA AND HANK are driving north on Route 5 to Hank's parents' house. The top is down on Hank's Ford Thunderbird, and the wind is blowing through Kayla's long black hair. Hank's wearing a pair of signature Elvis sunglasses and an open button shirt. Kayla looks over at her handsome boyfriend and ribs about how much he's a dead ringer of Elvis. She always feels so happy when she's with Hank and his family. Although her family and his family are miles apart, in some ways, they are very similar. Both parents' social lives revolve around their children.

Everything so far is going great between Kayla and Hank; however, now and again, she wonders about her future with him. She knows she adores him and that he adores her, but there's never been any serious talk about marriage or any mention of commitment. She hopes there should be no doubt in Hank's mind that they are perfect for one another. They are both well educated, share each other's interests, are very down-to-earth, and are also both homebodies and family-oriented people. Kayla doesn't want to be let down, nor does she want her family to be disappointed if things don't work out between Hank and her. Unbeknown to Kayla, Hank shares the same insecurities but from a different point of view in that Kayla's parents are very well educated and have accomplished a lot in their lives.

Hank's father and mother attended state universities, worked at Pratt & Whitney together, where they met. At that time, Hank's father was a junior engineer. They married young, and soon after, Hank was born. They decided to stay in California and raise a family. Kayla's father graduated from Stanford and went on to work at Dun & Bradstreet, where he met Kayla's mother at a seminar for young business professionals. Kayla's mother graduated from Georgetown and was pursuing a career in microbiology. They were both career minded but not career obsessed. Kayla's father left Dun & Bradstreet and founded a small mutual fund investment firm with a former Stanford College classmate. After fifteen years of seventy-hour weeks, they finally hit it real big in the early eighties with Microsoft stock. Today, Kayla's father's net worth is around $50 million; however, you would never know it. Kayla's mother was as equally successful, but when Kayla was born, she decided to devote her life to Kayla and then to John; and after John, it was Kate. With these comparisons, Hank is concerned about the cultural difference between the parents; however, he feels this can all come to past. Being an only child, Hank enjoys the benefit of Kayla's large family and is looking forward to a commitment with Kayla as soon as he's more financially stable.

They arrive at Hank's house around 7:30 p.m. Hank's father comes out to the front yard as soon as he hears Hank's Thunderbird drive up to the driveway. Kayla is greeted with open arms by Hank's mother, father, and grandfather. Kayla is always so moved by their affection. Kayla and Hank's grandmother get along wonderfully. Hank's grandma reminds Kayla of some of the eccentric people she met while she was attending Georgetown.

Hank's house is big enough so that Kayla has her own bedroom when she visits. That night, they have a quick supper; and by 10:30 p.m., they are all in bed. Hank is tired from his trip, so he dozes off in a matter of seconds. Kayla, on the other hand, lies awake, tossing and turning and revisiting her thoughts about her relationship with Hank. She feels somewhat insecure about not having some kind of a commitment from Hank, and here she is sleeping in his house. Kayla finally dozes off at around 12:30 a.m.

They are up by 8:00 a.m. Mary is cooking breakfast with Hank's grandmother. Hank is getting things organized for the party with Henry. While having breakfast, they discuss the festivities of the day. Grandma keeps reminding Hank that he is getting along in years. Hank laughs it off but deep down inside knows that things will have to change for him if he wants to keep Kayla around.

The birthday party is in full swing by 3:00 p.m. The entire Hunk family, friends, and neighbors are all over the backyard, in the garage, in the house, on the front lawn, and on the sidewalks. There must have been eighty people at the party. Hank's family has food and drinks spread all over the place. There are hot dogs, hamburgers, nuts, chips, fruits, candy, coffee, soft drinks, beer, and wine. The fried calamari is being deep-fried, and tuna is on the grill. There is something for everyone.

Hank has a couple of friends who has a rock band, and they are whiling away all afternoon. Everyone is dancing and carrying on. It is a great time. After about three hours into the party, Mary thinks it is time for Hank's birthday cake, so they roll it out and ask Hank to say a few words. Hank is not good at giving speeches, so he just thanks everyone for coming and mentions how good it feels to be in his early twenties. To save him from his lackluster speech, Hank's grandmother goes into the house and gets Hank his Elvis sunglasses and his acoustic guitar. She hands them to him and asks the band to play "Don't Be Cruel." Hank gets into the role immediately, and within seconds, all eyes are on him. He is an instant hit. His voice is good, but his looks are the showstopper. Kayla is feeling a little tipsy from the wine and the California sun, and the sight of Hank driving the crowd wild excites her.

Hank's mother and father join the group with their guitars, and the party becomes a jam session. When Henry and Mary were in there twenties, they played a lot together and were quite good. Hank would dance around the floor when he was a little boy while they played Elvis's songs. Hank, Mary, and Henry play three sets of music, with Hank singing along perfectly. Kayla and the entire group are totally entertained. The guests don't want them to stop. The three of them look so very happy together, especially Hank. At that moment, Kayla looks at Hank and knows he is the one for her. When Hank finishes his last song, he walks over to Kayla, laughing and joking and carrying on like it was all a big act. But down deep inside, Hank knows that this is no act and that his up-and-coming trip to Las Vegas is going to be a much more engaging performance than the one he just finished in his backyard. He knows something big is going to happen on his next secret trip to Las Vegas. His special friends will be waiting for him, and he is ready for the event. His trip has already been planned.

Chapter 8

Bobby Shrimp

BOBBY SHRIMP MAKES his last phone call, and now he is assured that everything is ready for the big event. He can now turn his focus on his latest acquisition. He still can't believe he actually found his dream car on the way to Lynn's mother's house. Even though the car was terribly tarnished, rusted, and weather beaten, he knows his crew will be able restore it to mint condition in a few short months. Getting parts for a car like this would pose as a problem for most restorers, but not for Bobby. He knows where to go for the parts that are needed to turn the wreck into a show car. Now all that's left is the interior work, and he has Jessie getting estimates from local shops that specialize in interior restoration.

At this point in his life, Bobby is getting skeptical about his future. The body shop is doing quite well, and his relationship with his Las Vegas friends is at an all-time high. The only thing that Bobby doesn't have under control is his relationship with Lynn. And this has been bothering Bobby for some time. Ever since they met, Bobby could not get a good feeling about their future. Their relationship began with a freak accident in front of Bobby's mother's house while she was visiting the neighbor next door. For some strange reason, the emergency brake on her standard shift car let go, and the car rolled down the hill and crashed into a hydrant. Fortunately, not much damage was done but enough that the car needed some body work. Bobby saw it all happen and went to help and offered to fix the car. She took Bobby up on his offer, and one thing led to another, and they soon became friends and then lovers. Lynn was five years older than Bobby, divorced, with no children. She liked him immediately. They've been living together in a rundown apartment building in a shabby section of the city for the past four years. Bobby could easily afford a lot more, but at this particular time of his life, he would rather be saving his money for bigger and better things. He's looking forward to having a family. Lynn admires and understands Bobby very well. She knows that his sometimes rough-and-tough get-out-of-my-way attitude is all a cover up for a guy with a very kind and generous disposition. Lynn saw through Bobby's act within a couple of weeks into their relationship. She immediately noticed that the way he smiles and how much people like him was his big giveaway.

Bobby has always been a hard worker, working twice, even three times, as hard in high school just to get average grades. After high school, he went on to vocational school, and it was there he was introduced to auto bodywork. He knew he found his passion as soon as he began using the tools. It was clear right away that someday he would have his own body shop.

His dream of owning his own business came to a reality at a very early age in his life. He opened his first body shop when he was twenty-six. At that time, he needed money to get things going. So he started doing small jobs for little or no profit. Most of them were favors for his friends and acquaintances and then for acquaintances of the acquaintances. Bobby was somewhat naïve, and before he knew it, he was taking apart and putting together cars at such a high rate that he had to work seven days a week, twelve hours a day. Bobby never asked any questions about where all the business was coming from, and that was his first big mistake. The money was coming in faster than he could have ever imagined. He kind of knew there was something not right about his newfound success. He surmised that some of the people that he was dealing with had to be involved in something illegal. He wanted to stop but was concerned about his well-being. Although Bobby was six feet three and 215 pounds of pure muscle, he knew he was no match for his counterparts. So to hide his fears, he would act a little tougher and a little more vindictive than the lowlifes that were bringing the cars in for a face-lift. Bobby knew it couldn't last. Something had to go wrong. He would either end up in the morgue or in jail. He was living in fear every day. He began hanging out with tough guys at the local bars and spent lots of time drinking, gambling, and spending time with women that would serve him no good. His world came crashing down on a Sunday in the middle of a winter night when one of his low-life cohorts brought in a new Mercedes-Benz with an unfamiliar accomplice. The deal was always the same: cash to rebuild the car with no questions asked. Bobby was a bit uneasy with the new guy. Somehow he didn't look like a two-bit car thief, and Bobby was right; he wasn't. The guy was an undercover cop. As soon as Bobby was handed the cash, the shop was overrun with law enforcement. Bobby was caught red-handed. It seems that Bobby's low-life customer got caught stealing a car and plea-bargained with the authorities and in doing so brought Bobby and the body shop down.

Bobby spent three years in state prison for grand theft auto and racketeering. At twenty-six years of age, Bobby's life was shattered. The three years in jail took its toll on him. It was a horrible experience to be with a bunch of hardened criminals. His dreams of owning a first-class body shop were over forever. The guys he was serving time with were a lot tougher and a whole lot more street smart than he. Turning inward, he became a recluse within the prison. Never imagining his life could come to this, it broke his spirit. He felt he let everyone around him down, particularly his mother and father, whose hearts were broken by his misgivings.

His parents were loving and caring parents. His father worked as a mechanic at GE, and his mother worked at the high-school cafeteria. Bobby had a sister who was extremely popular and very bright. His mother and father loved their son and daughter very much, and knowing that he had a learning disability, however, his work ethic made them even more proud of their son. Most of his preteen and teenage years, Bobby had minimal friends. He spent most of his time doing homework and keeping company with his mother and father.

While in prison, his mother and father and sister would come to visit him on the weekends. Every time they came in, Bobby would look in their eyes and immediately know how difficult it was for them see their loving son behind bars. Bobby made a promise to himself that one day they would look up to him and be proud of their son.

Through all of the terrible experiences in prison, an extraordinary relationship with a fellow inmate occurred that would change the path of Bobby's life forever. Bobby knew his new friend was no criminal. He was just some unfortunate drunk who hit a pedestrian, panicked, and left the scene of the accident. He turned himself in, was tried, and sentenced to serve two years in prison. It was during his second year that he met Bobby. They immediately befriended each other. Bobby didn't know much about him. He did, however, know that he was a lot older than him, married, and owned a used-car business with his wife and brother. They were running the business while he was doing time. A couple of things drew them together: one was they both knew a lot about auto bodywork; the second thing was they were both scared stiff of the other prisoners; the third and more engaging thing was their passion for rock-and-roll music, particularly Elvis's music. But their obsession was not just the music but rather with Elvis himself.

The inmate's name was Ray Cook. He was a self-made man who made a lot of money selling used cars and had a boatload of friends. Ray talked to Bobby about setting him up in the business when they got out. Bobby was convinced that this would never happen. Ray also talked about his fascination with Elvis Presley and how much Bobby reminded him of Elvis. He explained that it wasn't his voice or his looks that caught his eye but rather his mannerisms. Bobby was really into Elvis's music, as was Ray. They had all his tapes, records, and videos of movies and television appearances.

After two and half years, Bobby was released from prison for good behavior. His mother, father, and sister picked him up at the gate. This day was to be the beginning of his new life. When Bobby arrived at home, he immediately tried to reinvent himself. In a matter of days from the time he was released, he received a letter addressed to his parents' home. Bobby's mother gave him the letter. The letter was from Ray Cook. Ray wanted to meet with Bobby to discuss setting him up in a small one-man body shop next to his used-car lot. Bobby couldn't believe what he was reading. The man whom he thought he would never hear from again was keeping his promises. Feeling guilty that he doubted him, he called Ray immediately. They met the next day and worked out a business arrangement, and from that point on, Bobby was on his way. After a few years, Bobby's reputation for doing excellent work got around, and Bobby had to move into a larger space.

Over these years, Ray was drawn into a very captivating cult. He convinced Bobby to join him on his next trip to his special event, and it was on that trip that he and Ray met three other guys. Their names were Jeremy Shrinks, Henry (Hank) Hunk, and Terance Best. It was by total coincidence that they met. Immediately, Bobby became very popular with the other three guys. He was drawn to one of them because of his fascination with vintage cars, particularly 1953 Cadillacs. They enjoyed one another's company immensely. The most interesting thing about their relationship was the engagement of the secrecy each of them practiced while attending these visits to Las Vegas. Bobby soon became the front man for the group.

Bobby explained his prison time to Lynn early on in their relationship, and it didn't faze her one bit. But he never explained his trips Las Vegas. He kept that a secret from everyone. The prison part was easy to explain, but what he did in Las Vegas was not.

Lynn and Bobby are going out to supper, and Lynn is at the body shop at 5:00 p.m. While she is sitting in Bobby's office, the phone rings; it is Ray on the phone. She calls over to Bobby and announces that Ray is on the phone and that he needs to talk him right away. Bobby takes a deep breath, walks over to the phone, and takes the phone. Lynn is sitting right next to Bobby as she hands him the phone. Immediately upon hearing Ray's voice, Bobby asks if he could call him back in two minutes. The phone call ends, and Lynn asks, "What did Ray want?"

"He needs a favor."

Lynn is puzzled but knows she shouldn't be prying into Bobby's business dealings. She grabs her pocketbook and heads out to Bobby's car, and as she does, Bobby gestures that he will be coming right along. Lynn just smiles and walks out. As soon as Lynn gets in the car, he dials Ray's number. Ray is calm, cool, and collected. Ray asks if everything is in order for the next event. Bobby's reply is "Yes, I have confirmed the day, time, and the date with Hank, Terance, and Jeremy."

Ray replies, "Then I'll see you all in Las Vegas?"

"You bet."

A tingle goes through Bobby's body. It is time for an excuse to get out of town.

Chapter 9

Jeremy Shrinks Receives a Phone Call and Gets Ready to Go

THE PHONE CALL comes early Monday morning just around the time Jeremy is getting out of bed. The voice on the phone is clear, direct, and friendly. A time, place, and schedule are discussed, and Jeremy and the caller enjoy friendly exchanges. Jeremy hangs up the phone, and an emotion of excitement rushes through his mind. It is now time for Jeremy to begin enjoying a little bit more of life. It is time for him to be with his special friends and lose himself in a very exciting and different world. He walks over to his locked closet in the empty room in his trailer. He keeps the key hidden in a pair of socks in his sock drawer. He opens the door and looks at the leather suit bag hanging on the closet pole. On the floor is a white box. On the shelf above the closet, there is a box in which Jeremy stores his cosmetics. Jeremy just looks at the contents in the closet for a moment and thinks to himself, *Other than my special friends in Las Vegas, I am the only one in my miserable world that knows what this is all about.* While looking at the closet's contents, he sees an image of someone on a stage performing for a large audience; the audience was completely overwhelmed by the performance.

To him, it's absolutely clear what he needs to do. Just thinking about it gives him extreme joy and motivation. He's going to a place where he is no longer the down-and-out store clerk. It's a place where he can enjoy a wonderful and enlightening experience with people who accept him for his character and principles. He begins his packing routine, which includes bringing enough clothes and toiletries to last him for fourteen days. He'll withdraw some cash from an ATM when he's on the road. Jeremy doesn't need to explain where he's going or what he's doing to anyone, including his low-life girlfriend who couldn't care less if he's around. He does, however, worry about his daughter, Marie, whom he will be conversing with via his mobile phone. Jeremy often thinks about Marie being so far away from him. It makes him feel very vulnerable and insecure knowing what an underachieving life has done to him. Ultimately, he would love to make Marie proud of him.

Maybe with this trip, with help from his friends, he may find his way to becoming someone special. Jeremy's innermost dreams are not that far from reality. He is blessed with a very unique voice and a very bright mind. He just needs someone or something to help him with his God-given gifts, and maybe then he will be able to bring enjoyment to his life. Suddenly, Jeremy snaps out of his dream world and returns to the kitchen, grabs a large Post-it, and writes on the pad: "I will be gone for about fourteen days. Take care of the dog. I'll see you when I get back. Jeremy." He sticks the Post-it on the refrigerator door. He loads his stuff into the Ford Falcon, checks his wallet and cell phone, and takes one last look around the dump he lives in and leaves. It's December 26, 2009. The trip should take him around twenty-two hours of driving time. He should arrive at his destination on December 28, 2009. A much different world awaits him when he arrives.

Chapter 10

Terance Best Receiving His Phone Call

TERANCE'S EXCITEMENT LEVEL has risen to new heights since he received his phone call. His agenda for the next two weeks will be completely different from his fast-paced business life. He often wonders why he does it. What makes somebody like him drop everything to participate in these unorthodox events? He wonders about it for a moment and keeps coming to the same conclusion time and time again. He's obsessed with accomplishing something he has no control over. It puts him on the edge the more he gets involved with his obsession. His obsession is something no one on earth would expect someone like Terance Best would even think about, particularly when it evolves being in the company of a group of misfits.

Thinking about all of his advantages, one would think that would be enough, but it's not. All of his accomplishments and good fortunes have, one way or another, been under his control, with the exception of this one very secret endeavor that he participates in Las Vegas. His principles, work ethics, and compassion for helping people have never let him down. The more he gave, the more he got back; and the harder he worked, the luckier he got. His life has been a quintessential bowl of cherries. So why then, he wonders, does he dress up in an emerald-studded jumpsuit and compete against fifty or so people just to end up losing? Losing is not something that he's not used to.

Terance once thought it was the mystique of it all, but as time passed, he realized it was something else attracting him to participate. He now believes that something else has something to do with the obsession he shares with his secret friends.

He knows he has no chance of ever winning the competition. So then what is it that draws him to Las Vegas? Terance believes that when he is in the company of his friends, something mystical happens. He can't describe what it is, but he knows that it energizes him. He believes that he and his friends share a common mission.

This trip will not be via his private jet, nor will there be the welcoming entourage waiting for him at airport. This trip will be different. Terance will drive downtown to the central parking garage, park his BMW in the long-term parking area, walk two blocks to the Hertz rental agency, and rent a Chevy Malibu, which he will drive to his out-of-the-way public storage facility, where he keeps his secret belongings. He will then drive to the Fort Myers airport, where we will park the rental car in the long-term parking lot. His flight was prearranged via the Internet. He has his boarding pass in hand, and it's just a matter of boarding the plane. The hardest part of this ordeal will be fabricating reasons why he will be out of town to Terri, his friends, and staff. In the past, it was easier, but now he has scores of people who depend upon him, and it's getting harder with each trip. He knows he has to be very careful about how he describes the reasons for his absence. Being well known to business travelers, he has to have an explanation for why he's where he is. He comes up with a very simple explanation: he's working on a very special deal with some very eccentric people who wish to stay anonymous. They meet in very offbeat places at unlikely hours of the day or night. His excuse includes the need to spend lots of time with them working out the details of the deal. He tells his staff that this deal could possibly end up being too much for him to handle or the best thing that could happen. Terance hates making up stories, but for now, it's what he needs to do until he is ready to tell Terri about his secret life. He's anxious to bring this part of his life to closure.

At breakfast, Terance told Terri that his eccentric clients have beckoned him to Nevada for another round of talks, including site inspections for this outrageous deal. Terance acts skeptical about the whole thing but comments that he has already put so much into this deal that he cannot back out. Fortunately, these trips only happen once a year, and Terri knows she can get through it. Terance is very, very special to Terri. He's given her a lifestyle way beyond her wildest dreams and, more importantly, a caring and loving relationship. She is extremely happy. And for this, she will wait with open arms for his return. Terance needs to get going. There are people who will be waiting for him.

Chapter 11

Hank Hunk Receives a Phone Call and Gets Ready to Go

THE DAY HAS finally come for Hank. He received his phone call from his friend last night. He was jubilant the moment he opened his eyes this morning. He quickly gets ready for his trip. While shaving, he looks in the mirror, and he wonders why he gets so much attention from people around him, particularly women. His looks don't impress him even though he looks a lot like the legendary Elvis. He is consistently reminded by his likeness from movies and Elvis paraphernalia his father has scattered all over the house. In Hank's mind, there must be hundreds of other guys his age that look like Elvis. He, however, hasn't met any of them other than his friend Bobby. Hank's lure to Elvis is not routed in his similar looks or the music. It's something deeper than that. There's something numinous that drives him to Las Vegas to compete against men twice his age. He's convinced that he may in fact possess Elvis's persona, passion, and charisma. If he could improve his voice and choreography, he could be a dead ringer for Elvis. Unfortunately, he hasn't been able to improve his performance. With a little help, this trip could be a pivotal point in his life.

Jeremy's voice is perfect. It's similarity to Elvis mesmerizes Hank. The fact that Jeremy looks nothing like Elvis doesn't matter. Hank doesn't watch Jeremy's performance. He closes his eyes and listens to Jeremy's beautiful voice and imagines that it's Elvis singing to him. When Hank watches Bobby Shrimp move across the stage, he sees Elvis not Bobby. Hank recalls watching a video of the young Elvis Presley performing with the Jordanaires on *The Ed Sullivan Show*. It left an everlasting impression. When Bobby is on the stage, Hank is concentrating on Bobby's choreography and hand movements and believes that if Bobby had Jeremy's voice, he could be the number-one impersonator. Hank feels he needs to watch Bobby's moves very closely and listen to Jeremy's voice very intensely in order for him to move up in the competition. Just thinking about what Jeremy and Bobby have to offer him makes his trips to Las Vegas worthwhile.

It's 6:00 a.m., and Hank's ready for breakfast. His mother and grandmother are busy in the kitchen making breakfast for him. Hank's grandma looks over at him and greets him with a big "Good morning, Elvis. I hope you had a good night's sleep."

Hank's mother and grandmother think they know what he's up to but don't have all the details. They think it has something to do with Elvis, but they're not sure exactly what it is. He could be involved in an Elvis fest but not as a participant. Hank keeps everything very low key; thus, he feels it's best to let things remain a secret. He doesn't know how Kayla or her family would react if they knew he was up on the stage with a bunch of wannabe Elvis Presleys.

Everything was packed in the car the night before. He'll say good-bye to his grandmother and mother and give Kayla a call on his cell phone at a more reasonable time in the morning. The time and location of his rendezvous with his companions were given to him last night. His absence will be explained as a job search seminar in Las Vegas and would be spending up to fourteen days interviewing and visiting design firms in the southwest part of the country. He knows that Kayla will understand his desire to find work in architecture. Hank is ready to go. He loves driving through the desert, particularly alone. The open space, the desert heat, and the landscape excite his senses. He is very excited about where he is going and the people that he will be with. Hank considers himself one of the luckiest persons on earth.

Chapter 12

Bobby Shrimp Getting Ready to Go

BOBBY IS ALONE in his office at the body shop organizing work assignments for the mechanics for the up-and-coming weeks ahead. He's extremely meticulous about the work schedules and writes everything down with easy-to-understand instructions. He has all the repair manuals to describe how long each repair should take. He leaves phone numbers of the customers. Bobby also writes detailed instructions for his part-time secretary/bookkeeper, Irene. Irene will happily work full time while Bobby is away. In her mind, she's the boss when Bobby's away, even though Bobby has not assigned that responsibility to her; he lets her think she is. The ultimate responsibility goes to Jesse, who willingly takes it on as testament to how much he cares about his brother and the body shop.

The mechanics, Bobby, Irene, and Jesse, all get along like one big family. Bobby has a way of making everybody feel important. No one ever quits. Bobby has natural managerial skills even though he never took a class at tech school for business practices. It all seems to come very naturally for him. Having a very down-to-earth, trusting, and good-hearted nature also helps. His disposition is what makes him so attractive to the people around him. All his employees welcome his presence. His customers keep coming back because they trust and like him. Most of the car dealers in the area refer their customers to him. His enthusiasm for his work precedes him. He's passionate about it. He's also very generous. He's been known to charge less for the work if he knows the person can't afford the going rate. Bobby is one in a million. He is constantly giving to others, but now it's time for him to be on the receiving end. He takes care of all the little details for his companions and trusts they will be at the meeting place at exactly the time he told them. He finishes making all the arrangements at the body shop and will now need to explain to Lynn why he'll need to be out of town for the next fourteen days. He simply explains that he is going to a car repair/restoration convention in the southwest part of the state and will be meeting up with some fellow body shop owners. The group will be visiting some state-of-the-art repair shops, and he'll also be on the lookout for vintage cars to restore, preferably another 1953 Cadillac convertible. Time is of the essence, and Bobby needs to get going.

Chapter 13

Jeremy Shrinks on His Way to Las Vegas and Thinking All the Way

JEREMY GRABBED A bunch of sandwiches, snacks, cookies, candies, and drinks when he left the convenience store the night before. He filled his cooler with ice cubes and ice packs and placed everything in descending order of consumption during the trip. The breakfast food was on top, the lunch food was in the middle, and his supper was on the bottom. The snacks were in the pockets on the outside of the cooler. Jeremy took along maps just in case he had to make a change in his plans due to weather conditions. The maps were arranged in the order of the states that he'd be passing through. Oklahoma is on the top followed by Texas, New Mexico, Arizona, California, and finally Nevada.

Jeremy is a creature of habit. He always prepares himself for unforeseen conditions. He's been like that all of his life. He wants to know where he is at all times while he's driving, how long it will take him to get to his next destination, how many miles it will be, and about what time he will arriving. His ex-wife would nag him to no ends about his traveling habits. He could not understand why she felt that way. It drove him up a wall. In his mind, it was the only way to go, particularly when you're trying to arrive somewhere at a specific time. This made all the sense in the world to him. He was once was tempted to buy a handheld GPS for his car but for some reason didn't follow up because he felt he would only use it once in a great while. However, he now wishes he had one. He's taking a big chance driving his "over the hill" car on such a long trip. Being a compulsive worrier, he consistently thinks about what could go wrong with the car—overheating, a flat tire, engine seizing up, and brake failures. There's nothing he can do about it now because he's on his way, and he's traveling alone with his insecurities, cooler, maps, and idiosyncrasies . . . what a way to travel.

For a moment, Jeremy wonders why he is putting himself through all this. He knows he doesn't have a chance in hell at finishing in the top ten after his recent failure of finishing thirty-fifth out of forty. He couldn't believe it. He knows he sounds just like Elvis. But for some reason, the judges didn't give him any credit for his extraordinary voice. This has been really bothering Jeremy for some time. It's not that Jeremy wants to win the competition; it's much more than that. There's something deep down inside Jeremy's perceptive mind that compels him to take these trips, compete, and be humiliated by the results of his performance. The truth of the matter is, Jeremy is actually looking for Elvis. He wants to see him there up on the stage in real life. He imagines himself as Elvis but is immediately withdrawn from his thoughts when he looks at his pitiful face in the mirror. If it's not him, then he will settle for someone else.

Life has not been good for Jeremy, and for that matter, life was not that good for Elvis dying at age forty-two. He wishes Elvis didn't die so young. Jeremy imagines how wonderful it would have been if he had a chance to meet Elvis and sing along with him. How exciting it would be to know that somewhere, Elvis's exact double is waiting to be discovered.

At this moment, Jeremy feels he is thinking too much about what could be when he should be thinking about what is immediately in his future. He is very excited about meeting his friends in Las Vergas. He enjoys their company and knows that they see something very special in him. There is a kinship he feels when they're together. Maybe they're also looking for Elvis?

Jeremy is now driving on Route 40 heading west. His car is the oldest one on the road. People passing him look at him and shake their heads as they whiz by. He pays no mind to their actions. He is on a mission, and there is nothing that will distract him from his mission.

Being alone on the road, or for that matter being anywhere alone, never bothered Jeremy. He spent most of his childhood alone. He played by himself in his living room. He loved building things. His mother bought him car kits, airplane kits, and miniature house kits. Jeremy was able to put them together in no time without looking at the instructions. He was in fact happy to be alone. People his age intimidated him, particularly the girls. He had no luck with the opposite sex when he was young, not that he had much success when he got older. The girls in school constantly ridiculed him to the point of getting an inferiority complex. Someone like him with a brilliant mind and a vivid imagination should not have had an inferiority complex.

All the other cars are passing him at over 80 mph. He should be paying attention to his driving rather than thinking about his past. Jeremy has his portable tape deck in his car plugged into the cigarette lighter. He feels he needs something to comfort him, settle him down, and take the worry off on what might go wrong with the car. He presses the play button on the tape deck and listens to the beautiful voice coming out of the cassette player's speakers. Jeremy starts to settle down as he looks around at the great expansion of land and thinks to himself how lucky he will be if the car makes the trip without incident.

Chapter 14

Terance Best on His Way to Las Vegas

IT'S A CLEAR, warm, and beautiful day for the month of December in Coral Gables. Terance will make the forty-five-minute drive to Fort Lauderdale via Route 95, where his paraphernalia is kept in a secret storage space next to the Fort Lauderdale airport. He arrives at the storage building at 6:45 a.m., punches in the access key code into the keypad, and drives to the door that leads to his ten-by-five-foot storage space. The lock on the rolling door is opened with the unmarked key on Terance's key ring. He turns on the light and looks at the trunk sitting on the floor next to a freestanding wardrobe. He carefully removes a leather suit bag from the wardrobe rack and one small carry-on case from the trunk. He checks the contents of the suit bag and the carry-on case to confirm everything is in good condition. He locks the storage room door and takes the suit bag and the carry-on bag to the car. The carry-on case is placed on the driver's side of the Malibu, and the suit bag is hung on the hook over the rear passenger's seat window.

It's now time to driver to Fort Myers International Airport via Route 75, also known as Alligator Alley. It's 7:15 a.m. The ride will take one hour and forty-five minutes with no traffic. With traffic, the ride could be two hours plus. Terance gives himself ample time to make it to the airport.

The trip becomes interesting after he passed by the town of Weston. This is where the wilderness begins. He loves the everglades. It's entrancing how it seems to go on forever into the horizon. The canals along the side of the highway are populated with fishermen in their bass boats. Beautiful birds are perched on trees along both sides of the canals, and every once in a while, he spots an alligator sunbathing on the banks. Terance loves nature; he cherishes its existence and wants to see it preserved for the generations to come. As a developer and contractor, one would think that Terance would be at odds with the conservationists and environmentalists, but that is far from the case. Terance has been very vocal toward preserving the natural environment, and it's for that reason he chose to be a developer. His projects have always received the highest acclaims and awards from public agencies, regulatory authorities, and nonprofit trusts. They recognize his sensitivity to the natural environment. Choosing a site to develop is done with extreme sensitivity. Understanding the value of sustainable land development and green building design is his key to success. He's committed to improving the quality of people's lives through environmentally sensitive land planning and innovative design. He's committed to his mission and is willing to accept less profit in the name of preservation. The entire team of architects, landscape architects, planners, and civil engineers are all committed to his mission. To ensure that everything goes in the right direction, he participates in the planning and design process from the very beginning of the project to the end. He never compromises his commitment to improving and protecting the natural environment. When completed, his projects add more to the ecosystems than when the land was undeveloped. Terance is very proud of his accomplishments, which include developing in urban areas that offer brown fields and large areas of previously developed underutilized buildings. Reducing the amount of hard services with permeable landscaping, vegetated roofs, and water features is SIVLE's goal for all of its commercial projects.

Driving north on Route 75, he passes through Naples and Bonita Springs. As he does, he can't help but notice all the gated communities that have sprung up along the highway and wonders if maybe Florida is getting overdeveloped. The next exit will be Corkscrew and then onto Ben Hill Drive. The last ten minutes of his drive take him past South Florida University and finally to the entrance to the airport. The entry road is a long sweeping drive to the terminal. The car will be parked in the long-term parking lot. He heads to the terminal with his carry-on bags, passes through security, and walks down to gate 5D, where he will board Jet Blue flight 514 to Las Vegas Nevada. It's now 10:30 a.m. His boarding pass was downloaded and printed out on his laptop in his office the night before. Traveling light, except for some cash and credit cards in his wallet, is the routine for his special trips. He looks like the quintessential businessman on his way to a business meeting or conference. How surprising it would be if people around him knew what he was really up to. The flight will depart at 11:20 a.m. and arrive in Las Vegas at around 3:00 p.m. Terance takes a seat at the gate, opens his newspaper, and scans through the paper quickly, stopping only at something that interests him. He pays no attention to the people around him and tries not to draw any unwanted attention. He feels somewhat vulnerable in the airport, fearing that he may run into someone who knows him and thus having to explain why he's in Fort Myers airport. Finally, he hears the flight boarding sequence over the gate's address system announcing his flight. He booked a seat in the rear of the plane in order to be one of the first passengers to board the aircraft. When his seat number is called, he quickly moves to the front of the line and hands his boarding pass to the gate attendant, purchases a set of headphones, and makes his way onto the plane. The suit bag is stored in the coat closet at the front of the plane, and the carry-on bag in the storage apartment above his seat. Immediately upon taking his seat, he sighs a breath of relief. There will be less pressure on Terance from this point on. As the attendants go through the emergency procedures, Terance drifts off into a deep thought, and it's only when the plane turns onto the runway and begins to pick up speed that Terance bounces back to his present state of mind.

Flying has always been very exciting. His eyes are glued on the ground. As the ground begins dropping below the plane, the more exhilarated Terance feels. Flying high above the ground, he wonders, could that someone he's looking for be somewhere down there? During the flight, Terance thinks about what lies ahead of him in Las Vegas. This year needs to be special. Time may be running out for him and his companions. It's a very stressful situation, which does not include the desire to win the competition but rather the ultimate experience to be present when the miraculous event happens. He's convinced that at least two of them share his passion for the event. He once tried to induce them into elaborating why they competed but backed off at the last minute. Terance was involved in a very enlightening conversation with two of his friends at which time they implied that they were not there to compete to be the next Elvis but rather they were *competing for Elvis*. To put it in context, Terance believes that he and his friends are attracted to the competitions by the expectation that they will bear witness to Elvis reincarnate. He will finally appear before them alive and breathing. It's this prophecy that keeps Terance coming to Las Vegas.

Chapter 15

Hank Hunk on the Way to Las Vegas

HANK IS ON his way, with the car packed with all the stuff he will need for his fourteen-day trip. He checked things out two or three times to be sure he had everything. Lately, Hank has been having trouble remembering things and has been writing a lot of notes down on Post-its as reminders. It seems he's been forgetting a lot for a guy his age. Hank dismisses his problem as a condition of an absent-minded professor who has too many things on his mind to remember every little thing. As soon as he settles down, his memory will come back, so he thinks.

Hank will drive the T-Bird to Las Vegas, navigating with his handheld GPS. A small CD carrier is in the passenger seat along with some snacks for the trip. The gas tank was filled the night before, and the oil and tires were checked, and now everything is ready. Hank's route will take him to Las Vegas via the San Bernardino Parkway, west to Route 15 through Victoria Ville, the Mojave National Preserve, and finally into Las Vegas. The trip is 280 miles plus or minus. It will only take around four and a half hours if he takes it easy and stops for lunch along the way, which he plans to do. Hank loves driving through the desert.

The desert has always been something special. When he was a teenager, he often visited his cousin Alan in Costa Mesa. Alan had a bungalow not far from Laguna Beach. They would spend weekends together. The fun part of his visits was driving Alan's pickup truck out to the desert with his two dirt bikes strapped to the truck's flatbed. Each trip, Alan could come up with new and exciting destinations where they could raise hell on their bikes. The desert air at dusk was rejuvenating. The cousins really enjoyed their time together. Those days have passed. Alan got married, and that was the end of Hank's bike-riding partner. They still see each other often but not to ride bikes. Kayla, Hank, Alan, and his wife, Jill, get along great. Hank is very tempted to bring all three of them with him to Las Vegas.

As Hank drives along Route 15, he recalls the time when he met his Las Vegas companions. Hank seems to recall that they were taken in by his likeness to Elvis. The competitors were standing around a bar at a lounge where the competition was being held. They somehow just found themselves next to one another and began talking about the event. The conversation was very light at first, but somehow it got very intense when each of the men began describing their disappointing performances. An immediate comradely developed between them. Hank surmised that misery loves company. The men left the bar and sat at the booth and began talking about their frustrations. Jeremy, the oldest of the group, complained that even with a perfect likeness to Elvis's voice, he knows he will end up at the top of the pack because of his looks. Bobby never expressed the same disappointments. Having Elvis's moves down pat didn't make a difference. It always goes unrecognized by the judges. Hank, the youngest of the group, with his mirror-image looks of Elvis, never got above the middle of the pack. Although it sounded like the men were complaining, the fact of the matter was they really didn't care about winning or losing. They accepted their fate that there was no possible way that either of them could win. However, there was something about the passion for the event, or more precisely the people in or around the event, that made it worth being there. With their newfound friendship, their gatherings went on routinely; and at one of their get-togethers, they attracted the attention of a very different kind of person.

Hank vaguely remembers how Terance became part of the group. He recalls that Terance was standing nearby with Bobby, Jeremy, and Hank and an older guy named Ray Cook. He was more of a friend of Bobby than Jeremy; at the time, all three men were talking about their performances. Hank couldn't help but notice that Terance was listening in on their conversation. Bobby, who is the most engaging of the group, looked up at Terance and offered him a big smile and an invitation to sit down and join in on the conversation. At first, Terance seemed reluctant to do so. Fortunately, Bobby's good nature convinced him to join the group. He sat down and went right into a dialogue about how he observed how they had perfected certain parts of Elvis's act and the trouble he was having with his performance. During the conversation, Bobby asked Terance why he kept performing. Terance was slow to respond. He couldn't offer a good answer other than to say that it had something to do with why everyone else was there and left it at that. Hank recalled Terance saying, "Too bad the three of you couldn't combine your talents and God-given looks into one person." The conversation then turned back to the reasons why they compete. Jeremy openly talked about Elvis's impact on his life and how he would have loved to do a duet with him. Jeremy sadly explained that there was a time when he thought his voice could bring him bigger and better things, but that time never came to be. Bobby also felt akin to Elvis. He really liked Elvis in his early years when he appeared with this Jordanaires on *The Ed Sullivan Show*. Elvis's audience attraction, his wholesome image, his youthfulness, and of course, his outrageous moves onstage were a big attraction for Bobby. Elvis was an anomaly. Elvis was a humble, good-hearted kid, blessed with good looks, a great voice, incredible music talent, and a very likable personality. Without those virtues, Elvis could not have become the king of the music industry and changed the direction of music forever.

Elvis's passing at a very early age was truly a tremendous loss to all four men. They would have loved to have seen him in person. Now all that they can hope for is that there is another

Elvis out there waiting to be discovered, and when he appears, they want to be present. Terance was moved that the men were talking openly and intimately about their inner feelings. He explained that he was attracted to Elvis because of his spirit and good-hearted nature. Terance felt that he could relate to Elvis's persona, and not to describe himself, he decided to introduce a third party to the conversation. This someone Terance described was very successful, very wealthy, and very happy. He was lucky and used his good fortune to bring happiness to others, just as Elvis did with his voice. Bobby, Hank, Jeremy, and Ray listened emphatically to Terance. He described how he felt that one day he would witness the reincarnation of Elvis, and that's why he competes. Terance brought to light the same attractions that Bobby, Jeremy, and Hank brought to the group. They were good-hearted, good-natured, and compassionate people, and that is what bonded them together. Now the attention was on Hank. Hank explained that he felt akin to Elvis even though he didn't know much about him other than the music and the movies he had watched at home. He explained that his mother and father often sang Elvis songs when he was young. Hank loved to sit around and listen to them sing and play their guitars. Hank wished he could have met the young Elvis. At the end of the conversation, the five men toasted to finding Elvis.

Chapter 16

Bobby Shrimp on His Way to Vegas with His New Friend

BOBBY HAD ALL his clothing apparel and paraphernalia packed the night before. He brought the stuff to his office at the body shop the night before so he wouldn't be seen carrying a suit bag. The travel arrangements to the airport were also made the night before. The Community Cab Company was scheduled pick him up at 6:00 a.m. at the body shop. He'll leave his car parked in the rear lot for the duration of his trip. Bobby is waiting at the window inside his office and watching for the cab to arrive. The cab comes promptly at 6:00 a.m., and Bobby walks out to the rear of the cab and waits for the driver to open the trunk. The carry-on is placed on the floor of the trunk, and the suit bag is carefully placed on top. The driver closes the trunk, and they are off to Logan airport. Bobby simply says "American Airlines," and the cabbie waves his hand and presses the meter button. It is still very dark in Massachusetts in late December and extremely cold. The trip to the airport would take only twenty-five minutes. Flying is not one of Bobby's favorite things to do, and he wants to get the plane trip over with as painlessly as possible. He hates to fly. If he could, he would have preferred to drive to Vegas; however, the five-day trip by himself during the winter months was not a good option. The lesser of the two evils was to fly.

Bobby immediately strikes up a conversation with the cabbie. Mostly small talk, but friendly talk nonetheless. Stirring up conversations with complete strangers all the time, no matter who they are, comes easily to him. People always seem to be very comfortable around him. His welcoming smile lights up his entire face. His persona is subtle but extremely inviting. The two men talk about everything under the sun. When the cab pulls up to the curb at the American Airlines drop-off, it seems like Bobby and he are long-lost friends. The cabbie's willingness to help Bobby with his luggage is a genuine gesture of his gratitude for his engaging passenger. Bobby pays the forty-five-dollar fare and tips the cabdriver ten dollars. They say their good-byes with compassion bestowed to caring friends. With his boarding pass in hand, he moves quickly to the security gate. The line at gate has minimal travelers. A warm greeting is offered by the security guard, and she smiles continuously as she looks at him and his driver's license a couple of times before she hands them back. He removes his shoes, watch, and belt and places them with his keys into the plastic containers and then places his carry-on suitcase and suit bag on the conveyer and moves through the security gate. The luggage and plastic containers are retrieved at the other end of the security area, where he puts on his shoes, belt, and watch and gathers up his bags and heads for gate 24, where his plane is waiting. It is a surprise to see how many people are waiting at the gate at this time in the morning. After a short wait at the gate, the attendant begins calling the row numbers to board the aircraft. Bobby always made sure he didn't reserve a seat over of the wings. This time he reserved a window seat in the back of the plane, a very good location for him. The window seat will help with his claustrophobia while on board. As soon as the plane starts gaining altitude, his vertigo kicks in. This, along with the claustrophobia, is nerve racking.

Soon after settling in, he is interrupted by a very good-looking middle-aged woman who takes the seat next to him. She is blonde, slender, very well built, and professionally dressed. She looks like a lawyer or a high-end professional. She looks around fortyish and has blue eyes, slight facial features, and beautiful clear skin. Bobby couldn't help but stare. He looks over at her and immediately says hello with the friendliest smile he could muster up. She returns a slight smile, nods her head, and clicks on her seat belt. The plane is filling up quickly, and the sun is now high enough in the sky to make everything visible around the runway. The attendant closes the hatch door and begins demonstrating the emergency equipment. Bobby thinks, if the plane were to go down over Rockies, what value would a seat belt have? Being obedient, he listened and watched the demonstration every time he flew. He was glad when it was finally over.

The plane pulls away from the gate and is on its way to the runway under its own power. As soon as the plane reaches the end of the taxi lane, the pilots power up the engines, and the plane starts making its way down the runway at full throttle. It's this moment when Bobby feels the most stress. As stressed out as he is, he doesn't want the attractive passenger sitting next to him to notice his lack of composure. As soon as the engines start to roar, his heart starts beating faster and faster. As the plane races down the runway, the tighter Bobby squeezes the armrests with both hands. He waits for that thump that signals the plane has left ground. The next few seconds are always the most difficult. He notices that no one talks when the plane is taking off. Maybe they share his fear of flying. If something were to happen at this point in time, it would be *adios amigos*. He contains his anxiety by looking out the window and staring down at the islands in Boston harbor. As the plane banks to the right and heads west, his fears begin to subside. The ride so far is as smooth as could be. The plane rises to six thousand feet and then to nine thousand in a matter of seconds. Relaxation only comes to Bobby when the seat-belt light is turned off and people begin moving about in the cabin. Lunch was scheduled to be served on this flight; this gave him something to look forward to. When the plane reaches thirty-five thousand feet and the seat-belt light is turned off, Bobby is finally able to compose himself and begins to read his newspaper. He quickly turns to the weather page to see what the temperature is going to be in Las Vegas today. To his delight, the forecast is for clear skies and seventy degrees—unseasonably warm for Las Vegas this time of year. He then turns to the attractive passenger sitting next to him, who, fortunately for Bobby, is not paying any attention to him during the takeoff. With an energetic smile, Bobby comments, "It looks like a beautiful day in Las Vegas. The temperature has been unusually warm for this time of year, and I understand it's going to continue for the next couple of weeks. What a treat!"

Her response is welcoming and friendly. "I am so happy to hear that. I get very depressed at this time of the year—you know what I mean, short days, cold weather, long nights, all that New England stuff."

Those kinds are the conditions that don't bother Bobby one bit. As a matter of fact, business always picks up for him when there are snow and ice covering the roads. Bobby doesn't want to explain why he feels this way, so he explains that he feels the exact same way. He also mentions how much he hates flying to which she replies, "I try not to fly unless I absolutely have to."

Bobby responds, "I think I have claustrophobia."

She responds, "I think I have claustrophobia and vertigo too."

Bobby replies, "You don't say. I think I have vertigo too."

Their conversation elevates to a level that makes Bobby forget about his flying discomforts. He is really encouraged to know that somebody else feels just as he does about flying and that someone happens to be a very attractive woman. Bobby notices that she has some paperwork on board and is reading through it prior to their exchange. Not wanting to pry into what she was doing, he asks if she had made the trip to Las Vegas before. Her reply is that this was her first visit, and she is really looking forward to it. Bobby asks if the trip is for vacation or business. Her answer is it is going to be both business and vacation. She glances down to her paperwork and then at Bobby and asks if he had been there before. Bobby replies, "I've been going to Las Vegas for the past seven years, and once in a while, I go twice a year."

She asks if he has friends, family, or owned a business in Vegas. Bobby replies, "It's part business but mostly friends."

She then asks if Las Vegas is really like it's made out to be. Bobby replies, "It's overwhelming, the lights, the buildings, the people—it's all just very exciting."

Bobby feels that now would be a good time to ask her if it is more business than vacation but wants to pose the question with an assumption rather than a question. Bobby comments, "I guess from the looks of things, you're going there more for business."

Her reply is somewhat mysterious. She answers, "You could call it that, but I hope to have more of a vacation trip than a business trip."

Bobby doesn't know how to follow up with that response without doing some serious prying. So he leaves it at that and says, "I think you're really going to enjoy it. It's different, it's exciting, and there are all kinds of people, extravagant hotels, great restaurants, and terrific shows. You'll have a great time. It took me a little time to get into the culture of Las Vegas coming from Boston. As you know, people are not quite as friendly as they are in other parts of the country."

"I've noticed that the Bostonians are not as open or engaging as I've been accustomed to in other parts of the country."

Her response makes Bobby think that she isn't from Boston. He wants to ask where she is from but hopes she would offer that information in her own time. To get a response, Bobby mentions that he has lived in the Boston area all his life and realized that the people were a bit standoffish but adds that once they get to know you, things are much different. Taking notice of his remark, she comes right out and says she had lived in Kentucky, Florida, North Carolina, and New Hampshire.

"Wow! That's a lot of places to have lived."

She explains that her father was a major in the air force and was stationed at airbases up and down the East Coast.

"Are you living close to Boston now?"

"No, I'm not right now, but I would like to be. I live in Portsmouth, New Hampshire. It's close to where I work."

Bobby asks where she works.

"I work for Northwestern Mutual at the headquarters building."

Since she offered that information, Bobby asks what she does there, and she explains that she is an actuary. Bobby knows what that is. Bobby says that he is in the automobile repair business and explains that he had his own business. Through all the small talk, he realizes that he never introduced himself. He stops in the middle of his sentence and says, "I'm sorry I never introduce myself. My name is Robert Shrimp. My friends call me Bobby."

"My name is Catherine. My friends call me Kate." Kate asks, "What kind of repairs do you do?"

"My body shop specializes in car restoration."

She immediately responds with "That's very interesting. My father was heavy into cars. He had a 1964 Thunderbird that he restored and proudly drives around in his gated community in Florida."

Bobby asks, "Do you like cars?"

"I love cars, particularly the older ones."

Bobby is beginning to get cautious about how much he revealed about himself to his new acquaintance, nor is he in no way trying to pick up Kate. She seems too sophisticated for that. Not to mention the complications that would arise if she suggests that they get together in Las Vegas. It may be difficult for him to try to explain the Elvis thing. But on the other hand, she, being from the South, now living in Portsmouth, New Hampshire, and with a father who's a car buff, it's possible the Elvis thing wouldn't sound so crazy; but then again, she looks too sharp to be attracted to a bunch of guys dressed up in white rhinestone-studded jumpsuits trying to be someone that they're not. Much to Bobby's surprise, she asks Bobby what hotel he was staying in.

"I'm staying at the Bellagio."

Bobby knows the competitions always take place at the lower end of the strip, away from the high-end hotels; thus, he revealing his hotel was not a problem. Kate responds, "Well, I guess we are going to be neighbors because I'm saying at the Bellagio."

Bobby is getting a little bit overwhelmed thinking that this very attractive woman is being exceptionally friendly to him. He has no other way to respond other than to say, "What a coincidence. I hope we run into each other."

Kate's response is "I hope we do."

At this point in time, the attendants are taking lunch orders. Bobby is worried that there is still one and a half hours left in their flight, and he is afraid if he continues the conversation, he might end up putting his foot in his mouth. When the meals come, Bobby thinks this would be a good time to break from the conversation; and after they finish, he would pick up the newspaper and pretend he is reading.

When Bobby and Kate finished their meals, Bobby takes up reading the newspaper, and Kate goes back to underlining paragraphs on the papers she brought on the plane. Not wanting to end the conversation awkwardly, Bobby thinks that it would be good to reopen the dialogue when they are close to landing.

Bobby looks down at the newspaper and wonders who would be waiting for him in Las Vegas. He doubts his ability to juggle his time between Kate his friends. Kate immediately overwhelmed Bobby. She seems so nice. However, at this point in time, there are some facts left unanswered. He has no idea if she's married, divorced, or has a boyfriend. He doesn't want to overreact to what he thinks is an opportunity for a relationship based on a trivial conversation he had with a passenger on an airplane. He wouldn't want to cause problems with his relationship with Lynn. Although he is also not sure of his future with her either, this is a catch-22 position. He thinks maybe he's reading much more into this encounter than he should be. To get his mind off Kate, he begins to plan his itinerary with his friends in Las Vegas.

As the ringleader, he sets up the agenda for his companions and makes sure everyone has a good time. This trip needs to be special because he feels the attraction may be wearing off for the other men and possibly him too. He hopes one of them will do well at the competition. It would mean so much to all of them. Somehow, Bobby can't see that happening unless something exceptional was to take place, and it wouldn't necessarily have to happen to them. It could be a newcomer to the competition, someone with Hank's looks, Jeremy's voice, and his stage charisma—a cloned Elvis. This would bring closure to Bobby's mission. However, at this moment, Bobby feels like a high-school boy with the best-looking girl in the school sitting next to him, and he doesn't have the courage to ask her out. If Bobby only knows what is in store for him.

Chapter 17

Jeremy Shrinks Arriving in Las Vegas, What a Trip

JEREMY IS NEARING the end of his journey. The trip was not delightful, particularly when he was driving through the mountains and desert in his junk box Falcon. At times, Jeremy felt anything could have gone wrong; the brakes could have failed, the engine could have overheated, the transmission could have seized up, or he could've gotten a flat tire. Anything could have happened. Luckily nothing did. The first stop was in Albuquerque, New Mexico, some five hundred miles into his trip. He spent the night in a cheap motel, enjoyed the sandwich he packed in his cooler for supper, and went to bed. He was up at 6:00 a.m. to get an early start on the four-hundred-mile drive to Lake Havasu City.

When he arrived in Lake Havasu City, he decided to splurge and spend the night at Hampton Inn. Before checking in, he treated himself to a Big Mac at McDonald's. To avoid anyone seeing him drive up in his shabby-looking car, he parked the car at the rear of the hotel. The Hampton Inn offered their guests a free breakfast, which he took full advantage of. Before leaving the hotel that morning, he made sure he had a couple of extra containers of milk, some extra muffins, a few hard-boiled eggs, and a copy of *USA Today*. These were extra treats for the remaining three hundred and fifty miles of his trip. The muffins, hard-boiled eggs, and milk would be Jeremy's lunch for that day. The last leg of his trip will take him around seven to seven and a half hours, depending on if he stopped to eat, fill the gas tank, stretch his legs, or whatever. The trip should take no more than eight hours. He left Lake Havasu at 7:30 a.m. He estimated that he should be on Route 95 N no later than 10:30 a.m., and his arrival in Las Vegas would be 3:30 p.m.

At precisely 3:45 p.m., Jeremy arrives in Las Vegas, Nevada. This was great planning on his part. His meeting with Bobby, Hank, Ray, and Terance isn't until 6:00 p.m. There's ample time to check into the hotel, get settled in, and maybe take a nap or walk around Las Vegas and enjoy the sites, the blue skies, and the droves of tourists.

Upon arriving at his hotel, Jeremy goes through the same tactics of hiding his car in the back of the building. He stayed at the Best Western a couple of times before and liked the friendly service and location, which is walking distance to the strip. The Best Western is a perfect location, and the cost of the room is real cheap. It all fits nicely into Jeremy's budget, which is minimal at best. Jeremy has to keep it that way because the little money he has will be needed to be expended when he is with his friends. He always requested a room on the top floor to avoid having people over his head. Being an extremely light sleeper, the slightest noise wakes him up.

The lobby at the hotel has a fifties look to it, which Jeremy likes. He feels very comfortable in this environment. The other bigger, newer, more expensive, and glamorous hotels don't interest him at all. He feels at home here. He is comfortable with everything, the accommodations and the friendly greetings he gets from the young people behind the reservation desk. As Jeremy approaches the desk, a young woman looks up at him and says, "Sir, are you checking in?"

Jeremy replies, "Yes, I have a reservation. I'm Jeremy Shrinks."

The young woman looks at her computer screen and then looks at the Jeremy and says, "Yes, Mr. Shrinks, I have you arriving today. You have a room on the top floor next to the exit stair as you requested. Is that OK?"

Jeremy replies, "That's perfect."

Being next to the stairs would allow Jeremy to come and go without being noticed. This would work out fine for him when he needed to use his car. The young woman asks Jeremy if he needs help with his luggage. Jeremy replies, "No, thank you, I can handle it myself. I only have the carry-on and a suit bag."

The young woman responds, "Thank you, Mr. Shrinks. The breakfast starts at 6:30 a.m. and ends at 11:30 a.m. Would you like a wake-up call?"

Jerry's responds, "No, thank you. I'm an early riser."

With that, Jeremy takes his carry-on case and suit bag and heads for the elevator. When he arrives at the elevator lobby, he is in the company of an older couple who is waiting for the elevator. From previous visits, Jeremy noticed that most of the hotel guests were somewhere in their late sixties to late seventies; they were probably just like him, all on very limited budgets. They exchange smiles and get on the elevator. He holds the elevator door open so they could get in. While pressing the button for his floor, he asks what floor they were on, and they reply, "The third floor."

As they leave the elevator, the old man comments, "Enjoy your vacation."

Jeremy replies, "And you as well."

Jeremy thinks it was peculiar that they thought he is on vacation, being alone, maybe so, but not likely. He enters his room and looks around. The room is perfect for him, a top-floor location, next to the exit stairs; thus, there is only one wall that sound could pass through. What makes it even more desirable is the headboard of the bed is on the stair wall. Not that loud noise would be a problem being the place filled with elderly people like him, who would be in bed asleep by 9:00 p.m. The suit bag and the carry-on are placed in the closet. The jumpsuit is left in the suit bag for fear that the cleaning girl would see it.

Being very tired from his long drive and all the stress just thinking of all things that could have gone wrong, he thanks God he made it in one piece. Thus, he decides to take a nap and then later on take a walk out to the strip to look around.

Jeremy lies down, and while looking up at the ceiling, he wonders if the other guys would show up as planned. Having no contact with any of them while he was driving to Las Vegas, he has no guarantee that they would be there; but from past experiences, he finds his companions to be completely reliable. Jeremy received his phone call from Bobby Shrimp; thus, he knows that he would show up. He is sure that Bobby had made contact with the other guys because Bobby is the guy that kept everything going and everyone together. His meticulous planning, reliability, and structured lifestyle are very appealing to Jeremy. Bobby is the one who would take care of all the details. Jeremy is much too lazy to take on that kind of responsibility. Bobby always made Jeremy feel very comfortable as he did with Hank, Ray, and Terance, but there is something special about Bobby that draws Jeremy closer to him.

Dozing in and out of sleep for around an hour is very relaxing. It is now around 4:30 p.m. and time for a walk. Jeremy leaves the hotel via the exit stairs and walks through the parking lot and onto the street that led to the strip. The walk to Las Vegas Boulevard took approximately fifteen minutes. The fountains at the Bellagio Hotel are first on his agenda and then a look at the gondolas in the man-made canal at the Venetian. A walk through the casino to check out the action would be next. He, of course, would not gamble. The strip during the daytime is exciting, but it isn't at its high point. That happens at dark, when all lights are illuminating the buildings and the marquees. That's when the strip takes on a spectacular look. Wandering around from one hotel to the other took about forty-five minutes, and then he walks over to the hotel where the group is scheduled to meet. The meeting place is none other than the Voodoo Lounge at the Rio Hotel. There they would talk things over drinks. Being curious about how long it would take him to walk from his hotel room to Voodoo Lounge, he checks his watch to see what time it is before he starts walking back to his hotel. When he arrives back at the hotel, he looks at his watch and sees that it took him exactly twenty-five minutes. Knowing that he has to meet the guys at 6:00 p.m., he plans on departing from his hotel exactly 5:30 p.m. This would get him at the lounge five minutes early. Jeremy is getting very excited.

Chapter 18

Terance Best Arriving in Las Vegas

TERANCE'S FLIGHT TOOK approximately four and one-half hours, and it is now circling over Las Vegas on its approach to the McCarran International Airport. Looking down as the plane flies east of Las Vegas Boulevard, he could easily identify the giant footprints of the Bellagio, Mandalay Bay, Caesar's Palace, Circus Circus, and all the other hotels and casinos along the strip. These sites are easy for Terance to recognize, for he had made many a trip to this destination over the past ten years. He marvels at the extent of the development that has taken place over the past twenty years. The hundreds of millions of dollars that is needed to package a project like the Wynn Hotel, the Bellagio, and the Mandalay Bay Resort and Casino is second nature to Terance. The trips are always very exciting whether it's for pleasure with his companions or for business when he's visiting his Las Vegas office to meet with his staff, real estate brokers, contractors, or public officials.

Terance enjoys being on the bottom floor of every one of his new projects and personally visits every site his development team feels has possibilities for success. Las Vegas is the new city in the United States he felt would undergo the most growth, and from the air, it looks like a sprawling megacity surrounded by an endless desert. It's a unique environment. During an everyday drive down Las Vegas Boulevard, one could easily reach the desert edge with in a ten-minute drive. Terance spends most of his time in the older sections of Las Vegas during his business trips. It's this section of the city that inspires him the most. These areas are on the fringes of the desert. Terance's choice of development locations has always been in the preexisting developments within the old city. The old antiquated or vacant buildings are ideal for his redevelopment projects.

His company's objective is to demolish or recycle the nonperforming buildings and replace or renovate them with energy-efficient green buildings. There are numerous sites in Las Vegas that have these opportunities, and that's why his satellite office is here on the edge of the desert that provide large areas.

The pilot alerts the attendants to prepare for landing. Terance raises his seat back to the upright position and looks down as the land begins to rise up to the plane. The routine is very simple. He will grab a cab at the McCarran International Airport and go a few blocks to the Mandalay Bay Hotel, where he will be staying for the next fourteen days. The Mandalay Bay was chosen as a precaution to avoid a perchance meeting with an associate or a business acquaintance. SIVLE Corp makes a practice of booking all their rooms for their employees and consultants at the Bellagio Hotel. Fabricating a story on why he is in Las Vegas alone if not for business is not what Terance wants, particularly if a perchance meeting were to occur when he is in the company of his diverse companions.

The cab ride to the hotel took just a few minutes. Terance stands impatiently behind the cab and waits for the trunk to open. The driver comes around the back of the cab and removes the carry-on suitcase and the suit bag out of the trunk. Terance pays the fare and gives the cabdriver a very generous trip, which prompts the driver to reach out and shake Terance's hand. They shake hands, and Terance smiles and says, "Have a nice day," and quickly walked into the hotel lobby. A medium-range suite was booked; a V Suite was his choice. If, for some reason, the guys needed to come over to visit, they would not be overwhelmed by his accommodation, or so he thought. Upon receiving his key cards, he immediately takes the elevator to his room, which is on the fifteenth floor of the hotel.

The room has a large living room, one bedroom, a sitting area, two bathrooms, a wide-screen TV in the living room and bedroom, a small bar area with stools, an under-counter refrigerator, and a large desk with a chair. The bathrooms are embellished with polished marble walls and floors and generously stocked with extra large white towels, all kinds of shampoos, soaps, body lotions, slippers, and a terry-cloth bathrobe. It all seems very accommodating to Terance, although he is used to much more luxury during business trips. It is early afternoon, and Terance wants to go down to the lobby to secure a safety deposit box for his cash. It is warm for December, so he grabs a light lunch at the cabana lounge at the poolside. Finishing his meal quickly, he returns to his room to read a book that he brought with him from home. He is very anxious to see who would be at the meeting. Terance is hoping it would be all of them. He is in for a surprise.

Chapter 19

Hank Hunk Arriving in Las Vegas

SO FAR, HANK'S trip from Los Angeles has been trouble-free. He made one stop at a restaurant in Barstow, California, and was in great spirits. He did, however, have a minor incident at the restaurant. The incident occurred in the dining room when someone shouted, "Look, it's Elvis, he's alive."

Hank hasn't experienced the Elvis recognition for some time. His young friends, particularly the girls, used to tease him about his mother and grandmother calling him Elvis. Even though they had no idea who Elvis was, it just sounded funny to them, and so the name sort of stuck with him for a while. When he was in his midteens, the Elvis thing fell by the wayside. And soon after, his nickname "Hank" prevailed. "Hank Hunk," or "Hank the Hunk," as some the young girls called him, was fine with Hank. To avoid being ridiculed by people who knew who and what Elvis looked liked, he would go out of his way to alter his looks. There was a time in his life when he tried a beard, a goatee, a mustache, and finally he settled for just parting his hair down the middle and wearing nonprescription horn-rimmed glasses when he was traveling outside his social circle.

The incident at the Barstow restaurant was instigated because that morning, Hank left the house in a rush and forgot his horn-rimmed glasses and didn't comb his hair with a part down the middle. Hank's good nature and engaging personality usually results in a friendly resolve from the gawking strangers. He's always been able to turn a hostile situation into a positive one with his God-given charm. He left the restaurant shaking hands and getting pats on the back from the would-be gawkers who wished Hank well. Feeling very good about the friendly resolve with the gawking strangers, he is now looking forward to his rendezvous with Bobby, Jeremy, Ray, and Terance. After leaving the restaurant, he continues on Route 15. He is now about halfway to Las Vegas. The entire trip should take him about four and one-half hours. The route will bring him through the Mojave Desert and finally to Las Vegas. While driving through the desert, he begins thinking about his four companions.

Thinking about each of them individually resulted in some unknowns. First, he wasn't sure if Jeremy was ever married. He never mentioned a wife. He did, however, talk about his daughter. Terance and Ray wore wedding rings, so that sort of confirmed that they had wives. Bobby may have been married, but he never mentioned a wife, past or present. Hank had no idea what each of them did for living. The closest he got to what they did was that Jeremy was in the retail business, and Bobby and Ray were in the car business. Terance was somewhat more mysterious. Terance didn't come right out and say what kind of business or profession he was in, but he did at one time hint that he was self-employed. Hank really didn't care if they were married or what they did for a living. His attraction to them was their good nature and interest in the competition. It seemed to Hank that his companions felt that he could aspire to being a good Elvis impersonator, not a great one, but good one. His friends Jeremy and Bobby had very special talents. Jeremy's voice was perfect, and when he performed, Hank would close his eyes and imagine that it was Elvis standing in front of him singing the song. Unfortunately, when Hank opens his eyes, he see a balding, skinny, old-looking dude with a black wig and false sideburns making a fool of himself upon the stage; the image is gone. The one thing Hank surmised about Jeremy was that he seemed to lack ambition. He was the follower of the group. Bobby, on the other hand, looks something like Elvis. His height, weight, hair, and facial features kind of fit into the Elvis image. It's Bobby's body rhythm, his presence, and his way of moving around the stage that set him apart from the rest of the competitors. Bobby's choreography is so perfected that once on the stage, you would swear it was Elvis. Hank often visualizes Bobby's routine on the stage. He sees the stage in darkness. A single spotlight moves across the stage, and Bobby appears with his back to the audience. He begins to move around, and as the music picks up, he begins his choreography, all the time with his back to the audience. Hank knew Elvis's moves from watching his movies and documentaries. He watched them over and over again. He even took dance lessons to improve his body rhythm, but he couldn't come close to Bobby. If Bobby had Jeremy's voice, he would have been a very good Elvis, not the greatest one but a very good one. Terance, on the other hand, really didn't have anything that came close to Jeremy or Bobby, except that his height, weight, and facial features were close to Elvis, but not enough to leave an impression.

Terance was a mystery to Hank. He seemed to be in Las Vegas for some other reason other than the competition. It was like he was on a trip to find himself or maybe to forget who he was. Hank couldn't figure out what it was, but there was something drawing Terance to Las Vegas. What Hank knew was that he was a dead ringer for Elvis, and with a little luck, a lot of practice, and a lot of time studying other performers like Bobby's, he could easily move up to the top and win some money. The money would be used to get things going in his life. He enjoyed competing but was concerned about how long Bobby and Jeremy could endure the letdowns. Hank knew he could keep going on but feared that Jeremy and Bobby may stop competing. If that happened, he would also stop coming to Las Vegas. To Hank's delight, while together, they feed off one another in a very positive way. They can ridicule one another and laugh about it without any feeling of discontentment. They seem to possess Dean Martin, Frank Sinatra, Sammy Davis Jr., Peter Lawford, and Joey Bishop's comradery when they dominated Las Vegas. They were the rat pack, some very big stars poking fun and making wisecrack jokes and colorful remarks about one another all for the enjoyment of the audience. It seems that Hank's companions do a little bit of the same thing, but it's not for an audience but rather for themselves. It's a very special relationship that Hank hasn't experienced other than with them. Hank believes that if he had met Bobby, Jeremy, Ray, and Terance under other circumstances, the magic and attention would not have been there. The passion to find Elvis is what draws them together. They somehow recognize their passion in each other, and it gives them a common cause, a reason to be in Las Vegas, and a desire for something miraculous to happen.

Hank is now driving on Las Vegas Boulevard and passes the Mandalay Bay Resort and Casino and is headed westward to Circus Circus, where he has a reservation. There will be ample time for him to check in, check out his room, and take a walk around the town. The excitement of the city inspires Hank. His knowledge of architecture tells him it's all fake, the Eiffel Tower, the sphinx, the gondolas, Disneyland, etc. The city grew up too fast to have its own image, so it borrowed multiple images from all over the world. And it's to attract the crazy ass tourists and gamblers who swallow it all up. However, there is another side of Hank that feels that these incredible hotels and casinos and the culture of Las Vegas somehow bring everything together and attract millions of people of all walks of life to enjoy the city. It's a virtual mixing pot of cultures, nationalities, the young, the old, the rich, the poor, and everyone in between. Hank imagines all these people looking up at these unbelievable buildings and saying, "Holy mackerel, I can't believe someone actually built these things in the middle of the desert!"

Hank arrives at his hotel and parks his car in the garage. He usually tries to avoid the valet parking to save money. He grabs his suit bag and his carry-on and heads into the hotel lobby through the side entry door. The lobby is packed with people. He goes in unnoticed. The reception desk has lines of people waiting to check in. Hank gets in one of the lines and notices two well-dressed women looking at him up and down. They look somewhat polished. They could be high-end hookers.

He puts their age at early to middle forties. He tries not to look straight at them but notices that they are staring at him. They are also saying something to one another while they are looking at him. He smiles, and they both smile back at him. Their line moves forward, placing them side by side with him. Now they're close enough for him to notice the gold jewelry, expressive clothing, and how well groomed and perfectly made up they are. They could be wealthy tourists. The closer they get, the more intense their glances become. It is getting a little bit uncomfortable. Finally, one of them breaks the ice and looks Hank straight in the eyes and says, "Hello, my name is Shirley, and this is my sister, Jackie, and you, I presume, must be Elvis."

With that, Hank smiles intensely and lets out a catchy laugh, which makes the two sisters and the rest of people standing next to them laugh with him. It's an instant bonding moment. The sisters are making overtures to Hank, and he is ready to oblige. It is now Hank's turn with the receptionist, who is acting very cool about the whole incident until Shirley says, "Elvis is staying with us."

Shirley's comment made the receptionist go from being very serious to be very giddy, all the while looking at Hank very intensely. Shirley and Jackie check in and wait for Hank to do so. When he finished, Hank walks over to the two sisters standing in the lobby and gives them each a big smile and introduces himself. "I hope you'll be having a good stay."

And with that, Shirley says, "We sure will. We hope to see you around."

Hank takes his luggage over to the elevator lobby and presses the button, hoping he could get there before Shirley and Jackie do. Luck is with him; the elevator comes, and he and some other guests get on. The other guests are carrying all kinds of stuff in their shopping bags. The room is on the fifteenth floor of the hotel. It has a great view looking down the strip and across the way to the magnificent hotels that punctuated Las Vegas Boulevard. After taking a quick shower, he gets dressed and combs his hair. This time, he parts his hair down the middle and puts on his horn-rimmed glasses and a polo shirt. He has a couple of hours to kill before his meeting with his friends. Hank spends the afternoon looking at buildings from the inside and out. Some are still under construction. The unfinished buildings held his attention for a much longer time. He wonders, if things could change in his life, maybe he could be the lucky architect that designed one of these glittering towers. Maybe things will change for Hank.

Chapter 20

Bobby Shrimp
Arriving in Las Vegas

THE PLANE IS making its approach to the McCarran International Airport. The pilot announces that they will be on the ground within ten minutes and requests the flight attendants to take their seats. Bobby feels relaxed when he sees the ground below and the beautiful weather outside the airplane. He's torn; he's glad the stress of flying is finally over but is unhappy that Kate and he will be departing company. It feels somewhat awkward. He would like to come right out and ask Kate if she would like to meet up with him when they are in Las Vegas but lacks the confidence to do that. There were many women interested in him throughout his life; however, none of them fell head over heels for him. Bobby has a very appealing look. He's tall, well built, and boyishly handsome. His appearance is somewhat on the earthy side. One's first impression is that he's a macho kind of guy. However, after just a few minutes of conversation, his charm comes out, and he becomes extremely appealing. His rugged looks have a touch of vulnerability that goes unnoticed at first glance. It's his vulnerability that is very comforting to the women in his life. The women who saw through Bobby's rugged macho appearance were rewarded by his good-hearted character. These women loved him dearly, and those that didn't dropped him like a hot potato.

Bobby tried to suppress his vulnerability by acting a bit tough with some of the people in his life but fortunately not all of them. Lynn saw Bobby's flaws and all his good qualities and immediately fell for him. Lynn had lived alone after a six-year divorce and was subject to all kinds of men, some almost good, some bad, and some very bad.

Lynn took Bobby up on the offer to repair her car from the damaged he witnessed at this mother's house. Lynn handed Bobby the insurance adjuster's estimate, and then she and Bobby went outside to look at the car. After looking over the damage very carefully, he made it known that the car would look brand new when the work was finished. Bobby and Lynn returned to his office through the body shop repair area. Lynn was very impressed by the size of the operation and the busyness of the mechanics. It looked very organized. All the mechanics were dressed alike. They wore shirts with the word "Bobby's" on the back. As Lynn walked by, each mechanic looked up and smiled at her warmly. They all seemed very proud to be part of Bobby's operation. Bobby showed no signs of ego, which was also impressive to Lynn. When they arrived back at the office, Lynn asked if she could use the phone to call a cab. Bobby replied, "Don't worry about a cab. Where do you want to go?"

Lynn answered, "I work at General Electric on Western Avenue."

Bobby replied, "No problem. I'll have my brother, Jesse, give you a lift."

Bobby's bookkeeper immediately called Jesse over the loudspeaker system and asked him to come into the office. When Jesse arrived, he smiled at Lynn and asked Bobby what he needed. Bobby first introduced Jesse to Lynn and then said, "Lynn needs a ride to work. She works over at General Electric."

Lynn and Bobby said good-bye. While Jesse and Lynn were driving to GE, they had an engaging conversation. At which time, Lynn said, "Jesse, your brother, Bobby, seems like a great boss."

Jesse replied, "Lynn, he is more than a great boss. He's a great friend to everyone in the shop."

Lynn wanted to come right out and ask Jesse if Bobby was married but didn't need to because Jesse made a remark that Bobby would make a great catch for some lucky woman. With that, Lynn began thinking how she could arrange a date with him. She really didn't need to make any effort because when Jesse got back to shop, Jesse announced that the good-looking woman with the Toyota may be interested in him. So Bobby took that as an invitation. One thing led to another, and Bobby asked her out on date, and they've been together for the past four years. However, in those four years, Lynn has never hinted about marriage. Bobby feels that Lynn may be still affected by her past difficult divorce.

The plane finally lands, and Bobby feels awkward again. Not wanting to be so bold as to say, "Maybe we can get together for a drink," he remains quiet. It's time to depart the aircraft, and Bobby doesn't know what to do. Kate stands up next to Bobby to grabs her luggage. Bobby lets Kate move out into the aisle of the plane. Bobby reaches up to give Kate a hand with the carry-on suitcase she is having trouble removing from the overhead compartment. Reaching over Kate's shoulder, he pulls the suitcase out on the compartment. He then retrieves his carry-on, and the two of them walk down the aisle. Kate is in front of Bobby.

Being confused, nervous, and feeling very insecure, Bobby knows something needs to happen if they are to continue their conversations. It would have to be Kate's assertion, not his. He begins to feel more vulnerable than before. He tries to guess how Kate would say good-bye to him: "Well, Bobby, you have a nice day now," or would it be "Enjoy your stay and don't lose all your money in the casinos." Any one of those comments would single a brush-off.

Kate walks off the plane without looking back or saying a single word to Bobby. His confidence sinks to the point where he thinks he isn't even going to get a good-bye at all. Bobby is used to these kinds of letdowns. It seems he always lost the opportunities to continue a relationship with a classy woman. Bobby lets Kate walk ahead of him to avoid an embarrassing situation if in fact there is someone waiting for her in the terminal. After a few minutes, Kate is outside, and Bobby is licking his wounds.

To avoid feeling sorry for himself, Bobby feels he should turn his attention to what is in store for him in Las Vegas. The expectation of seeing his companions immediately lifts his spirits, and he is getting back to feeling good about himself. Picking up the pace, he begins walking briskly toward the ground transportation area when he hears a voice to his left side.

"Bobby, are you taking a cab to the hotel, or is someone picking you up?"

The voice is Kate's, which takes him by surprise. Kate's question is very sincere because of her acknowledging that someone could in fact be picking him up. It is all very innocent but very effective. Bobby looks over Kate with a beaming grin and says, "I'm not being picked up. Would you like to share a cab?"

Kate replies, "That would be great."

Bobby and Kate grab the first cab in line at the sidewalk. They load their luggage in the trunk. Kate makes a remark about Bobby's suit bag, "Don't see much of them around anymore since casual Friday became casual Monday through Friday."

Bobby smiles and says, "It's a good way to get more stuff on the plane without checking it in."

"I would have never thought of that."

They get in the cab, and off they go. Bobby leans forward toward the driver and says, "The Bellagio Hotel."

The cabdriver waves his hand in acknowledgment. Bobby asks the cabdriver how the weather has been, and the driver looks in the rearview mirror and says, "It couldn't be better. It's been unseasonably warm for this time of year."

Bobby turns to Kate and says, "Well, now that we know the weather couldn't be better, I can't wait to get to the hotel after being in Boston."

Kate replies that Portsmouth is no different and that she is looking forward to being outside. Bobby takes that as an encouragement for him to also be outside, hopefully with her. Bobby is now feeling a lot more at ease but is still not 100 percent sure of himself. He begins telling Kate that he has four male friends waiting for him. He explains that they met several years ago in Las Vegas and that they are all going to meet that night. Kate looks over at Bobby and says with a laugh, "Is this an old friends' reunion?"

Not being sure how to answer the question, he says, "Well, kind of. We met at a craps table sometime ago when I was on a roll, and as the chips started piling up, we all started buying each other rounds of drinks, and before long, these guys started pumping my enthusiasm up, and we all ended up winning money. I guess we thought we brought luck to each other. Soon after, I started running into them individually at different times and places."

Wanting to keep the group together, he planned a dinner party at an Italian restaurant so they could get to know each other. From that time on, they all became friends.

Kate asks, "How many of your friends are married?"

Bobby thinks that this is a perfect lead-in question for him. He answers, "One of them is like me, single, two are married, and one I think is divorced and has a daughter in Miami."

Kate remarks, "Divorce is no fun."

Now Kate knows that Bobby isn't married, and he knows she may be divorced. Kate asks, "You have never been married?"

Bobby answers, "No, but I would like to be."

Not wanting to ask her if she is married, he decides to change the subject and asks Kate if she is going to spend more time working or relaxing. Kate says she doesn't know yet; she would have to see how it goes and goes on to say that she isn't much of a gambler, although she does admit that she had played a couple of times but not with much luck. Bobby says that he isn't much of a gambler either. There would be some gambling in Bobby's agenda but very cautiously, and he would limit his losses to one hundred dollars a night. Bobby admits that he's been lucky and has walked away from the roulette table with close to a thousand dollars.

The cab pulls up to the Bellagio Hotel lobby entrance. Kate is overwhelmed by the size and splendor of the building. Looking at Kate, he says, "If you think the outside is something, wait until you see the inside of the hotel. It's going to knock you off your feet."

Bobby offers to pay the cab fare, but Kate wouldn't let him. She insists that they split the fare down the middle, and so they do. They get out of cab and head toward the lobby. Kate walks ahead of Bobby and toward the reception. Kate gives the receptionist her name and reservation number, and the receptionist gives Kate a packet that holds her key card and hotel information. Bobby is hoping to hear the reservationist tell Kate what her room number is, but that doesn't happen. Kate immediately turns and walks to middle of the lobby to allow Bobby to check in. Smiling at the reservations clerk, he announces, "I am Bobby Shrimp. I have a reservation."

The clerk looks at Bobby with a half smile as if she knows something is going on between him and Kate and says, "Yes, Mr. Shrimp, I have you here on my computer. I have you booked for a single on an upper floor. Do you need help with your luggage?"

Bobby replies, "No, I can manage everything myself."

The clerk asks Bobby how many key cards he needs, and Bobby requests two. The receptionist hands him his packet, and he immediately walks over to the middle of the lobby to join up with Kate. Kate comes right out and asks Bobby what room number he has.

"I'm in room 1615."

Bobby asks what room number she has.

"I have room 1715."

"You're right over my head."

"Maybe in more ways than one."

Not knowing how to take Kate's response, he just laughs and says, "You're probably right."

"Well, Mr. Shrimp, I hope to see you around."

"I hope I will be able to find you."

"You don't have to worry about that. I will make it very easy for you to find me."

They say good-bye, and Bobby walks to the elevator lobby. Their rooms are close together but not that close to cause a problem with his other activities.

While riding up on the elevator, he wonders if Lynn is back home thinking of him. Lynn has been very trusting. Things could get very dicey, so he better watch what he is doing. Bobby decides that nothing is going to happen between him and Kate. Arriving at his room, he inserts the key card, opens the door, and walks in. He immediately hangs up the suit bag and places his carry-on luggage on the folding luggage rack, checks his watch, and sees that it's 4:00 p.m. He'll take a shower, rest for a while, and then head off to his rendezvous with Terance, Jeremy, Ray, and Hank. So far it's been a wonderful trip for Bobby.

Chapter 21

Jeremy Shrinks Getting Ready for the Meeting

JEREMY IS READY to go. He's already confirmed how long it would take him to walk from the motel to the Rio Hotel's Voodoo Lounge. He'll take a quick shower, dress, and head out the door at exactly 5:20 p.m. to make his 6:00 p.m. meeting in ample time.

While in the shower, he lets the water rinse through his thinning hair and thinks about how shabby his accommodations are compared to the luxury resort hotels that his companions are enjoying. But then again, he's aware that he's one hundred times better off here than at his dumpy trailer back home in Yukon, Oklahoma.

Jeremy steps out of the shower, dries off, clears the steam off the mirror with his towel, blow-dries his hair, plugs in his electric shaver, and quickly shaves. While looking in the mirror, he thinks how quickly age caught up to him and how little time is left to accomplish the things he wanted to do. If it wasn't for his loving daughter, his life would have been a complete waste. However, there is hope, being here with the possibility that something extraordinary could happen to bring meaning back into his miserable life.

On the way down the elevator, two older women who are all dolled up for a night out on the town accompany him. Jeremy is wondering where the hubbies are then surmises that they are probably in the room by themselves watching TV. Jeremy pays no attention to them. But they seem to be staring at him for whatever reason. Maybe it's because he has a slight smile on his face that they could have taken as flattery. The elevator door opens, and Jeremy allows the women to exit first. They thank him graciously. He wishes them well and waves good-bye to the pleasant young desk clerk and begins his walk to the lounge. At first, he walks somewhat slowly and mindlessly; but after a while, he picks up the pace as his adrenaline begins to run through his body. Jeremy is hoping everyone would show up. He has no clues on what the agenda would be. He knows that he, as always, would take a backseat and be more of a listener than a conversationalist. He has nothing interesting to say. But that's going to change.

Chapter 22

Terance Best
Getting Ready for the Meeting

TERANCE'S SUITE AT the Mandalay Bay Hotel is very comfortable. The accommodations are high end; however, he's been in the highest of the high-end suites all over the world. However, for this occasion, the suite is perfect. This afternoon, he'll take a quick shower and get ready for the meeting in just twenty minutes' time. Dawdling is not one of his traits. He shaves, takes a shower, gets dressed, and quickly checks himself out in the mirror. There's always a lot on his mind, which distracts him from paying attention to his appearance. He's always on the go, except when he is home with Terri and the kids, where life takes on a whole different meaning. Oddly enough, he's a multimillionaire homebody. Tonight he'll dress semicasual-dress slacks and button-down light-blue shirt and loafers. His appearance doesn't seem to portray his reason to be in Las Vegas.

Terance can sense that he is more educated and is better off financially than Bobby, Jeremy, Ray, and Hank. Their cultural differences mean little to him. Here, they're all absolutely equal, and that's refreshing for Terance. His diverse friends accepted him for his character and principles, and for that, he embraces their friendship. Terance feels that he has been very lucky. He works sixty hours a week and takes enormous risks that turn into enormous accomplishments; nonetheless, he is humbled by his good fortune.

Terance's presence brings a sense of confidence to the group and a feeling of legitimacy to their cause. Terance enjoys being with Jeremy, Hank, Ray, and Bobby. Being with them takes his stress level miles away from that of his daily business life. While in Las Vegas, he is no longer Terance Best, the successful entrepreneur. He's just one of many friendly competitors giving it their all. Terance knows he can never finish in the top ten. Finishing at the top is not his priority. Terance compares his life to Elvis's. They were and are very lucky people in many ways. Terance's business skills came easy for him, as did Elvis's music talent. Terance admires Elvis's for his music, his contribution to rock and roll, his devotion to his mother and father, and his humanity to his fellowmen. Terance leaves the hotel, quickly grabs a cab, and heads to the lounge. What could be in store for Terance?

Chapter 23

Hank Hunk
Getting Ready for the Meeting

HANK'S BEEN KILLING time in the hotel and outside on the Las Vegas Boulevard. But now he's back in his room looking out the window at the sites below. Hank enjoys Las Vegas and would love to have Kayla come along on his next trip. Maybe next time he will. However, he's not sure how she would react to his involvement in the Elvis competition. He hopes she would understand. But then again, maybe she wouldn't. Now is not the time for Hank to be thinking about these things. It's time for him to get ready for the meeting. He quickly gets ready. He'll wear a pair of black chinos, a casual shirt, and a pair of black loafers and white stockings. This look should get him into the swing of things.

Hank is ready in just thirty minutes. He grabs his wallet and watch but has a problem remembering where he placed the key card when he came into the room. He checks his wallet, his clothes he was wearing when he arrived at the room, but the keycard is yet to be found. He also checks the dresser next to the bathroom and a large desk opposite the bed. Obviously, the key has to be in the room, or he would not have been able to get in. A slight panic is taking form because he doesn't want to be late for his meeting with Bobby, Terance, Ray, and Jeremy. Retracing his steps from the beginning at the time he entered the room should locate the key card. Every possible surface where he could have placed the key was checked out, but to no avail.

It seems the key disappeared off the face of the earth. In a last moment of desperation, he opens the closet door where he had hung his suit bag and checks the shelf above the closet pole, thinking he may have set it down when he hung the bag, but it isn't there. Panic is now overtaking him. He slides the suit bag frantically to one side, and in his amazement, there it is on the floor of the closet. The assumption is he dropped the keys when he hung the suit bag, but he isn't sure. Now is not the time to worry about things like this. He must've been in such a hurry when he came into the room that he just forgot what happened. Maybe, maybe not. It is now time to leave. Feeling much better about things, he is looking ahead and hoping he isn't going to be the first one to show up at the lounge. He is never one to hang around in bars and lounges. That would be a little bit awkward, standing there alone and waiting. Presumably Bobby would be waiting for the group to show up. Driving down Las Vegas Boulevard with his radio blasting and taking in all the sites raises his spirits. The car will be parked in the garage one block up from the Voodoo Lounge, and he'll walk the rest of the way. These next two weeks are going to be very exciting for young Hank in more ways than he could have ever imagined.

Chapter 24

Bobby Shrimp Getting Ready for the Meeting

BOBBY'S VERY ANXIOUS to meet with Terance, Hank, Ray, and Jeremy. He feels exuberated from his encounter with Kate on the plane and later on at the hotel. He's on cloud nine. Now it seems Bobby has two very exciting and wonderful adventures going for him in Las Vegas. The first one being his planned meeting with his colorful friends, and the second one is his great expectations with Kate. Bobby, however, couldn't help feeling that Kate's presence could somehow throw a monkey wrench into why he is in Las Vegas. Being able to hold her at bay while he's planning and carrying on activities with his friends may be possible. Should Kate ask about his itinerary, he could use the same excuse he gave to Lynn. Kate's not a sure thing, and Bobby knows it; the guys, however, are, and in no way would he jeopardize his relationship with them if the thing with Kate gets out of hand. Some very serious juggling may be in order. He hopes that these extracurricular activities don't throw him off course.

Planning to be the first one to arrive at the Voodoo Lounge, he gets himself ready in a flash. His attire tonight will be a pair of blue jeans, an open-collar button-down shirt, and the extra sport jacket he brought from home. He's excited being in Las Vegas, and he senses something big is going to happen.

At exactly 5:30 p.m., he'll leave the room, and the estimated ten minutes by cab to the lounge will give him about a twenty-minute lead time before the other guys arrive.

Up until now, he hasn't received any indications that any of them will actually show up. Bobby, Hank, Ray, Terance, and Jeremy share little to no communication when planning these trips to Las Vegas. They try to keep everything a secret, except, of course, for Ray. Oddly enough, the guys have never discussed why they have chosen to be out of touch with one another. They could have easily communicated via telephone, letters, or e-mails. That way, they could have confirmed their whereabouts at a precise point in time. Other than Bobby's phone calls, there is no other contact between them until they arrive at the Voodoo Lounge. Bobby surmises that they are all here under the same pretenses. It's their sense of secrecy that bonds them together. These elusive meetings are particularly exciting for Terance, Jeremy, and Bobby. Hank and Ray don't seem to share the mystique in all the secrecy. Bobby knows that Ray and Hank don't need to be as accountable as they are. Ray's wife is involved in all of his activities, and Hank is young, has little responsibilities, and no one to answer to. Thus, he could be expected to do something outrageous.

Bobby is just about ready to leave when his cell phone rings; it is Irene, Ray's wife. This is somewhat unusual because Irene has never called him before. Irene's voice sounds very distraught. She explains that Ray asked her to call him and let him know that he had suffered a major heart attack. Bobby is shocked and in disbelief. He asks Irene what Ray's condition is and when it happened. She informs Bobby that Ray had the attack two days ago, and he is recuperating at the Massachusetts General Hospital. She gives Bobby the phone number for the room and says he should give it a couple of days before he called. He asks Irene if there was anything he could do, and she says that the only thing Ray wants him to do is to keep him posted on what happens in Las Vegas. Bobby says he would call in a couple of days, and until then, he would have Ray on his mind. Bobby asks if his condition is real serious, and Irene says at first it was touch and go, but now he seems to be stable. Bobby confirms that he would call Ray at the hospital in two days, and if he can't get through, he will call her back. With that, Bobby and Irene say good-bye.

It's now exactly 5:30 p.m., and Bobby is on his way to the Voodoo Lounge via taxicab. He arrives at exactly 5:40 p.m. Immediately after paying the fare and tipping the cabbie generously, he heads into the hotel and straight up to the lounge. The turnout in the lounge is light at 5:30 p.m. Bobby's choice of seating at the bar gives him a clear view of the entry into the lounge. He orders a pineapple and Malibu and immediately takes up a conversation with the bartender. When the bartender moved to the other side of the bar to serve a customer, Bobby leans back in his chair, looks around the lounge, and takes a deep breath. He's ready for his friends.

Chapter 25

Jeremy Shrinks Arriving at the Voodoo Lounge

JEREMY ROUNDS THE corner onto S. Las Vegas Boulevard and heads to the Rio Casino, where he's anxious to meet his friends at the Voodoo Lounge. The strip is bustling with traffic, and the sidewalks are packed with pedestrians walking feverishly in both directions alongside the overpowering high-rise hotels. Remembering back some years ago when he first visited Las Vegas with his ex-wife, Karla, just before Marie was born, he recalls how things looked then. It's nothing like that now. Back in the early seventies, it was just a couple of casinos and hotels. Not that long ago, the *James Bond* movie had Bond scaling the Sands Hotel and ending up sitting in the bathroom in the hotel room. Las Vegas was a very different place then. It was just emerging from a desert frontier town with a couple of midrise buildings and a lot of honky-tonk. Somehow the craze caught on, and the city transformed itself from a small, prostitute-ridden gamblers' retreat to a vacation destination. There are still hookers aplenty if you know where to look, but of course, Jeremy wasn't interested in that. Tonight he was going to be with his friends, enjoying a very engaging experience that is not available back home.

Jeremy picks up the pace as he nears the hotel. Immediately upon rushing into the hotel, he heads straight up to the lounge. He's very anxious to see who's arrived, if anybody. Being a couple of minutes early, he thinks he could be the first one. To his delight, he immediately recognizes Bobby's jet-black hair and masculine build sitting at the bar. Bobby is into an animated conversation with the bartender and a not-so-busy cocktail waitress. Jeremy would have expected nothing less from his energetic friend who can make friends with anybody at any time and any place. Jubilantly, he heads right over to Bobby, who at the time is sitting sideways with his back toward the approaching Jeremy. As he approaches the bar, the waitress looks over toward him, at which time Bobby notices that she's been distracted and immediately swings around on his bar stool to see his oncoming friend. Bobby jumps of the stool and, with a big beaming smile, wraps his arms around Jeremy and says, "Jeremy, my man, how are you?"

Jeremy smiles and says, "As of now, I couldn't be better."

These kinds of greetings are not offered to Jeremy, except for when he is with Bobby, Terance, Ray, and Hank. It's the Las Vegas magic that does something to their chemistry. Jeremy responds, "Bobby, I am so glad to see you. Are Hank, Ray, and Terance going to join us?"

"I don't know for sure about Terance and Hank, but I know Ray will not be joining us this year. I will explain when Terance and Hank arrive. I bet they will be walking through that door any minute."

Bobby gestures to Jeremy to sit down on the stool next to him, and Jeremy happily does so; and as he does, he brushes against the young waitress standing next to Bobby who reacts with a very pleasant smile and a warm "Excuse me."

Bobby introduces Jeremy to the bartender and to the waitress and orders him rum and Coke with a twist of lime. Jeremy replies, "Bobby, it's amazing you remember what I drink."

The bartender prepares Jeremy's drink in under a minute. Jeremy settles in on the bar stool, takes a long slow drink from his glass, leans back in his chair, smiles at Bobby and the waitress and the bartender, and says, "It's so nice to be here."

While Jeremy is sitting at the bar, he listens to Bobby carrying on with the cute waitress; Bobby is talking to her not so much as a man on the make but rather as an interested friend. He's not one bit threatening. As a matter of fact, it seems to Jeremy that the waitress is trying to be very accommodating. Some guys have it, some guys don't. Bobby definitely has it, and he's so glad that he's his friend. Bobby now turns his attention to Jeremy and comments, "Well, my good and reliable friend, how is life treating you?"

"Life here is great. Need I say more?"

And with that comment, the two men raise their glasses and toast one another. Now all they need to do is wait for Hank and Terance.

Chapter 26

Terance Best Arrives at the Voodoo Lounge

TERANCE IS RIGHT on time. He arrives by taxicab at the Voodoo Lounge, graciously pays and tips the cabbie, and walks quickly into the lobby and up to the lounge. Upon recognizing Bobby and Jeremy sitting at the bar, he rushes over them, places his hands on both their shoulders, and says, "It's good to see you two guys."

With that, Bobby spins around on his bar stool, looks at Terance, and gives him a welcoming embrace. Jeremy follows suit, and the three men take their seats at the bar. They're finally together again. Terance senses that Ray and Hank are not present and mentions it to Bobby. Bobby responds, "Well, Terance, you know how it is with these young good-looking guys, particularly here in the city of heavenly delight."

Terance jokes and says, "I know all about that. You think Ray will also be late?"

Bobby responds, "Ray won't be joining us this year. I'll explain all that when Hank arrives."

Terance comments, "Maybe Hank is having a difficult time saying good-bye to somebody, if you know what I mean?"

"I sure do know what you mean. Hopefully he will be arriving soon."

Bobby turns to the bartender and orders drinks for his friend and then gestures to them to move over to the booth to the right of the bar. This particular booth has a clear view to the lounge entry. Bobby expects Hank to be coming right along, and from where the booth is, he would have a clear shot of him entering the lounge. Terance could sense that Bobby was somewhat concerned about Ray and Hank. So to lighten things up, Terance remarks, "Well, guys, it's only five minutes past six. Hank could be right outside the lobby and joyfully on his way in."

With that, the three men raise their glasses and make a toast to one another. Bobby once again looks over to the entry to the lounge for just a second so as not to seem disappointed that only Jeremy and Terance showed up. To keep positive, Bobby looks at Terance and says, "Terance, you look great. Don't you think so, Jeremy?"

"If he looked any better, there'd be two of him."

Bobby picks up on Jeremy's comment and says with a mischievous grin, "I wish during this visit, there could be two of me."

His facial expression suggests that maybe something is going on. Fortunately, his companions don't pick up on his comment, which is lucky for Bobby because he knows he'd slipped with that remark. Terance has an inquisitive grin on his face as he looks over at Bobby. It is a kind of look that suggests maybe he knows something. Jeremy is shaking his head and looking across at Bobby. Bobby is smiling and looking at his two friends as they are shaking their heads at him. All in all, it is a very good moment for the three men. Now if only Hank would arrive.

Chapter 27

Hank Hunk Arriving at the Voodoo Lounge

HANK IS RUNNING about five to ten minutes late because of his problem locating his key card and is very upset with himself for being late. Being prompt is one of Hank's many virtues. Heading east on West Flamingo Drive, he passes the Voodoo Lounge's hotel-casino and parks the T-Bird in the parking lot a couple of hundred feet from the entry. He hands the attendant in the kiosk a ten-dollar bill and drives to an empty parking space in the rear of the lot. He routinely parks his car as far away from the other vehicles so as to avoid the risk of careless drivers slamming their doors into his mint car. After locking the car, he is mindful of what pocket he put his car keys in.

Hank quickly walks past through the lobby and heads straight up to the lounge, where he immediately sees his friends Bobby, Jeremy, and Terance sitting in the booth off to the right of the bar. As he walks toward his three companions, Bobby catches a glimpse of him coming into the lounge. Upon seeing Hank, he immediately gets up, rushes over, and greets him with a warm embrace, and says, "I'm so glad you made it. You had all of us worried."

Hank, in fact, is only fifteen minutes late; however, to a group of very punctual men, fifteen minutes is a long time. Jeremy and Terance are now on their feet waiting for Hank to approach them, and when he does, they both give him a warm pat on the back and express how happy they are that he made the trip. The cute young waitress, who is watching all of this with a big smile on her face, comes over to the foursome and asks Hank what he would like to drink. Bobby responds, "Give my young friend a tequila sunrise."

The four men return to the booth and thank one another for taking the time to be together again. Jeremy and Hank admit that they have much more free time than Bobby and Terance. Terance, of course, has the least amount of free time than the other men but never lets on how important his time is. At these meetings, they give one another their undivided attention, which, to an outsider, looks completely out of context. This year, they will celebrate Elvis's seventy-fifth birthday. Bobby calls for a toast and says, "The four of us are so lucky that we're able to be with one another on this historical year. However, there is some sad news. Ray's wife, Irene, called to let me know that Ray will not be joining us because he suffered a heart attack."

Terance, Jeremy, and Hank immediately grow very sober. Bobby goes on to say that Irene is optimistic that Ray is going to pull through and that he is going to contact him in a couple of days. Bobby's companions express their sorrow over the news of their friend. Bobby then offers a toast to Ray, wishing him a speedy recovery and their success in this year's competition. They raise their glasses and toast to Ray, "Get well, Ray, and let this be our year."

Chapter 28

Jeremy, Terance, Hank, and Bobby at Graceland

THE ENGAGING FRIENDS buy rounds of drinks for each other and settle right into the groove of socializing. Hank starts off by explaining his reason for being late because he misplaced his key card in his hotel. The guys comfort Hank, encouraging him to pay no mind to being late and acknowledge how lucky they are to all be together again. Bobby, being the self-proclaimed toastmaster, immediately gives it his best shot and says, "We are all gathered here as a declaration to our friendship and our mission to find Elvis."

With that, they cheer and drink up. Bobby starts right in, jubilantly explaining what an exceptionally good time they are going to experience in Las Vegas this year. The schedule of events he has planned for his companions would be enlightening, entertaining, and motivating. The itinerary will help them get ready for the up-and-coming competition. They have been through the prep work before; however, this time, things need to take on a new direction. What they could have done, or what they should have done and why they finished where they did, doesn't matter anymore. There would be no more ending their meetings elaborating on their failures. Bobby comments, "Guys, we all know what our shortfalls are. Thus, we should not be dwelling on them. This year will be different. This will be our year. Tonight we should begin energizing one another with optimism and positive thinking."

Terance interjects by saying, "Bobby is right. Sometimes you just have to accept things for what they are and make a positive out of a negative. Life is too short to think about our failures. We are here to think positive. By the way, I think much more positive on a full stomach, so let's drink up and head out to Bobby's restaurant choice for tonight—which is?"

Bobby smiles at Terance and answers, "Interesting you should ask, my friend. I found out about this restaurant that's off the strip. I just happened to overhear these two guys sitting on the aisle across from me on the plane. One of them may have been a guy who competes, but the other guy looked much too conservative for that kind of stuff. They were talking about this restaurant called Graceland. They described it as being unbelievable, the food exceptional, the service terrific, and the motif like something you've never seen before. The place is filled with Elvis memorabilia."

Jeremy cuts in and says, "I wonder why we never heard of it until now?"

Bobby shakes his head and says, "Maybe we're not in touch because we are here only once a year."

Terance wonders, "I've been here a lot, and I never heard of the place."

"Obviously none of us have been to this restaurant. It should be an interesting experience."

"What time is our reservation?" Hank asks.

"At 7:30 p.m. It'll give us ample time to get there if we leave right now."

"How long do you think it's going to take to get there, Bobby?"

"To be honest, I don't know. I was going to ask the people at the reservation desk, but I forgot. However, it shouldn't take any more than thirty minutes."

Terance asks, "Why don't we ask the waitress if she knows anything about this place the next time she comes by?"

"I will do it."

Within a few seconds, Bobby catches the waitress's attention and waves her over to the booth and asks with an inquisitive smile.

"Do you know where Graceland restaurant is?"

The waitress looks down at him and says, "It's somewhere way off the strip in the industrial area."

"How long should it take us by taxicab to get there from here?"

"No more than a half hour."

Hank asks, "Are we dressed properly?"

"I don't know. I have never been there. I just know where it is. Why, are you guys planning on going there?"

Bobby answers, "Yeah, we are."

"Let me know what it's like. I've heard all kinds of things about the place."

Bobby responds, "OK, I'll give you a full report the next time I come by. But now we need a check."

Earlier, Bobby set up a running tab at the bar and requested the bartender and waitress to give him the bill. When the check came, it is handed to Bobby; and all three guys insist on chipping in, but Bobby refuses to let them and just leaves with it.

"You guys can pick up the next round when we get back."

Bobby pays the bill in cash and leaves a generous tip for the waitress and bartender. The four men leave the lounge and get a cab for the ride to the restaurant. Bobby sits in the front seat with the cabdriver, and the other three men squeeze into the backseat. Bobby looks at the cabdriver and says, "We're going to Graceland restaurant do know where that is?"

The cabdriver, looking straight ahead, says, "I sure do."

So they are off, and in a few short miles, the glimmer of the Las Vegas strip starts to dissipate, and the working part of the city begins coming into view. For Bobby, Hank, and Jeremy, this is a new experience, but not for Terance. As a matter of fact, Terance is very familiar with this part of the town. He's in the process of negotiating a deal to buy a rundown industrial building and is waiting for the owner's response. Hank looks out the window and says, "This is the part of Las Vegas you don't see featured in movies or in the magazines."

Terance adds, "That's right. This is the working part of the city, where everything that's needed to keep the megahotels operating twenty-four hours a day, seven days a week, and 365 days a year."

Bobby cuts in and says, "This looks like my kind of a town."

With that, they all laugh. They arrive at the restaurant in just under thirty minutes. From the outside, it looks like an abandoned 1950s warehouse. Bobby could only make out a miniscule sign over an unlit door. The sign has only one word on it: *Graceland.* The cabdriver looks over at Bobby glancing at the sign and comments, "That's not the entry door to the restaurant. You need to go around the side of the building, through the parking lot, and then you will see the entry."

Bobby thanks the cabdriver for his directions and pays the fare. Terance, Hank, and Jeremy offer Bobby money for the fare, but Bobby refuses the offer. With a big smile and a confused look on his face, Bobby comments to the driver, "I thank you again. I hope this place is good."

The cabdriver turns around and looks at the three men sitting in the backseat and says, "If you guys like Elvis and exceptionally good restaurants, then believe me, you will not be disappointed."

With that comment, all four men show signs of excitement. They get out of the cab and walk around and through the parking lot and, to their surprise, find a much more inviting entry. They notice that there are groups of people going in, with some of the groups being very large. The four men walk quickly to the entry and into the building. They are accompanied by a group of young men and women who look like they could have been on spring break from college. Bobby enters first. The waiting area inside is nondescript. The hostess asks with a warm smile, "Welcome to Graceland. Do you have a reservation?"

Bobby replies, "Yes, for Bobby Shrimp."

"Are all the members of your party here, Mr. Shrimp?"

"Thank goodness, yes."

"Then please follow me."

The four men follow the hostess down a dimly lit hall that turns a ninety-degree angle into the main dining room. The sight of the dining room all but knocks them off their feet. Hank's response is "Holy mackerel! Look at this place."

The hostess turns and smiles at Hank when she hears his comment. The four men stop in their tracks and just stand for a moment marveling at what lies before them. The main dining room has a forty-foot-or-so high ceiling with an enormous skylight, which is artificially lit from the outside. The skylight sends beams of light down into the middle of the dining room. There is mezzanine seating on all four sides, and in the middle of the dining room right directly under the skylight is a perfect replica of Graceland, with trees, grass, and a driveway with Elvis's Cadillac. It is unbelievable.

There are thousands of people sitting everywhere. There are tables on the patio, at the rear of house, along the driveway, and in the front yard and side yard. The whole thing is truly overwhelming. The four guys look in silence until Bobby says, "Now I know what the cabdriver meant when he said, 'Believe me, you won't be disappointed.'" The hostess leads the four men to a table just to the right side of the mansion. The location is perfect. Hank is wondering who had the imagination to come up with something like this. The dining room is bustling with activity. The waiters are dressed up like Elvis in one of his Hawaii movies. There are Elvis memorabilia everywhere. There are huge pictures of Elvis when he was young and when he was performing in Las Vegas. It is all done in perfect taste; nothing looks tacky or out of place. Everything is very well thought out. The whole theme of the restaurant is a celebration to the late Elvis Presley. The restaurant has a museum quality to it. It is truly unique.

The four men sit down at their table still looking around and gleaming with delight. Jeremy looks over Bobby and comments, "This place looks like a retreat for all of the fans of the greatest rock-and-roll star ever. You really outdid yourself with this choice, my friend."

Bobby responds, "Remember what Terance said earlier about thinking positive? So I did, and look where it got us."

As soon as the men sit down, a waiter immediately comes over to their table. He is a young, handsome guy with sideburns and wavy black hair. He looks like Elvis without really trying. He makes eye contact with the four men and announces that his name is Johnny. Johnny says, "I'm glad you're here with us tonight, gentlemen. Anything you need, just let me know. I can get you your drinks now, or you can wait until you order your meal—whatever you choose. As you read through our menu, you will see that the food selections are grouped into categories: large portions and medium portions. A lot of the people who dine with us choose the large portions so that they can share them. In that way, they can sample two entrées."

With that, Terance looks around the dining room and notices that most of the food on the tables look like it was probably large portions being served family style. Bobby smiles with delight and says, "What do think, guys?"

Terance responds, "Let's take a look at the menu and then see what we want to drink."

They all agree. The waiter smiles and says, "Take your time. I'll be here for you when you need me."

And that he is. He stands between the tables in the section, looking at each and every table for a patron's request. Terance comments that you don't see this kind of service anymore.

The men again compliment Bobby on his choice of the restaurant and then begin looking over the menu. The entrees selections consist of steaks, chops, poultry, and seafood. The food selections are very down home American, which complement the culture of the restaurant. The menu also describes in detail the way in which the entrées are cooked. The men are undecided, and the waiter senses their dilemma immediately. He walks up to the table and says, "Sometimes it's difficult for people to make a selection when it's their first time at the restaurant, so I would like to make a suggestion: you may want to try large portions from each category and split them four ways. I can have the kitchen prepare your orders that way so that you won't have to pass plates of food to one another, or I can have the food served family style. Whatever you prefer, I can do it."

They all agree to family style, and then the waiter comments on what the favorite dishes are. The restaurant's entrées are nothing out of the ordinary, so making a selection is easy. Once they had ordered their food, they also ordered two bottles of wine, one red and one white. They hand the menus over to the waiter and spend a couple of minutes just looking around trying to take it all in. Hank comments, "It looks like there are people eating in the house and all around the house at a big family get-together."

After pouring the wine, the waiter leaves the table and, within a few minutes, comes back with four skewers of barbecued meats, which surprise the men because they didn't order them. The waiter says, "Try this and let me know what you think."

But before they could respond, he is gone. About ten minutes later, he comes out with four cups of soup and asks, "How did you like the skewers?"

The response from all four guys is "They were the best we ever had."

The waiter doesn't place the soup on the table, so they think that the soup is probably for somebody else. But to their surprise, he places one bowl of soup in front of each of them and comments, "This is a specialty of the house. It's a vegetable soup with a little something special. Try it and let me know what you think."

They start in on the soup immediately. It is unbelievable, like nothing Terance had ever tasted. They all compliment how exceptionally good things are so far. The waiter returns in ten minutes to announce that the main course is on its way, and if they would like a salad now or when the meal is served, the choice is theirs. All four men request the salad with the meal and then ask what the salad dressing choices are. The waiter responds, "It can be almost anything you want," and leaves it at that. He then turns and looks toward the house and says, "The salad bar is in the main dining room of the house."

Going into the house is a real treat for the guys. They had all been to Graceland and wondered what the inside house was going to look like. As they get closer, they realize the house is an exact replication of Graceland inside and out, with the exception of the large salad bar in the middle of the dining room and the exit signs over the doorways. The salad bar has everything one could possibly imagine. The men bring their stacked plates back to the table just in time for the waiter to arrive with the food. Two other waiters help with placing the dishes on the table. The portions are just unbelievable, and the aroma of the food is out of this world. The entrees are cut neatly into four portions. Each plate could feed at least three people. Now the men understand why the restaurant is so popular with the young and fast. Four people could order two meals and have enough food for all of them with a doggie bag to boot. The moment of truth is upon them. The $64,000 question is, is it quantity or quality the restaurant offered? That question immediately disappeared with the first bite. The food is simply the best. The cuts of meat, seasoning, garnishes, the variety of vegetables, the sides of sauces, everything is just like home cooking, except it is ten times better. The men dive into the food with gusto and celebrate their dining experience with compliments to Bobby on selecting the best restaurant for their first meal together. The men drank, ate, talked, and joked, all the while looking around and admiring their surroundings. Bobby remarks, "At this point in time, I am so full, I should stop eating right now, but this steak is the best I have ever had, so I'm going to force myself to finish it."

The other guys all feel the same way. The waiter is always nearby to offer assistance. He comes over every now and then to ask how everything is. The reply is always the same: "The food here is unbelievably good." The waiter asks if they would like coffee and dessert. They all answer at once, "I'm stuffed."

He then asks if they would like the leftovers. Their response is they are staying at hotels. The waiter understands. Actually, Jeremy would have liked to have taken the leftovers back to his room but was embarrassed to say so. The waiter says that he would be right back with the check. When he returns, he places the check in the middle of the table. Bobby reaches over and opens the leather check holder. He goes through the check carefully and realizes the food is not cheap but certainly worth every cent. Terance asks Bobby how much the bill is. Bobby responds, "Three hundred and ten dollars."

They all pull out their wallets and place a one-hundred-dollar bill over the check. The $400 will cover the cost of the bill plus a generous 30 percent tip. The waiter comes back to the table, picks up the check and the cash, and asks if they need change, and their reply is no. He thanks them each for the generous tip and shakes each of their hands vigorously and says good-bye. They all remark to the waiter that the service is impeccable, the food is outstanding, and the decor is beyond belief. The waiter remarks, "I hope to see you all again."

Bobby answers, "You will."

And with that, the four men leave. They grab a cab and head back to the Voodoo Lounge for a nightcap. They are certainly not disappointed.

Chapter 29

Back at the Voodoo Lounge

THE MEN ARRIVE back at the Voodoo Lounge at 10:00 p.m. for one last round of drinks. They settle into the booth they were sitting in earlier that evening. Bobby glances around the room to see if the young waitress that served them earlier that evening is still working. It seems she wasn't. A cheerful older waitress approaches them and asks, "What will you have, boys?"

The guys order their drinks, and Bobby asks, "Where's the young waitress that was working the lounge at around 6:00 p.m. today?"

The waitress answers, "Which one? At 6:00 p.m., there were two or maybe three waitresses working the lounge."

Bobby replies, "She had this section. She was young, blonde, and very cute."

Immediately, the waitress answers, "Oh, that must be Irene. She got off today at 9:00 p.m. She works 3:00 p.m. to 9:00 p.m. on Tuesdays. She will be back tomorrow."

Bobby thanks her for the information, and with that, the waitress heads over to the bar to pick up the drinks for the men. Bobby reaches into his sport jacket pocket and pulls out four neatly folded sheets of paper and hands them to his friends. They immediately open the folded papers, and while they are doing so, Bobby comments that this itinerary is his best guess on what they could be doing for the next fourteen days. Bobby watches as each of them reads down the activities outlined on paper. The outline includes meeting rehearsal times, trips to other destinations, precompetition times, and preparation times for the final competition. Terance, Hank, and Jeremy don't have much to say except for Terance's remark: "Well, you seem to have thought of everything. This is very much appreciated."

Jeremy and Hank also join in to praise Bobby's efforts. Bobby obliges with "Thanks, guys, but please, if any of you wish to modify or add anything else, I wish you would do so, and please feel free to mark this up so we can talk about it the next time we meet, which, as you can see, will be almost every other night."

Terance, Jeremy, and Hank nod in agreement, fold the papers up, and place them in their shirt pockets. Bobby is about to do the same, but he takes another look at his piece of paper and comments on the scheduled trip to Reno.

"Reno has similar competitions taking place in a week."

Terance picks up on Bobby's comment and says, "That's a great idea. Maybe we can pick up some pointers."

The waitress is now back with the drinks and is placing them in front of the four men and then asks, "Will there be anything else?"

They look at Bobby for direction, and he says, "No, I think this is about it for me. What do you guys think?"

Each of them agrees that this would be it for them tonight. The waitress then says, "I'll be right back with the check," which she does immediately. Bobby is about to reach for the check but is overcome by Terance, who insists on paying the bill and does so with cash. The four men sit around talking about how much they enjoyed their experience at Graceland. Bobby offers up one more toast, "It's great to be together again, guys, but I'm kind of tired and need to get some rest."

The other three men agree. They all down their drinks quickly and briefly talk about the Reno trip. Hank offers to drive his friends up to Reno. Bobby doesn't think that would be such good idea because of the time it would take to make the round-trip ride. Bobby explains, "Maybe we should look into flying. That would give us more time to look around a bit and see if there is anything else going on that we should know about. Maybe there are other Elvis events?"

The men finish their drinks, and Hank offers to drop them off, but they all decline his offer. Hank comments that he is going back to his hotel to call his girlfriend, Kayla, and with that, they all get up at once, give each other pats on the back, and head out. They are all going in different directions, so sharing cabs doesn't make much sense. Jeremy could have shared a cab with Terance but does not want him to know where he is staying. So they all leave alone. Jeremy is exhausted from the long drive through the desert and the night's events. The walk back to the hotel isn't going to be pleasant. Terance also feels a bit tired, but it isn't from the evening's activities. Terance is an early riser and is usually in bed at 9:00 p.m. So the trip back to his hotel via the taxicab is very relaxing for him. Bobby, on the other hand, is somewhat tired but not exhausted. On the ride back to the hotel, he couldn't get Kate out of his mind. He thinks about how she might react if he were to take her to Graceland. Bobby knows he might be reading too much into his encounter, and to avoid getting disappointed, he concludes that she is in fact an acquaintance and that's all. Bobby feels that he should call Lynn and let her know that he arrived OK.

Hank walks briskly to the parking lot to pick up his car. When he arrives, he couldn't for the life of him remember where he parked it. The lot isn't that big, so he decides to walk up and down each row until he finds his T-Bird. He is hoping it isn't stolen. Finally, he sees the car parked up against the far side of the hotel. Hank has no recollection of parking the car in that location. He knows that he has a habit of parking as far away from other vehicles as possible. But this time is different.

As tired as he is, Jeremy walks briskly back to his hotel. He now, however, wishes he had accepted Hank's offer. Maybe next time he would. It is now around 10:30 p.m., and the strip is bustling with people. However, once he reaches the street where his hotel is, the numbers of people dropped off drastically.

Fortunately for Jeremy, the walk took only about twenty-five minutes. He walks quickly through the lobby, takes the elevator up to his floor, and is back in his room by 10:55

p.m. He is in very good spirits. He thinks he should give Evelyn a call, and as soon as he settles down on the bed, he dials up his home phone number. The phone rings a number of times, and then finally it picks up on Jeremy's recording greeting: "Hello, this is Jeremy. Leave your name and phone number, and I'll get back to you." The recorded greeting was taken from Jim Rockford's phone-machine greeting on the popular TV series *The Rockford Files*. Jeremy doesn't leave a message; he just hangs up and heads to the bathroom to brush his teeth, take a whiz, and get ready for bed. He gets into bed, and within a matter of minutes, he is sound asleep.

When Hank arrives at his hotel room, he immediately calls Kayla. She answers her cell phone with "Hey, Hank." She had Hank on caller ID.

Hank replies, "How's everything back in LA?"

"It's OK, but I miss you already."

Hank says, "I've been thinking of you."

Kayla says jokingly, "You had better be thinking of me, big boy, particularly when you're surrounded all those vacationing single women with the infatuation that anything goes in Las Vegas."

Hank laughs and comments, "You're absolutely right. I will keep thinking of you when I'm surrounded by all those beautiful women."

Hank goes on to say that the ride to Las Vegas was very relaxing, and he had no problems whatsoever. He mentions that his hotel is very nice, but tonight, he and his group went out to eat at an incredible restaurant. Kayla says in a sarcastic way that she is very happy for him and that she is going to head down to her family's house for the weekend. She would call Hank when she arrives in Laguna. He comments that he'd be anxiously waiting for the call, and with that, they say good-bye.

Terance gets back to his room and immediately calls home. He knows it is kind of late, but he wants to talk to Terri and let her know that he was OK. He had already brushed his teeth, washed his face and hands, and was in bed. He presses 1 on his cell phone, and Terri picks up the phone on the first ring and says, "Terance, I was wondering when you were going to call."

Terance apologizes for being so late. He explains that his discussions with the people he was meeting with went later than he would have liked it, and he unfortunately left the cell phone in the hotel room.

Terri says, "I knew something was not right because I tried calling at 6:00 p.m. and got your voice message."

Terance knows she had called because he felt the vibration on his cell phone. Terance remarks, "Things seem to be going OK here. How's everything going back home?"

"The kids are already in bed. I was just falling asleep when the phone rang."

Terance apologizes again for calling so late and says that he is very tired and would call again tomorrow. With that, Terri says, "You take care of yourselves and don't worry. I'll be back here holding down the fort until you return."

"I know you'll take care of everything, you always do. I will be thinking of you until I return." With that, they said good night.

Terance places his phone on the night table next to the bed, rests his head on the pillow, and within a few minutes, is sound asleep.

Bobby's cab arrives at the Bellagio Hotel at 10:45 p.m. The place is bustling with people. There are groups of people everywhere. Young couples, old couples, groups of men, groups of men and women, groups of just women, and groups of all kinds. Bobby is kind of hoping he would by chance run into Kate. But he doesn't. Maybe it is for the best. He would have been upset if he had seen her with some other guy. He is beginning to get a little paranoid about his overreacting to someone he just happened to be talking to on an airplane and shared a cab with. He is getting all worked up over nothing, and that is not like him. He begins to worry about his obsession with Kate. He takes the elevator up to his floor. When he arrives at his room, he immediately takes out his cell phone to call Lynn. He hits the speed-dial button, and Lynn picks up the phone on the first ring and says, "Hi, Bobby, how have you been, and where are you? I called you earlier today." Bobby explains that he had turned off his phone at the request of the seminar speaker and just now turned it on. Lynn asks, "How did it go?"

"Very good."

Lynn then replies, "I was on the phone with my mother and sister, and then I tried calling you. Other than that, that's it for me. It's freezing here. What's it like in Las Vegas?"

"It's around sixty degrees. I guess it couldn't be better."

"That's great. I'm just so happy for you."

"The hotel is just wonderful. I wish you were here."

Lynn then asks how the flight was. Bobby is somewhat nervous about answering that question. He doesn't want to get caught lying about of his carrying on with Kate.

"You know how I hate to fly, but this flight was very relaxing."

Bobby is not happy with his response because he is feeling very guilty about leaving a lot out. Lynn replies, "You take good care of yourself. I wish I could talk longer, but I need the get up at 6:00 a.m. tomorrow."

"Of course, you do. I will call you again at an earlier time."

With that, they end the conversation. Bobby goes into the bathroom, washes up, brushes his teeth, puts on a T-shirt, and gets into bed. He turns off the light on the night table next to the bed, closes his eyes, and spends the next couple of hours thinking about Kate and then finally falls asleep.

Chapter 30

Jeremy Shrinks Getting Around Town

JEREMY IS UP early after his night out with his friends. He takes a quick shower, gets dressed, and heads down to the hotel restaurant. The free buffet breakfast is a delight. He usually treats himself to coffee and a muffin at the convenience store before he begins his shift. This morning, however, Jeremy will be enjoying the hotel's buffet with everything from scrambled eggs to cornflakes without having to work.

He grabs a cup of coffee and a container of milk. He doesn't like the small cream containers. Jeremy prefers a lot of milk in his coffee, and he also has a habit of drinking a glass of juice while standing in front of the juice dispenser and refilling it when it's empty. He carries his coffee and juice to an empty table and heads right over to the buffet and fills his plate with everything available, which includes eggs, cereal, fruit, Danish, sausages, and waffles. The waffles are made in the waffle iron at the end of the buffet table. The food is taken to the table at the far corner of the room so as not to be noticed. There he takes a sip of coffee and looks around the room at the other guests sitting around him. His first impression is that it looks like a nursing home or an assisted-living facility. He then begins to wonder what will become of him when he is their age. He's now fifty-eight and will be fifty-nine in March. Unfortunately, he doesn't have a penny to his name, nor does his girlfriend, Evelyn, who mostly sponges off of him. His only consolation is that his daughter, Marie, could help him out if she gets a good job; however, he really doesn't want to depend on her for his well-being. He realizes that he's totally responsible for his predicament. Consequently, in his later years, it will have to be up to him to make things right; and at this point in time, things don't look that good for old Jeremy. His insurance benefits will end when he retires, which is not that far away. His voice is his only hope. It would get him some extra cash, but now he realizes that he needs more than Elvis's voice to cash in on the competition.

To avoid getting himself totally depressed, he decides to change his train of thought and now begins to think about what's up next with his companions. After finishing breakfast, he heads out to the back of the restaurant and walks around the pool. The pool area looks OK but not great. He didn't pack a bathing suit because he wasn't planning on using the pool. He thought he could just hang out in his cutoff blue jeans and get some sun and maybe get a little tanned before the big competition. Visiting some of the newer hotels and casinos just to see how the other half lives was on his list of things to do. This would need to be done with some caution because he doesn't want to run into Bobby or Terance and have to explain where he is staying. With Hank, it wouldn't matter. Hank is young, a free spirit, and doesn't seem to be affected by all the glitz. Hank would be a good choice to hang around with. Jeremy is caught up in an awkward situation. He wants companionship but feels that if he looks outside the group for it, he could end up being the center of attention, which would not fare well for him. Being very protective of his low-life lifestyle, he feels he needs to keep a low profile while he's in the company of his friends. His conversations are at a minimum so as not to expose himself. Fortunately, their secret behavior includes their personal lives back home.

When his walk around the pool ends, he heads back to the dining room, picks up a cup of coffee, a container of milk, a copy of *USA Today*, and heads back to his room. Once there, he tries to call Evelyn again, but there is still no answer. It's a beautiful, exceptionally warm day in Las Vegas, and Jeremy wants to go somewhere and do something different. He decides to go out to the parking lot to check on the car. The trip to Las Vegas left a big coat of dust on which someone wrote across the rear window "wash me." So Jeremy decides to do just that. He goes back into the lobby and asks the reservationist where the nearest car wash is. She tells him to go two blocks south to the Mobile gas station and buy eight gallons of gas so that he could get a car wash for two dollars. That sounds perfect to Jeremy. He drives to the Mobile station, buys ten dollars' worth of gas, and takes the Falcon through the automated car wash, which does a decent job of cleaning the car. Now with the car a bit cleaner, he can drive without feeling the least bit embarrassed. Most of the people who look at it think it's an antique. There are lots of people in Las Vegas driving around in antiques, and Jeremy seems to fit right in. The exterior of the car could pass for one; however, the interior is ripped to shreds and has a distinct odor of motor oil. This would not be the norm of a restored car. Nonetheless, the outside is in not that bad a shape, if you overlook the faded paint and the rust under the front and rear bumpers.

While driving down the Las Vegas Boulevard, he gets the urge to drive by the high-end hotels. As he passes by the Bellagio, Mandalay Bay, Caesar's Palace, the Excalibur, and the Venetian, he wonders if his three companions are staying in one of those plush hotels. He wishes he had the money to do so. He drives by two enormous construction sites and wonders to himself, *Where the heck are all the people going to come from to fill these hotels?* Will it be like the housing boom of years 2008 and 2009, where developers overbuilt apartment buildings, condos, and retail strip malls, and then the balloon burst, leaving empty buildings scattered everywhere for years? Jeremy knows it is going to happen again.

These predictions worry him, not for himself, but rather for his daughter, Marie, who will be looking for a job after graduation. As Jeremy drives around, he begins to sing. His voice is so much like Elvis's that even he is mesmerized by it. If only he could have cashed in on his gift, he wouldn't be in the situation he's in now, and he could have been more help to his daughter. He feels sorry that he let her down. Maybe, he thinks, this time will be different. But what changes will he have to make to change his life drastically? He begins to feel like a loser again. He needs to get hold of himself and do as Terance says: Think positive.

Chapter 31

Terance Best
Looking for an Opportunity

TERANCE IS UP early this morning. The night before, he placed his room-service menu on the door latch before going to bed. A pot of decaf coffee, two soft-boiled eggs, toast, and orange juice were his choice for breakfast. A 6:30 a.m. shower, and he is ready for the day. At exactly 7:00 a.m., the breakfast arrives, and he enjoys it while watching the news. Recalling his wonderful experience at Graceland restaurant the night before, he couldn't help thinking what it would cost to build something like that; being the businessman that he is, he wonders how much one could gross each night and what the profit would be. Thinking about things like this all the time isn't unusual for him; looking at a building under construction and quickly running the numbers through his head to see if the project made sense is the kind of thing he does all the time. Coming up with conclusions on whether a project would be a success or doomed to failure is second nature to him. He is a genius when it came to numbers.

It is all very simple. He assigns a cost for land acquisition, costs for financing, unforeseen conditions, real estate commissions, taxes, consulting fees, construction costs, vacancy expenses, and every other cost imaginable to develop a project. He would then factor in a realistic selling price and come up with the gross profit. If it was rental property, he would figure in the rental income by the square foot, factor in a vacancy cost, operating and maintenance costs, broker's fees, etc. and arrive at a gross profit per square foot of leasable space. Terance keeps his wheels spinning all the time, and he constantly updates his numbers, which keeps him from making bad decisions. Never allowing an ego to control him or acting out of compulsion or gut feelings keeps him out of trouble. Everything he does is totally methodical. The restaurant operation is very interesting to him. Estimating that the restaurant seats at least one thousand people per sitting, it was amazing things went on going smoothly. There were no signs of any hectic moments all the time the men were dining. He watched the waiters and the busboys very closely and noticed a synergy between them that kept things moving and the dining experience totally enjoyable. It seemed it was one for all and all for one. Everyone paid the utmost of attention to the diners. There was no rushing anyone out or keeping anyone waiting. Someone thought about everything, from the portions of food served, the manner in which it served, and how the tables were cleared after each sitting. The portions of food were so large, you were compelled to leave immediately after you finished the main dish. The service was impeccable, and the little treats they served before the main course came out were a great way to keep the diners occupied while the food was being prepared. The culture of the restaurant was unique. It seemed all who worked there, the waiters, busboys, and hostess, were like one big family who were happy to make you feel special.

It was a fitting memento to the late Elvis Presley that everything was strategically thought out so that the diners knew that they were getting more than their money's worth. The restaurant opens at 4:00 p.m. and serves meals until midnight. That's about eight hours of operation, give and take time-out for busing and setting up tables. Terance also noticed how quickly two busboys could clean and reset a table. The whole thing took under forty seconds. This little noticed task of getting the table ready for the next sitting was very impressive. He estimated that the waiters and busboys and kitchen staff were able to turn the tables over at least five times a night. One other thing that caught his attention was that nobody was waiting outside the dining room. The patrons kept moving through the restaurant unnoticed. He surmised that maybe there was more than one of those dark halls that he and his friends were escorted down into the dining room. This would allow multiple hostesses to seat diners in different areas in the dining room without passing by the same tables over and over again. Terance also summarized that the wine and beer were purposely offered at very reasonable prices, while the mixed drinks were pricey. He knew that there was a lot less work serving wine and beer than there was to preparing mixed drinks. The profit on the beer and wine was very good. The salad bar also cut down service time, and the menu was somewhat limited, which gave the kitchen the opportunity to prepare repetitive meals more quickly. He keeps thinking about all this stuff while he is eating his breakfast. Terance, Bobby, Jeremy, and Hank were there on Monday night, which is not usually a busy night for a restaurant; however, Graceland was packed.

Other than word of mouth, the restaurant needed no PR. He thinks that this is the best-kept secret for millions of people, and that's what made it so special. He begins to run the numbers through his head and estimates that there were around 250 tables for parties of four, plus or minus. He assumes $200 per table, times three turnovers per night, being conservative; it would put the gross income for Monday night at around $125,000. It didn't seem possible, but the numbers proved him right. He does the math over again and comes up with the same conclusion: $100,000 per night. He is impressed. Someone came up with a restaurant operation that seems, at face value, to be making money hand over fist. He wonders what kind of person or persons are responsible for this; he has to know. He thinks what an opportunity this would be for him and his wife, Terri—particularly for Terri, who was in the restaurant business before they got married. He wants to know more about it. He decides to do some research and find out who the owner or owners are and if they would be interested in talking to him. He would immediately get someone from his office to do some research. He has to know who the people are behind this enterprise. Getting involved in something like this could be a great opportunity for him and the people around him. Terance likes to spread his wealth.

Chapter 32

Hank Hunk's Idle Time with Special People

HANK IS UP around at 9:00 a.m., a little late for him. He opens the draw drapes to allow the sunshine and the view of the city to come into the room. The view immediately motivates him. Looking at buildings and particularly ones that are under construction is enjoyable to him. There's a big construction project one mile down the strip from his hotel he wants to visit. At the moment, breakfast is his priority. After showering, shaving, and getting dressed, he wonders if he should jump in the car and find something that's just off the strip or head down to the hotel restaurant. Taking the car and checking out some local spots is his choice. If he likes what he finds, he may want to bring one of the guys the next time. Before leaving the room, he makes sure that the key card is in his wallet, his cell phone is in his shirt pocket, and his car keys are in his pants pocket. Now he can leave. With a little effort, he locates the car in the parking lot.

As soon as he gets in the car, he checks himself out in the rearview mirror and realizes that he isn't wearing his glasses. Luckily, he sees them on the console in front of the glove box. He has no idea how they got there, but at the moment, he could care less. He puts on the glasses, starts the car, and heads out to the strip. Driving up Las Vegas Boulevard South, he decides to turn onto East Sahara Avenue, where he finds nothing. He then heads south onto South Maryland Drive and finds a Denny's restaurant across the street from the Sunnis Hospital. It isn't exactly what he is looking for, but it is now after 11:00 a.m. He parks the car out front where he can see it. The restaurant is nearly empty, so he is able to get a table near the window where he can see his car. Looking over the menu, he notices that there are fifteen Denny's in Las Vegas alone. Suddenly, there's a cute young waitress waiting to take his order. He orders a cup of coffee, a bagel, a glass of orange juice, and a bowl of cereal. The waitress is very friendly, and Hank couldn't help but notice that she is looking at him very intensely. He is used to this kind of behavior but not at this time of the day. But then again, he is in Las Vegas. Hank eats his breakfast quickly, pays his bill, leaves a generous tip for the waitress, and heads out the door. It is now around 11:45 a.m., and Hank isn't ready to go back to the hotel just yet. A drive around the city would be inspirational. Heading east on Sahara Avenue, he drives for a couple of minutes and finds himself in a residential area, where he doesn't want to be, so he decides to head west to Las Vegas Boulevard and back to his hotel. Maybe a little R & R around the pool will be good for him.

Not having any reading material, he turns into a strip mall and parks his car in front of a big box store. Browsing around for a few minutes, he finds himself confused and lost. The bookstore seems to have everything except for what he wanted. So he chases down a clerk and asks where the top-ten bestsellers are and is instructed to head back to the checkout area at the front of the store. After a little searching around, he finds a small counter with the top-ten bestsellers. To his surprise, there is only a small selection of new books in a building that could have housed millions of volumes of reading material. He wonders, *Who are all these other books for?* No matter. He finds a book that he thought he would like; it is titled *Los Angeles Police Stories*. Now he has something to read for the next fourteen days when he is alone.

The drive back to the hotel is only a few minutes. With his book in hand, he heads straight to the pool area. He is surprised to see how beautiful it is. It features one large swimming pool and a couple of small pools and a beautiful cabana with tables and chairs set up all around the bar. Hank thinks he could have saved a lot of time if had chosen to have breakfast. But no matter, this morning, he is trying to kill time. He is getting very excited about the hotel's amenities. The weather is exceptionally warm for this time of year, so he heads up to his room to get changed into something he could wear around the pool. However, on the way up to his room, he realizes he doesn't have anything to wear around the pool. For some reason, he didn't pack a bathing suit. Not a problem, he thinks; shorts and a T-shirt are all he needs for now, and tonight or tomorrow morning, he could buy himself a bathing suit. In a flash, he changes into his pool attire and quickly heads back down to the pool. While he was looking for a place to read, he notices that there is a mix of guests at the hotel. The mix includes families, young and middle-aged women and men in groups of three and four, the young and fast with boyfriends and girlfriends, and of course, the baby boomers. A place away from the families is his choice. Finding three empty chaise lounges, he spreads the towel he picked up at the pool gate and places it on the back of one of the lounges. Now is the time for him to relax, catch a few rays, and read his book. His sunglasses are placed on the small table next to the chaise lounge. Closing his eyes, he feels the warm sun on his face and chest and then wonders if he should have put on some sun block. It is too late for that. All he wants to do now is to be alone and relax. To avoid having someone sit next to him, he thinks he should spread some of his clothing on the two empty chaise lounges on either side of him so that he would have some breathing room. But he has second thoughts about his actions if in fact he is being watched. It would be embarrassing when after a while no one showed up.

While he is drifting into a semi sleep mode, he is distracted by a voice that sounded familiar to him but he couldn't place. The sun is right in his eyes, so he couldn't make out who it is. He ignores it for a moment, closes his eyes, and then suddenly feels the presence of someone standing right in front of him. When he opens his eyes to check out who it is, the sun blinds his view. A split second passes, and Hank hears a familiar voice say, "Look, Jackie, it's Elvis. Are we in luck or what?"

Immediately, it all comes back. It is Shirley and Jackie from the check-in incident in the hotel lobby yesterday afternoon. Hank looks up and smiles and says, "How are you ladies today?"

"We are just doing fine, and how are you doing?"

"As good as can be expected."

Hank is not trying to encourage an invitation. But no matter, Jackie and Shirley drop their towels on the two chaise lounges on either side of him. Jackie asks Hank if there is anyone using the lounge chairs. He wants to say yes, but for a number of reasons, he says, "By all means, help yourself."

With that, the two women take off their terry-cloth beach attire and begin applying sun block on their arms and legs. Hank couldn't help but notice that the two middle-aged women have bodies of women in their late twenties and that they are wearing $300 sunglasses, $200 swimsuits, and lots of expensive gold jewelry. Being in this good of shape, these women must spend a lot of time in the gym—lucky husbands or boyfriends, if there were any.

Shirley looks down at Hank and asks if he wouldn't mind rubbing a few dabs of sun block on her back. He happily obliges. She turns her back to him so that he could apply the sun block without getting up. As she moves closer, he couldn't help but notice how wonderful a fragrance her perfume has. It too must've been very expensive. After he is finished with Shirley, Jackie asks to have Hank rub the sun block on her back. As she moves up close to Hank, he notices a second wonderful fragrance of perfume. He is beginning to get aroused. After he finishes applying the sun block on Jackie, Shirley asks Hank if he needs any sunblock, and Hank says that he did. She hands him the tube, and he applies it on his chest, legs, and face; and when he is finished, Shirley asks if he wants some on his back. He says he does, and Hank gives her the tube. She tells him to sit sideways on the lounge chair, and as he does, she moves up very close to him and begins rubbing the lotion on his back with slow, caressing movements. Her touch is so sensuous He is glad that he is sitting down. Jackie looks over at Shirley and laughingly says, "OK. That's enough of that. You're going to give the young man the wrong impression of us."

Shirley giggles in a very suggestive way and slowly slides her hands off Hank's back. The moment is special. Hank couldn't remember when he was so turned on. He is completely overwhelmed. Jackie looks over to Shirley and says, "Let's go do a couple of laps in the pool."

Shirley agrees, and the two sisters head over to the main pool. As they walk away, their bodies are so tantalizing, he couldn't help but wonder, if they ever put the moves on him, would he oblige? The answer is that he doesn't know. All he knows is that the more he looks at them, the better they look. Watching them in the pool reveals how good swimmers they are. Both women are like conditioned athletes, performing underwater turnarounds at the deep end of the pool and swimming in perfect form from one end of the pool to the other. When they finished their swim, they walk back toward Hank. Their hair is slicked back from being in the water, which gives them a very girlish look that is very comforting to him. He wonders why he didn't see all this the day before but then remembered that he was very tired and his glasses sometimes blurred his vision indoors. All of this gives Hank a feeling of vulnerability and excitement at the same time. Convinced that Shirley and Jackie could easily pass for late twenties or early thirties, not the mid to late forties he guessed yesterday, he begins looking at them in a very different way. The sisters return to their chaise lounges, grab their towels, and begin to dry themselves off. Hank compliments them on their swimming performance. Jackie comments that they both swim at Miami, which Hank understood to be the University of Miami. Hank says, "You two were great."

"Thanks. We needed that."

Not knowing how to take her comment "we needed that," he decides not to push it. Shirley looks over at Hank and asks how he liked the hotel and if he had lunch or supper at any of the restaurants. He replies that he is very impressed with the hotel, but he hasn't tried any of the restaurants yet. He wants to tell them about *Graceland* but cautioned himself against it. However, by coincidence, Shirley asks Hank if he had heard about this new restaurant in the industrial area of town called Graceland. Hank answers, "I was there last night."

"Jackie and I have reservations there tonight."

"You two are in for a real treat."

"What is it like?"

"I'm not going to tell you, but you will absolutely not be disappointed."

Shirley reaches over for her beach bag and pulls out an orange and a book. The book looks to be a textbook on business management or entrepreneurial procedures. After peeling the orange, she offers half to Jackie and the other half to Hank. Oranges being one of Hank's favorite fruits, he accepts her offer. She then pulls out a tangerine, peels it, and places the peeled fruit on the table next to her chaise lounge, lies back, crosses her legs, and begins reading her book. The conversation between the two sisters becomes very serious as soon as Shirley picks up the book. They begin talking about a business deal that they need to work out in the next couple of days and how important it would be to brush up on some procedures they need to follow. Their conversation becomes very serious very quickly.

The way in which they engaged each other is very eloquent. Hank just listens to avoid saying something dumb around his two very sophisticated new friends. Shirley then says something to Hank that is completely out of context from her dialogue with her sister. What she says catches Hank by surprise and makes him feel a bit sorry for how he had falsely judged these women yesterday. Shirley says sincerely, "You know, Hank, today's world does not allow people to be friendly with each other anymore. If everyone had your disposition, there would be a lot more smiling faces around here."

Hank knows exactly what she is talking about from his relationship with his good-natured companions. Shirley comments that everyone should read Dale Carnegie's book *How to Make Friends and Influence People* at least once in their life; the world would be a much better place. Hank is now becoming very interested in Shirley's perspective on life. She is saying the kinds of things that draw him to Bobby, Terance, and Jeremy. Hank enjoys people, and he knows they like him, but he doesn't see that much of it outside of his family and his circle of friends. Hank contends that Shirley is right. Everyone's too busy to be friendly. Shirley looks down and begins reading her book, and Jackie asks Hank if is enjoying Las Vegas, where he lives, and what he plans on doing for the rest of the week. Hank is reluctant to explain exactly what he is up to in Las Vegas, so he answers by saying, "I have no real plans. I'm just vacationing."

"Shirley and I are here on business, and we don't have a lot of spare time during the day. But maybe we can all have a quick lunch together tomorrow—let's say, around 1:00 p.m.?"

Having lunch with these two very exciting women would be inspiring, so he agrees. Shirley immediately looks up at Hank and says, "Great! Lunch would be perfect for tomorrow afternoon, but right now, I have to get back to my room and make a few calls."

The poolside gathering ends, and the newly proclaimed friends say good-bye.

Watching Jackie and Shirley disappear into the crowd, Hank reminisces what his grandma used to say to him: "You can never judge a book by its cover." Hank thinks how true that is. He wants to learn more about them but is concerned about his attraction to them. The attraction is somewhat physical, though not entirely. It is their worldliness, maturity, sense of humor, and most of all, their inspirational personalities that captured his attention. All of which is something that he hardly ever experience, except with his special companions. He wonders how this is all going to turn out—hopefully for the best. Good things happen to good people. What could be in store for young Hank?

Chapter 33

Bobby Shrimp Pleasantly Thrown Off Course

BOBBY WAKES UP somewhat tied; thinking about the consequences of an unplanned meeting with Kate while being with his friends kept him tossing and turning all night. What he would say or do keeps him thinking about this while he lies in bed looking up at the ceiling. Bobby is very good at focusing in on a situation and following up with a positive action. However, this thing with Kate is way out of his control mentally. His concerns need to be differed if he's to be of any benefit to Terance, Jeremy, and Hank. So now it's time to get out of bed and get ready for a new day.

The time is now 8:30 a.m. By the time he is ready to leave the room, it is almost 9:30 a.m. This is a late start for him; a normal day at the body shop for Bobby begins at 7:00 a.m. Making it a habit of getting into the shop before the mechanics and his secretary arrived is his routine. Being the first one to arrive, he makes the coffee and gets things rolling so that everyone could get right to work when they get in. He is also the last one to leave. He likes being alone with all the equipment and the cars stretching out over his ten-thousand-square-foot work area. He marvels at all he had accomplished. Starting from nothing, he feels he's very lucky. However, he often quotes, "The longer and harder I work, the luckier I get." Could his lack of success with women versus his business success be his quagmire with Kate?

Disappointing relationships with women, particularly with those who were more sophisticated than him, his easygoing and everyone's-my-friend attitude work like a charm in the business world and with close friends and family. But unfortunately, once he strays outside his comfort zone, he loses confidence in himself, and things go downhill very quickly, and most often with women who have something to offer. His charisma and disposition always helped him in the early stages of a relationship with socially attractive women. Unfortunately, after a short period of time, they tend to lose interest in him, which ultimately ends up as a rejection. He doesn't want this to happen with Kate.

This morning, he'll grab a light breakfast in the hotel in one of the several restaurants on the ground floor. He'll go over his itinerary to see if there's anything he should be adding to his list of things he's planned for the group. There're crowds of people meandering around the restaurants and in the hotel lobby, which gets him thinking about Kate. Knowing he has to get her off his mind, he focuses on why he's in Las Vegas, and immediately his thoughts about Kate subside; and after his second cup of coffee and his review of his itinerary, Kate is all but gone.

Bobby now focuses on the trip to Reno and what might be gained by attending the precompetition trials. Reno is no match for Las Vegas when it comes to the competition, but for some reason, Bobby seems to be drawn to the Reno competition. There could be someone new in the competition that will give his companions and him some inspiration, or it may not be inspiring at all, and that may give his companions a boost in confidence. Everything is up in the air. Maybe if the first round of performers weren't that good, then they may be able to finish close up to the top. Or maybe not. Bobby is somewhat nervous about the outcome. If they do decide to go forward in Reno and finish in the bottom of the pack, they would lose confidence, thus hurting their chances for success in the Las Vegas competition. This is a very deleterious situation. If the first group of performers are real good, then the guys would be nervous about the Las Vegas show because they would know that the top contenders would move on to the

Las Vegas competition for the big money. A more disastrous scenario would be if the Reno contenders are not that good, and he and the guys decide to compete and end up in the bottom of the heap, then their chances of doing well in the Las Vegas competition would be out of the question. Bobby's only hope is for the first group of competitors to do fair, and the four of them decide not to compete and leave Reno with hopes of finishing in the top ten at the Las Vegas competition.

Where he finished in the competition didn't matter to him. He knows better; his bets are on Hank. If only Hank could master Elvis's voice and choreography, he could be the one. Bobby believes Elvis's clone is out there ready to be discovered. It could be anyone—someone who's never competed before, or maybe it's someone that has evolved into Elvis. Maybe it's someone close to him, someone who doesn't think that they have what it takes to become Elvis. That someone could be Hank, and that would be Bobby's salvation. Not being sure how Terance and Jeremy feel about their chances of success is a big unknown. He knows he has no chance of making it to the top and assumes that Terance and Jeremy feel the same way about their chances. His mission will be to groom Hank for the title, hopefully with help of Terance and Jeremy. He's been thinking about this for a while. Terance's attraction to the competition is a mystery and, for that matter, so is Jeremy's. Coming to Las Vegas with any hopes of winning can't be what compels them to come. He believes that Jeremy comes just to socialize with the rest of the group. Terance is a mystery. He hopes that Hank thinks he could have a shot at a high score but doesn't know how to get there.

Being in very deep thought for the past half hour, he doesn't realize that time had passed so quickly until he looks up and realizes that he is the only one left in the restaurant. Feeling good about his present state of mind and satisfaction with the itinerary, his spirits are in high gear. It's time to take a look at the pool area, the restaurants, shops, the theater, and last but not least, the casino. He waves to the waitress, who comes to his table promptly; and when she arrives, Bobby gives her a beaming smile and asks her for his check, which she immediately retrieves and places on the table. He leaves a generous tip and heads out to the lobby and down the mall to the pool area. The sheer size of the open space makes it look like a man-made park built on top of a concrete building. He guesses that there must be at least three acres of landscaped grounds. From Bobby's point of view, it's this part of the hotel's amenities that would keep him coming. He's convinced that it's all not by chance that the hotel's focus has gone in this direction—attracting families along with casinos players.

The city is rich with excitement, and the hotels and casinos are a big part of that enrichment. The casinos are loaded with wannabe high rollers. Most of them never achieve their financial dreams. Bobby, however, has. Through long hours and hard work, he made his body shop the largest and most successful shop in the area. Having a reputation for being fair and dependable has been another reason for his success. Thus, he keeps twenty mechanics busy fifty weeks a year.

Over the years, Bobby has been able to save a lot of money by living way below his means, being very frugal, and possessing no expensive addictions, except his hobby restoring vintage Cadillacs. Jesse has always been there to lend a helping hand. Over the years, he and Jesse have restored ten Cadillacs to mint condition and kept some and sold some for huge profits, which Bobby has no problem splitting with his brother. The body shop alone brings in enough income for Bobby to live comfortably, and the car restoration business adds to his wealth. He shares his profit with all his mechanics. With all this financial fortune, he now wants his lifestyle to change. He would like to move out on the crummy apartment and move up to a new custom-designed home with a garage big enough to hold all of his vintage vehicles. He's even drawn up a plan of the perfect home. He's been taking photos of the homes he thinks would fit his culture. He cuts out magazine clippings of kitchens, living rooms, and family rooms he likes. His dream would be to have a home large enough to have all his friends and family over for the holidays. He also wants a lot of children. Bobby can see this all happening for him. But as of now, nothing has materialized because there seems to be something missing, something preventing him from fulfilling his dream, and he knows what that is.

Not paying much attention to what's going on around him, he suddenly hears a pleasant and familiar voice from behind him. Looking over his shoulder, he sees Kate. She calls out his name and walks right up to him and announces with an extremely enthusiastic tone, "Bobby, I am so glad we ran into each other. Is this place unbelievable or what?"

Bobby is a little surprised to see Kate and for a second didn't recognize her. She looks different. Her hair isn't pulled back like it was on the plane, but rather it is hanging down almost to her shoulders. She has little or no makeup on and is dressed like the quintessential vacationer with shorts, sandals, and a Las Vegas T-shirt. If Kate didn't single him out, he would not have recognized her. Bobby is inspired with Kate's new look. Kate looks very outdoorsy and very wholesome. Bobby feels much more confident, so he immediately puts his arms around her and gives her a big warm embrace and says, "Were you trying to avoid me?"

"Of course, I was, and that's why I called your name so that you wouldn't notice me."

Bobby likes Kate's witty response and adds, "I just came in from outside, and I couldn't believe how beautiful everything looks like out there. The pools, the landscaping, the restaurants, everything is wonderful."

Kate agrees one hundred times over and adds, "This place does something to you. You know what I mean?"

Bobby doesn't know how to take her comment, so he just agrees and adds, "That's so right, this place does something to you."

Kate asks Bobby if he would like to meet her tonight at the main restaurant in the hotel. Bobby obligates immediately.

"How does 8:00 p.m. sound, Bobby?"

Bobby replies, "That sounds fine."

"Good, I have some stuff I have to do this afternoon. I can meet you, but I don't know where?"

"I'll pick you up at 7:30 p.m. wherever you want."

"Let me give you directions. Take the elevator to the fifteenth floor and head to room 1515. If my mother answers the door, tell her you made a mistake and leave—only kidding."

Kate's sense of humor and wit are very refreshing, and now Bobby is feeling very good about things. There's now something else for him to look forward to. Tonight, he'll be with a wonderful young woman who is in no way intimidating to him. Something very exciting is in store for Bobby, but he doesn't know exactly what it is right now.

Chapter 34

Jeremy Needed Something New in His Life and Found Something Wonderful; It's a New Beginning

JEREMY ARRIVES BACK at the hotel room around 10:30 a.m., kicks off his shoes, and makes himself comfortable in the chair next to the window. Feeling a bit lonely, he realizes he needs something to do to occupy his time between now and tomorrow evening when he meets with the guys. So he opens the drawer in the night table next to his chair to retrieve the outline that Bobby gave him the night before and glances over the activities. One of the planned activities includes a trip to Reno, Nevada. At first, he didn't pay much attention to that destination, but now he begins to wonder, why on earth would they be going there other than to watch a competition that doesn't include them? The idea of going to Reno doesn't bother him, and as a matter of fact, he's looking forward to spending a couple of days with his friends. Being a loner most of his life hasn't bothered him until lately. Now it seems he feels that he needs more in his life. While he's in Las Vegas, he would like to spend more time with Bobby, Terance, and Hank; however, too much time spent with them could reveal how much of a lowlife he is. The companionship his friends offer him is the motivator that transforms him into a more confident person. He feels like a totally different person when he's in their company. They treat him as an equal, which is very encouraging for someone with such a low self-esteem. Being very bright, he can, at times, sound very convincing and interesting, particularly when he gets going on one of his rants. He can speak articulately about politics, the economy, and the world's influence on the United States, and vice versa. Jeremy reads the *Wall Street Journal* cover to cover. He has also read numerous books on philosophy, art, history, and economics. If one didn't know Jeremy's present lifestyle, he could easily come off as being a worldly and a very accomplished person. But that's far from reality.

Keeping his intelligence undercover and never pushing himself outside his comfort zone have all but eliminated any worthwhile accomplishments other than his trips to Las Vegas.

After reading Bobby's itinerary, he realizes how lucky he is to have his Las Vegas friends and immediately begins to feel better about his life. Not a lot better but at least better. Recalling Terance's philosophy of always thinking positive inspires him to do something adventurous. From this point on, he will push himself beyond his comfort zone. Jeremy notices that Bobby, Terance, and Hank listen emphatically to each other's opinions and suggestions, and they always offer supporting advice and encouragement to one another. The synergy between them is enlightening. If he's going to be involved in their conversations, he's going to need to offer something more interesting than his job at the convenience store.

It's now time to think about doing something interesting with his idle time, something he can talk about when he and his friends get together tomorrow night. Glancing around the room, he looks over at the desk up against the wall, walks over to it, and opens the drawer to find the hotel's directory of restaurants, shops, special points of interest, guided tours, etc. He begins thumbing through the pages to see if there's something he could do or somewhere he could visit that could be a topic of interest during his next meeting with his three friends. The topic would have to be something different, adventurous, or something interesting. It would have to go beyond what they do together in Las Vegas. Looking over every page carefully and reading every description in the hotel's guest information book, he realizes that there's nothing in the book that would be of any interest to him or his friends. In returning the guest book to the drawer, he notices the Las Vegas Yellow Pages telephone book. Not having any other options, he begins going through the pages, starting with the listings under the letter *A*, which includes automobiles and have the biggest ads in the whole book. The next group of listings is the *B* sections, which covers millions of beauty salons and everything else under the sun. Before long, Jeremy begins to get frustrated until he gets to the *E* section, which includes escort services, which has more pages than automobile and beauty salons combined. Jeremy couldn't believe it. There are full-page ads for the discreet males looking for companionship to private party groups looking for adventurous couples. He begins to read every ad and wonders to himself, *How legitimate could all of this be?* Convinced that the whole thing is a front for high-end prostitutes is of no interest to him. Flipping through the pages, he quickly he comes upon the *M* section and finds himself reading through page after page of massage parlors. Now these ads seem a little bit more interesting. Each ad has something special to offer. They all advertise total satisfaction, a most relaxing experience, muscle therapy for the young and active, deep body massage, hot stone massage, pre—and post-sports massages, therapeutic massages, and exotic massages with names such as German, Swedish, French, and Russian massages. Jeremy wonders what a Russian massage would be like with those heavy-handed Russian women. For every massage, there is a country of origin of those people giving the massage, including Korean, French, German, Chinese, Indian, and so on and so forth. Dwelling on the Korean massage for a moment because of something he had heard about them back at home interested him. The Korean girls are kind of petite, thus would not be intimidating to him, and they probably couldn't speak that much English, which would be good because he had nothing interesting to say. And last but not least, it would probably be the least expensive adventure for him. Jeremy dwells over this for few minutes and weighs his options, which at this point in time are none. He concludes that maybe a massage may not be such a bad idea. Who knows, it may make him feel better, and besides it's time for him to think positive, and what could be better than to have some cute little Korean girl fussing over him? *Why not?* thinks Jeremy, *I'll do it.* Being somewhat cheap, he needs to find out how much it will cost before he totally commits to going through with it. If it's not that much money and it makes him feel good, then it certainly would be a worthwhile adventure. Unfortunately, it may not be the kind of adventure that he could elaborate in detail with his friends, but who knows, maybe it could be? The call is made to a Korean massage parlor on his cell phone. A woman with a very heavy accent answers the phone and asks, "How can I help you?"

"I would like to know how much the massages are?"

The woman answers within a nanosecond, "They start at sixty dollars and go up."

Jeremy follows up by asking, "What does a sixty-dollar massage include?"

"Why don't you come by, and I can explain everything we have to offer and what it will cost you?"

Jeremy mentions that he is staying in a hotel in the city but doesn't want to mention which one. The woman interrupts and says, "Oh, you want a girl to come to the hotel. I'm sorry we don't do that."

Jeremy replies promptly, "No, no, I will come down there. Please give me directions," which she does. Jeremy then asks, "When can you fit me in?"

"Within a few minutes when you arrive."

Jeremy writes down the directions on the back of the phone book in pencil, transfers them onto the pad of paper stored in the desk drawer, and erases the directions on the back of the phone book. Pausing a moment, he thinks about what he was getting himself into and begins to become leery of his plans, imagining the place is a dive or a front for a ring of prostitutes. *Maybe I should skip the whole thing.* Just as he is ready to throw the directions into the waste paper basket, he hears voices outside his door; it is the old couple he rode up on the elevator with the day before. He hears the old guy say that he is going to take a nap for couple of hours because he is very tired, and then he hears the old guy's wife say, "That sounds good. Maybe we can fool around a bit before you collapse? You old goat." That's all Jeremy needed to hear.

The place is three miles east of the strip just at the edge where the new meets the not so new. Knowing quite a bit about the "not so new," he imagines a shabby storefront with the sleazy rooms within. But to his surprise, the address is at a respectable building in a nice part of the not-so-new section of the city. Street parking is available not that far from his destination. The name over the entry is simply "The Parlor." The outside of the parlor seems legitimate enough to Jeremy. Being suspicious, he keeps coming back, assuming that it is all a front for cathouse. Hesitating a moment before going in, he feels the need to come up with an exit excuse if he doesn't like what is going on inside. If for some reason, he gets bad vibes, he would simply say that he is with a couple of other guys, and they would be back later on that evening and then never return. With that, he opens the door and walks in. The outside of the parlor is no indication for what is in store inside. To his surprise, it looks very professional, nicely appointed, and well furnished. There are groups of very respectful looking people waiting in the large nicely decorated parlor. He surmises that's how the place got its name. The inside of the parlor is like a posh hotel lobby with an assortment of sofas, upholstered chairs, coffee tables, interesting artwork, and beautiful flower arrangements placed tastefully throughout the room. There are men and women seated everywhere, which made things look very much on the up-and-up. The person Jeremy notices first is an absolutely beautiful young Korean girl standing behind a reception desk. Obviously, she isn't the woman he talked to over the phone earlier. In a moment's time, an older, very well-dressed, and well-groomed Asian woman greets him with a warm smile and a friendly introduction, "Hello, my name is Kim. Can I help you?"

Jeremy answers without hesitation or suspicion, "Yes, you can. I spoke to someone on the phone this morning about the kinds of massages you have and how much they cost. And you suggested that I come down and talk things over with you."

"Of course, I recognize your voice. You're person who called from the hotel."

"That's right. My name is Jeremy."

"Were my directions OK?"

"They were perfect."

Kim then requests that Jeremy follow her into the parlor and take a seat. As soon as Jeremy sits down, Kim walks over to a small end table, opens a drawer, and removes a classy-looking brochure and handed it to Jeremy. The brochure describes all the different types of massages the parlor offered its patrons. It describes in detail what each massage includes, what therapeutic values it offers, how long it takes, and how much it costs. Glancing over the brochure, he asks when he could schedule a massage, and Kim's answer is immediately. With that, Kim gets up and offers her arm to Jeremy. She escorts him over to the desk where the beautiful young girl is working on her computer and introduces Jeremy.

"Lin, this is Jeremy, and this is his first time with us. Please make him feel at home and explain our procedures and see what massage fits his liking."

With that, Kim leaves to visit with the other patrons waiting in the parlor. The mood is friendly and casual. People are conversing with one another or reading books, newspapers, or magazines while drinking spring water or juices. Jeremy watches Kim as she walks toward her waiting patrons. The friendly atmosphere is very reassuring. Jeremy notices a young Asian male entering the parlor and greeting a woman who is sitting on a sofa. The woman immediately stands up and shakes his hand and greets him by his first name. Having a massage by a young Asian male is not what Jeremy had in mind; thus, he begins to get a little nervous. He approaches Lin and asks her if there are only male masseuses, and Lin replies, "No, Jeremy, you have your choice of a male or female. Most

COMPETING FOR ELVIS

of our clients find someone they like and consistently schedule an appointment with that person. It sometimes takes a couple of times to find a good match."

Lin explains the procedure to Jeremy. She explains that once he enters the massage area, the massage therapist will ask him what kind of massage he desires while she is showing him around the therapy. Lin asks, "Do you prefer a male or a female masseuse?"

"A female would be good."

"OK, Jeremy, that's great. I will have someone for you in just a few minutes. While you're waiting, would you like a soft drink, mineral water, coffee, tea, or juice?" Jeremy requests mineral water. Lin reaches below the reception desk, removes a bottle of mineral water from the refrigerator, and hands it over to Jeremy. With that, he heads over to the parlor with his bottle of water and takes a seat. A few feet away, he can see Kim carrying on in a friendly conversation with her clients. So far, Jeremy is very pleased that he decided to go through with all of this. Kim looks over at Jeremy and nods with a welcoming gesture. He returns her welcome with a pleasing smile. Wondering how he's going to pay for all of this, he quickly glances through the brochure; and to his joy, he reads that the parlor accepts all major credit cards.

Jeremy is just about ready to pick up a magazine when he notices a very beautiful Korean woman heading in his direction, and as she does, Kim walks over to Jeremy and makes the introduction, "Kie, this is Jeremy. This is his first time with us. Please take very good care of him and explain what he needs to do before you give him his massage."

Kie looks directly into Jeremy's eyes, smiles, and shakes his hand warmly. Kie is wearing a white smock and toting a clipboard with what looked to be written instructions on a piece of paper. Kie beckons Jeremy to follow her through a door that leads them into the therapy area. It is very impressive. It looks like a high-end health club. Kie and Jeremy pass by a number of therapy rooms before entering what look like a combination of male and female locker rooms, which they are not. Kie points out the men and women have their own shower and locker areas. The locker and shower rooms are elegant, the walls are finished in clear wood, and the floors are polished tile. Each room is lit with wall sconces, and washroom area features solid marble countertops with four lavatories and a wall-to-wall mirror.

Kie stands outside the shower and locker room area while Jeremy takes in all the amenities. When he comes out, she hands him a bathrobe, a pair of disposable slippers, a small bottle of shampoo, a small bottle of body lotion, a bar of soap, and a key attached to a wristband. Kie instructs Jeremy to take everything into the locker area, get undressed, place all his belongings in a locker, put on his bathrobe, and head over to the shower area for a shower, and after he showers, he should go to room 3A with just his bathrobe and slippers on. Kie instructs Jeremy take a hot steam bath to loosen up before he takes a shower. The room is next to the shower area. With everything in hand, he heads over to the locker area, takes off his clothes, places them in the locker to which he has the key, heads over to the steam room, hangs his bathrobe on the hook on the wall next to the shower, and enters the steam room. As he steps into the room, he takes a couple of deep breaths, waits a moment, and then heads over to the shower. The shower area has individual showers and dressing rooms for each patron. While under the shower, he stands peacefully alone as he washes his hair, rubs soap all over his body, and closes his eyes to enjoy every minute of his experience. After applying the body lotion, he dries himself off with the soft extralarge white towel Kie gave him. He's now back in his robe, and once again as he looks around marveling at the accommodations, says to himself, "I already feel like a new man."

Wearing just his bathrobe and slippers, he heads over to the lavatory, where he dries his hair and then goes about finding room A3. The door to the room is open. The room is dimly lit and is arranged with a massage table in the middle of the floor and a small end table next to it. He stands there for moment until he hears someone coming up the hallway toward the room. He turns to face the door, and there is Kie. She has on the white smock she was wearing when she met Jeremy in the parlor. She asks him how he enjoyed his shower, and he replies, "It was wonderful." Kie is wearing a two-piece leotard, which emphasizes her beautiful slender body. Kie gives Jeremy a large white terry-cloth towel and asks him to put it around his waist under his bathrobe, which he does. Kie then removes Jeremy's bathrobe, hangs it up on the wall, and asks Jeremy to lie facedown on the massage table. Kie moves over to the front of the massage table and removes her smock. Her body is now in full view for Jeremy to marvel at. He now could hear very soothing music in the background. Kie asks Jeremy if he has any allergic reactions to body lotions. Jeremy replies, "No, I don't think so?"

"Well, Jeremy, let's try this lotion."

As Jeremy lies on the massage table, he could smell the tantalizing fragrance of the rubbing lotion Kie is applying on her hands. She immediately begins massaging the back of his neck, the underside of his ears, and the top of his shoulders. She does this for a while and then asks Jeremy to turn over. Now she is gently massaging Jeremy's forehead, eye sockets, nostrils, ears, chin, and temples, putting him in total bliss. He couldn't believe how wonderful he feels. Kie asks Jeremy to return to his stomach, which he does immediately. Moving to the bottom of the massage table, she begins rubbing his toes, the bottom of his feet, his ankles, and his calves. While doing this, she almost put Jeremy to sleep. Kie's touch is the most relaxing therapy Jeremy has ever experienced. Not that he has had that many therapeutic experiences. Her hands and fingertips are warm and soft, but she is able to apply enough pressure to Jeremy's body so that he gets a true therapeutic experience. She seems to float and drift above and around him like an angle. She asks Jeremy to turn over again, and as he does that, Kie pushes down on the lotion dispenser and, without missing a stride, applies lotion ever so gently on Jeremy's shoulders and back. At times, she is leaning so close to Jeremy that he could feel her breath rolling off the back of his neck. At first, he thought it was unintentional but soon realized it was not. He could also feel her long, silky hair sliding across his back and shoulders, causing his body hair to stand on end. Kie asks Jeremy how he is doing. Jeremy replies, "You've got me in a trance."

She chuckles and asks him to turn over onto his stomach. She begins rubbing the inside of Jeremy's legs so softly and gently that Jeremy gets a tingling sensation up and all the way down to his feet. Appling more lotion on her hands, she begins slowly rubbing ever so close to Jeremy's private areas. As she gently passes her hands between his legs, she moves her body very closely to the back of his neck so that he could feel her breath around his ears. Never experiencing anything like this in his entire life, he becomes enslaved to her touch. Repeating her movements, she gets closer to Jeremy and whispers, "Is this good?"

"Wonderful."

With every soothing movement of her hands, Jeremy becomes more entranced. His breathing begins to intensify, and his legs start to stiffen. Kie intensifies the moment ever so masterfully. Being in total ecstasy, he begins to fantasize. Within a few seconds, Jeremy is floating above the massage table. Kie continues rubbing Jeremy gently down as he lies motionless on his stomach. To bring closure to the massage, she slides her hands down the entire length of Jeremy's body and says, "I'm finished. How do you feel?"

"I feel like a new man."

She hands Jeremy his bathrobe and asks him to place the bathrobe in the large basket next to locker room after he has finished dressing, and she informs him that she would be waiting in the hallway.

Jeremy does exactly what she said, and in doing so, he gets a strange feeling that she had taken complete control of him. He couldn't stop thinking how this beautiful Korean woman gave him a new and exciting experience. While getting dressed, he is already planning a return trip. He knows he will be back again before he leaves Las Vegas to enjoy one more exhilarating experience with Kie. With that, he begins to fantasize on the possibility of a relationship with Kie if not more than a friendly acquaintance between him and his masseuse. This could be new direction for him; however, the more he thought about what he was getting himself into, the more he questioned his sanity. This could turn out to be a big letdown for him based on his past experiences. It is so far-fetched, he wants to end his fantasy, but he recalls Terance's remark about positive thinking. So he does, but in doing so, he begins to think, if it does work out, how would his daughter, Marie, feel about it, and to add to his problem, what would his ex-wife think about him carrying on with a woman twenty years younger than himself and an illegal alien to boot? He could deal with his ex-wife's badgering but not if his daughter is upset with his actions. Being alone for such a long time in a world that hasn't been very good to him, he begins to wonder maybe he's pushing the envelope little too far with this thing with Kie. Maybe she treats everyone exactly the same way she treated him. It could all be a typical day's work for her. Now he's beginning to feel that any type of involvement with Kie is a losing proposition; nonetheless, with all his negative thoughts, he still wants to come back one more time.

Forcing himself back to reality, he notices Kie is waiting for him in the hallway with a sealed envelope and a folded piece of paper. As Jeremy approaches her, she hands him the piece of paper and asks him to give it to the girl at the front desk and then hands him the sealed envelope. He is so thrilled by all that has happened to him, he thinks about how big a tip he should give her. Without thinking twice, he reaches into his pocket and pulls out twenty dollars. He does this awkwardly as if to say, is this enough? She clutches the money in her hand without looking at it, smiles, and walks him to the door that led to the parlor. They say their good-byes, and Kie warmly embraces him and says, "Thank you very much. Take good care, and I hope to see you soon," and turns and walks back to massage area.

Jeremy is standing alone in the parlor with the folded piece of paper and the envelope in his hand. He opens the folded piece of paper to see how much the most wonderful fantasy he'd ever experienced cost. It was sixty dollars for the base massage plus twenty. It was as simple as that. One hundred dollars including tip for a moment in time that he will never ever forget as long as he lives. He gladly pays the bill and thanks Lin, who asks if everything is to his satisfaction, and then she thanks him sincerely for his patronage. Walking out the door, he holds the sealed envelope tightly in his hand. With his head up high, he walks over to his car as proud of himself as he could possibly be. And to think it all started with feeling sorry for himself. He places the envelope on the car's dashboard and thinks about waiting until he is back in the room to open it, but anxiety is too much for him. He needs to see the contents even if it's no more than an advertisement for the parlor with a written thank you across the bottom. So he opens the envelope and is surprised to see a small piece of plain white paper folded in half. At the top of the paper is the date. The note read:

"Dear Mr. Jeremy, I hope I was able to make you feel relaxed and in better spirits so that when you come back next time, you will ask for me. Sincerely yours, Kie."

Jeremy is now on cloud nine, summarizing that this is a written invitation for him to request Kie when he returns to the parlor. Maybe his tip is more money than she is used to getting; thus, the note was written for that reason. However, thinking back at what transpired, Jeremy remembers that she had handed him the sealed envelope before he gave her the twenty dollars.

For now, Jeremy is a new man. He doesn't know how long it is going to last, but it certainly feels good. There's something wonderful to look forward to for the remaining fourteen days of his visit to Las Vegas. Jeremy's unplanned adventure is a big confidence builder for him. He actually feels lucky to be alive. Thinking about his exposé, he realizes that for just one hundred bucks, he feels great. What could be better? Driving back to the hotel, he sings jubilantly to Elvis's "I'm All Shook Up." This has been a great experience for him, but it's not enough to engage his friends in a stimulating conversation. Thus, he feels he should keep it under wraps for the right moment. Something else will need to be in place to enlighten his companions.

At 12:30 p.m., he is back at hotel, changes into his shorts, sandals, and T-shirt, and heads out to the pool. The temperature is exceptionally warm for this time of year in Las Vegas. Feeling relaxed and refreshed, his outlook on life has improved immensely. Finding an empty lounge chair next to the pool, he spreads his towel down on the chaise lounge, lies down on his back with his eyes closed and a slight smile on his face, and fantasizes about Kie. Now it's time to figure out what his new and interesting experience is going to be. Maybe some new clothes would help?—a sport jacket like Bobby's, a new pair of slacks, shoes, and a shirt. A visit the tourist information office this afternoon should be in order. There should be some interesting things he could do at the spare of the moment.

Jeremy now has a plan; he's thinking clearly and feeling really good. He closes his eyes and dozes off into bliss. One hour later, he wakes totally refreshed. Knowing he needs to get things moving, he leaves the pool area and heads over to the front desk, where he's greeted cheerfully. Jeremy asks, "Could you please tell me where the tourist information center is?"

The receptionist immediately pulls out a small map of downtown Las Vegas and points to the location of the tourist office and explains that it was in walking distance of the hotel. After thanking the girl, he folds up the map and heads out the door. He arrives at the tourist information center within fifteen minutes. Looking around, he positions himself behind a young couple that was going over a map with a woman who was standing behind the counter. A few seconds later, another woman comes to the counter and asks if she could help him. Jeremy explains that he wants to do something different, something interesting, and it has to be within a half a day's time. The woman asks if he has a car, which Jeremy said he does. She reaches behind the counter and grabs a pamphlet and asks Jeremy if he has ever been to the Hoover Dam. Jeremy replies he hadn't, but it seems very interesting to him. While showing him the map of the dam, she explains that getting there would be very easy. All he would need do is take Route 215 east to South Boulder Boulevard then turn east onto the

Nevada Highway, which is Route 93, and then follow that route through Lake Mead National Recreational Area and onto the Hoover Dam. She notes that the dam is only forty-five miles from Las Vegas, but one should give oneself a good hour to get there. It sounds perfect. After thanking the girl, he picks up the map and walks back to his hotel. Tonight he'll pick up his new clothes, and tomorrow he'll drive out to the dam early in the morning and be back to the hotel by late afternoon, which will give him plenty of time to get ready for his meeting with the guys. He'll be the new Jeremy, all buffed up with his new clothes and all excited about his adventures at the Hoover Dam. This could be a big couple of days for Jeremy, and he's ready to take it on.

That evening, he grabs a quick supper at the Denny's around the corner from the hotel and then drives off to find a mall. While in the car, he notices that he had left Kie's note on the dashboard, so he picks it up and reads it one more time, and the memory of his experience at the massage parlor comes back to Jeremy, enlightening his smiling face. Finding a mall is easy; there are so many of them in Las Vegas. He comes upon a factory outlet strip mall and decides to drive it. Noticing that there is a large selection of stores, he singles out Ralph Lauren as his first choice. Being accustomed to discount stores or Walmart, he isn't sure what he is in for. The plan is to look for the sport jacket section, which he does, and pick up a great-looking jacket that will fit him like a glove. The jacket is marked down 75 percent off the ticket price, which is $350; thus, Jeremy is able to buy it for a mere $52 and change. There are also great deals on slacks and shirts. When he is finished, he leaves the store spending a mere $145. The next stop is the Rockport outlet, where he picks up a pair of casual shoes for $25. This purchase brings Jeremy's total dollar amount to around $170 and change. All these bargains are adding to Jeremy's delight; thus, he couldn't wait to get back to the room to try it all on. Immediately upon arriving at his room, he undresses and puts on his new clothes and shoes and looks at himself in the mirror. He is amazed at how good he looks, however there is something he overlooked, and that was a belt. The one he is wearing looks real shabby with the new clothes. Not a problem, he thought, he could pick one up tomorrow morning or that afternoon on his way back from the Hoover Dam. A snakeskin belt from an Indian outpost store would be perfect. After neatly hanging up his new clothes, he gets ready for bed. It is now 10:00 p.m. An early start for his trip to the dam is his game plan. As he lies in bed, he fantasizes about Kie, and what he has accomplished in one short day is rejuvenating. This has been a glorious day for Jeremy. Sleep came easy.

Life back home for him was filled with disappointments. It seemed like a lifetime looking through the glass cooler at all the lucky people going about their business and living life to the fullest, while poor Jeremy loaded milk on the shelves. His way of living was the harbinger of all his hardships, disappointment, and insecurities. But that's all behind him now because tomorrow morning, Jeremy Shrinks will wake up to a new life.

Jeremy gets an early start and is very anxious to be on his way to the dam. He grabs a quick breakfast at the hotel and is on the road by 8:00 a.m. The hotel's carry-on bags filled with breakfast goodies are on the counter in the lobby for the guests. It is a nice touch for the people on the go. The time schedule for the tours was read the night before, and the plan is to sign up for the 10:00 a.m. tour, which gives him two hours to get to the dam, more than enough time even if he encounters some traffic or somehow lost his way. He would still have time to spare. He thinks seriously about taking on one of the guided tours the brochure advertised but doesn't want to get bogged down if, for some reason, the tour leaves later into the afternoon than scheduled. It's time to leave the hotel. Driving south on Las Vegas Boulevard, he turns onto Route 215 and drives east for ten miles and then it's south onto Route 515 for about twelve miles. The city of Las Vegas is now behind him. On Route 93, he passes through the desert and then through Boulder City where 93 heads north up to Lake Mead National Recreation Area. The drive through the mountains is breathtaking if only he had someone to enjoy it with him. Kie immediately comes to mind, and he wonders how she would react to visit the Hoover Dam. The distance to the dam is now approximately ten miles. He gives himself two hours, and at this point in time, he's been on the road for only forty-five minutes, so he decides to drive the rest of the way at a slower pace to take in the scenery. Within a couple of miles of the dam, Route 93 loops around a high hill and heads north down the long steep hill. At this point in his trip, he can see the massive concrete structure holding back the man-made lake. The sight of the dam is exciting. The construction of new highway bridge through the high ridge area just south of the dam was now in sight. The new bridge will allow traffic to bypass Route 93 over the dam. The view should be spectacular when the bridge is finished. As he approaches the dam, he checks his map and notices that there's a multilevel parking garage on the Nevada side. The map shows that the Nevada-Colorado state line passes straight through the center of the Hoover Dam. Nearing the dam, he spots the garage and decides to park. He heads over to the tourist information center on the east side of old Route 93 via a pedestrian tunnel, which passes under 93. The tourist information center is the first thing he sees when he exits the tunnel. At the information center, he's joined by large groups of tourists walking along the same route. He notices that there are a number of mixed groups of people made up of foreigners, Asian mostly, Germans, Canadians, and lots of young kids, probably from local schools and small groups of families who decided to take in the dam as he did. He walks briskly away from the crowds and toward the ticket counter where he requests a ticket for the 10:00 a.m. tour. The woman at the ticket counter asks Jeremy how many are in his group, and Jeremy replies, "One please."

"One it is. That will be twenty dollars, and you have forty-five minutes before the tour starts. You should visit our gift shop or head directly into the amphitheater to watch the show. There's one every twenty-five minutes."

"What's in the show?"

"The show contains a lot of information on why the dam was built, how it was built, and all kinds of other information."

Jeremy thinks that would be worthwhile watching, as do everyone else. The crowds of tourists follow him into the amphitheater. A show is already running but is nearing completion. The large group of ticket holders and Jeremy wait for the show to end, and when it does, they all rush through the doors to grab a seat. The young kids rush by Jeremy, almost spinning him around as they brush by him. He finally enters the amphitheater, sits down, and by chance, ends up sitting next to a young Asian girl who seemed to be with her parents. He is looking at her up and down and notices how plain she looks in comparison to Kie.

The show is both educational and entertaining; there are movies of how the dam was built and editorials describing how many men the project put to work during the Great Depression. The dam was named after Pres. Herbert Hoover. The construction began in 1930 and was completed in 1940. All the statistics and the historical facts enlightened Jeremy. All the information was easily stored in Jeremy's head. The concrete mix specifications, the amount of concrete used to build the dam, the cost of the project, the amount of men it took to build the dam, the amount of kilowatts the dam produces, how many gallons of water are in Lake Mead, and so on and so forth, could be recited in specific facts and figures. His high IQ never lets him down. Unfortunately, it never did any good for him when it came to advancing his social and financial status. He blames insecurities and his unwilling attitude to take chances for that, along with laziness and lacking self-confidence.

It wasn't always like this for Jeremy. There were opportunities. His father-in-law recognized his intelligence and offered to finance his college education. He could have attended any college of his choice but didn't follow through, and before long, he was divorced. Soon after, Jeremy became weary of his future. His terrible childhood and divorce took its toll. He turned inward and never pushed himself, never took chances. But that's all in the past, and this is now; and after yesterday's experience and today's adventure, things are going to change. He's looking forward to positive future, and that future is now, and now is beginning to take place for the better. And to think it all started with a one-hundred-dollar massage and some new clothes. Or maybe not? Maybe there's something else in the very near future that will bring even more enlightening changes to Jeremy's life.

The show ends, and everyone heads out to the lobby, where they are assembled into groups for the tours through the dam. The group of people that Jeremy joined looks to be around his age, maybe a bit younger. They all head over to the elevators that bring them down into the enormous generator room. The tour guide explains that the rushing water from the Colorado River that passes through the turbines is producing hundreds of thousands of kilowatt-hours of electricity. It is perpetual energy. What could be simpler, cleaner, and more cost effective? Nothing, Jeremy thinks. Without the Boulder Dam, there would be no Las Vegas, which in turn meant no jobs for thousands of people, no one contributing to the state's economy, and no one building and rebuilding in areas that were once a desert. There would be nothing but desert without the dam. And it's all because of water flowing through a big pipe. Jeremy is impressed. He fully enjoys every bit of information about the dam. What really excites him is the sheer size of the place and enormous spaces within. Who could have ever imagined there would be so much space inside a structure that was holding back a man-made lake and supporting a two-lane highway above? The whole thing is an amazing feat of imagination, engineering, and construction know-how. It is all somewhat intimidating to be standing at the bottom of a massive wall, knowing it is holding back an enormous lake.

As the group moves through the chambers within the dam, Jeremy overhears a couple talking about the riverboat tour down the Colorado through the Black Canyon. They are saying that the tour takes around two and one-half hours, and the next tour is at 11:45 a.m., which gives Jeremy about thirty minutes to purchase a ticket and get down to tour boat dock. The trip up and down the river would return him back to the dam at approximately 2:15 p.m. to 2:30 p.m., which would give him plenty of time to make the trip back to Las Vegas. Jeremy has underestimated the travel time to the dam and feels he could squeeze in one more activity. So he introduces himself and asks what the procedure is. They gladly explain that he needs to purchase the tickets at the tourist information center then follow the groups down to the docks where the inflatable boats are. They also explain that he will be overwhelmed by what he will see during the twelve-mile rafting expedition down the river and the twelve-mile ride back. The next tour leaves at 11:45 a.m. Jeremy decides to do it. He purchases the tickets and heads down the canyon walls to the boat dock area and is lucky enough to end up in the same group of people who gave him the info about the trip.

The tour guide is already waiting when everyone settles in on the dock. Jeremy and the rest of the people take their seats, and the excitement begins to mount. Looking around, he could see the massive structure of the dam and the high cliffs on the Black Canyon surrounding the Colorado River. It is truly overwhelming. The raft leaves the dock at exactly 11:45 p.m. at which time the tour guide begins explaining the ecology of river—how the Colorado gorged its way through thousands of feet of the rocks for millions of years to form the canyon. The views are breathtaking; the experience rafting down the fast-moving river is indescribable. The friendliness of the people on the raft adds to the delight of the trip. The tour guide is a character, which makes everything that more pleasant for Jeremy and his fellow rafters. Jeremy again is very proud of himself for making the decision to take the tour.

At every bend in the river, nature swallows him up and lifts his spirits with delight. The ride down the river is rejuvenating. The air, the wind, the water, the cliffs, all of it gives Jeremy a new appreciation of nature. There are bighorn sheep grazing on the walls of the canyon. There are rapids, still pools of water, and gravel riverbeds that are populated with deer. All of this is so refreshing and exciting, and the sound of the inflatable boat skimming across the water is totally invigorating. Jeremy takes it all in. With the wind rushing through his hair, the spray from the river in his face, the clean fresh air, the joys of the people, and the bouncing and rolling of the raft add more than he could have ever imagined. The incredible natural scenery, the overwhelming power of the rushing Colorado, and the feeling of being totally mesmerized for the once-downhearted Jeremy punctuate it all. He wonders where he's been all his life. For just under $300 for two days of total satisfaction, he's found a new life, a reason to live. It is nothing more than inviting adventure into his life. He recalls his revelation all happened within two days. It is all too simple. But what else could it be? Jeremy keeps on coming back to the same conclusion: "positive thinking," and as soon as he embraces that mind-set, *life could no longer hold him hostage.*

The trip back to the dam is equally exciting. Jeremy observes the excitement of all the other people on the raft. He notices the joyous looks on their faces, their congenial spirit, their enthusiasm for life, and the excitement. Jeremy knows that this is one of the more exciting events that he will never forget as long as he lives. He is refreshed, anxious, and impatient to get back to Las Vegas to tell his friends about his wonderful adventure. The trip back to Las Vegas is equally as exciting as a trip to the dam. His only regret is that he had no one to enjoy his excitement with. On the way back, he makes a stop at a Native American gift shop, where he picks up a snakeskin belt for thirty-eight dollars, one of his more expensive purchases. But what a great conversational piece it is going to be. At 3:45 p.m., he is back at the hotel with plenty of time to get ready for the meeting with his friends. And what a meeting it will be. Tonight will be a new beginning for Jeremy. He earned it.

Chapter 35

Terance Best's Meeting with the Restaurant Owners

TERANCE SPENDS HIS second day in Las Vegas relaxing around the hotel. The next morning, Terance notices a text message on his cell phone. The message reads, "We were able to track down the owners of the restaurant and will keep you advised about a meeting with them." At 11:30 a.m., Terance receives a second text message that reads, "We made contact with John from the restaurant. Please call him at this number 1-751-631-6666, Fran. Good luck."

Not being one to waste time, Terance immediately makes the call. He knows the number he is calling is a cell phone number from the area code. The phone rings twice, and a friendly voice answers, "Hi, this is John."

"Hello, John, my name is Terance Best."

John replies, "Hello, Mr. Best. I spoke with your people just this morning about arranging a meeting with you. What's your schedule like?"

"Anytime this morning or early this afternoon. I know you're probably a lot busier than I am, so you let me know what is good for you."

"That's very true, Mr. Best, but my partners and I would make time available to meet with you at any time up to 3:00 p.m. today, and the same goes for tomorrow and the next day."

"Today or tomorrow, anytime in the morning or early afternoon is good for me. How about today?"

"Sounds good. Let me run it by my partners, and I will call you back with a time. Oh, by the way, Terance, would you mind meeting at that restaurant? Do you know where it is?"

Terance answers, "I sure do, I was just there two nights ago."

"Oh, that's great. I hope you enjoyed the restaurant."

"The experience was more than I could have ever imagined."

John responds, "I'm very happy to hear that, Mr. Best. I will call you back within the hour."

Terance returns his cell phone back in his pocket and heads over to the hotel's café, where he has an early lunch. Terance feels very relaxed and somewhat excited about his meeting with the restaurant people. But at the same time, he's feeling a bit isolated. He's a man of simple pleasures. He prefers to be with his family and plans his life around them. Thus, the restaurant deal could be very exciting not only for him but also for his wife, Terri. Being very motivated about the meeting, he rushes through lunch so as to be ready as soon as he receives the phone call from John.

It's a beautiful day in Las Vegas, and Terance wants to enjoy every second of it before things become hectic. The meeting with John and then later on with Bobby, Jeremy, and Hank will consume much of the day. He decides to take a quiet walk around the pool area to get himself ready for the meeting. Terance is a meticulous businessman. All the i's are dotted and t's are crossed before he enters into a business deal. His arrangement with Bobby, Jeremy, and Hank is completely opposite from his regular routine, and his time here with his family is even more diverse from his normal life.

Suddenly, his cell phone rings; it's John's voice on the phone.

"Hello, Mr. Best, it's John from Graceland. How does 2:00 p.m. today sound?"

"At 2:00 p.m. sounds good. I'll see you then."

John replies, "Great! When you arrive at the restaurant, please come through the front door. I will be waiting for you."

"OK. I'm looking forward to meeting with your partners and you," John replies.

"And we are looking forward to meeting you."

The conversation ends. The anxiousness in John's voice is surprising. He seems to be going out of their way to meet with a complete stranger on a deal that involves a very successful restaurant. Maybe they've done a little checking on him and found out through the grapevine that he's a heavy hitter. Nonetheless, the meeting is scheduled, and Terance is looking forward to talking about his ideas to the owners.

It's now 1:00 p.m., and Terance heads back to his room. He has an hour to get over to the restaurant. While he's getting ready, he finds himself in the walk-in closet staring at the suit bag containing his Elvis suit and wonders, what would they think of him if he showed up dressed as Elvis? He chuckles to himself. He grabs a light sport jacket and black slacks and a button-down shirt and lays them on his bed. He grabs a pen and paper that's conveniently placed in the desk drawer next to the bed and writes down a few questions, which will be his agenda for the meeting. It's now 1:20 p.m. and time for a quick shower. He showers, and in ten minutes, he's out the door. It's now 1:30 p.m., and he is standing next to the valet. Terance requests a taxicab, and the valet immediately hails a cab, and he's on his way to the meeting. As soon as he's in the cab, he asks if the cabdriver knows where Graceland is.

The cabdriver replies, "I do. Do you know it doesn't open until 4:00 p.m.?"

"I'm aware of that. I'm not going to dinner."

Twenty-five minutes later, the cab turns into Graceland's parking lot at exactly 1:55 p.m., five minutes early. He's always on time for meetings. The cab fare is paid, and Terance heads to the front door, where he eyes two young men standing at the entry. They are very casually dressed. They must be restaurant employees who will be escorting him to his meeting with the owners. As soon as Terance approaches the entrance, both of them walk up to him smiling and say, "You must be Mr. Best. I'm John, and this is my brother Frank. Steve and Carl are waiting for us inside."

Now Terance understands why he's referred to as Mr. Best. The two guys he's meeting with couldn't be any older than twenty-five to twenty-eight years of age. Terance shakes both their hands firmly and says, "Please call me Terance. Mr. Best makes me sound too old." With that, they all chuckle and enter the restaurant.

The restaurant looks wonderful in the daytime with the sun shining through the skylight over Graceland. The main dining room is bustling with activity. People are setting up tables, vacuuming the floor, arranging the salad bar, setting flowers on tables, and dusting off chairs. Everyone seems to be on his or her toes. John asks Terance to follow him through the main kitchen. The kitchen is much larger and more sophisticated than he had imagined. The kitchen that the diners can view is only a small part of the kitchen's operation. The floor is spotless, and the lighting is perfect. Everything is stainless steel, and there are five or six pieces of every possible type of kitchen equipment. Terance now sees the big picture. The part of the kitchen the diners can see is the window dressing, and behind the walls is the moneymaker. John gives Terance the cook's tour. He explains the whys and hows the kitchen operated and how it is organized to mass-produce large amounts of food in a very short period of time. Terance gets the impression that John is very proud of his kitchen. All the equipment is strategically located. The prep tables, walk-in coolers and freezes, dry goods storage, and so on and so forth, are all coordinated for mass production based on a cruise ship restaurant, where vast amounts of food have to be served at predetermined sittings. The big difference between Graceland and the cruise ship is that Graceland serves four sittings a night at multiple intervals. Everything has to go perfectly in order to move as many people through the restaurant seven nights a week. Terance is impressed.

John, Frank, and Terance arrive at a small office that is raised about four feet above the kitchen floor. The office has a glass window walls so that whoever was in the office could see all that was going on in the kitchen below. Sitting in the room are two other young men and two young women. The women seem to be busy at work. Terance assumes that the two men are Stephen and Carl. John immediately calls over to the two young men to meet Terance.

"Steve, this is Terance Best from Coral Gables."

With that, Carl and Steve immediately get up and walk over to Terance and shake his hand rigorously. Carl turns toward the two young women working in the office and gives them some instructions, and before long, the five men are alone.

They all sit around a large desk in the middle of the office. Terance notices that the desk is positioned so that one could view the kitchen through one glass window wall and the dining room area through a second glass window wall. It is a very clever way of keeping an eye on everything going on in the restaurant. John apologizes to Terance for not introducing all the people present by their last names. With that, he makes his introductions.

"I'm John Olson. This is my brother Frank and my other brother Carl and our cousin Steve Olson. We are all very happy you came to meet with us."

Terance is surprised by John's remark. He asks if his office has given them any indication of why he wanted to meet with them. Their answer is that they are informed that he wanted to talk to them about a business opportunity. They also mention that they are aware of Terance's projects in Las Vegas. He surmises that the four young guys decided to check him out before they would sit down and talk to him. Terance is now feeling more confident about the meeting. With his pad of paper in hand, Terance opens the meeting with "Shall we begin?"

John replies, "Where do you want to start?"

Glancing down at his pad of paper, Terance replies, "Let's start at the beginning. How did this all come together?"

John, who seems to be the spokesman for the group, begins telling the history of *Graceland*. He explains, "It all started with their fathers—John Senior and Steve's father, Tony. John Senior and Tony ran a small restaurant in Las Vegas for years.

All the brothers and cousins worked at the restaurant, while they attended high school and college. Steve worked only a couple of summers and then went off to work at the Sahara Hotel. Frank and I attended Johnson and Wales in Miami, and Steve, of course, went to the University of Miami and then went on to get his MBA at Boston University. Frank and I worked on cruise ships for a couple of years and at various hotels along the strip. It was a great experience for us. Unfortunately, our uncle, Steve's father, passed away suddenly four years ago, and Dad lost interest in the restaurant. He asked if we were interested in carrying on in their footsteps, and at the time, we told him that we were not. Fortunately for my father, the restaurant's location, the land area, the liquor license, and a few slot machines scattered in the lounge had a lot of value. He was able to sell the restaurant for a surprisingly large sum of money to a group of people who saw its potential. They knocked it down and built a midrise hotel and casino. It all seemed to happen just at the right time for my father. The liquor and slot machine licenses were in his name. To keep the licenses intact, the new owners gave my father a modest interest in the deal, and within two years, he was making more money than he ever believed possible. At the time, he was sixty-two years old. Being a workaholic, needless to say, he got bored real fast doing nothing and wanted to do something with his newfound money. So he came to us. His plan was to set the four of us up in the restaurant business with the understanding that the restaurant had to be something special. That appealed to us. To give you a clue why the restaurant took on its look is because the Caddy that you see parked outside the house is his. So with his vision for the restaurant and his passion for Elvis Presley, the whole thing came together almost immediately. With the help of some very creative architects, historians, interior designers, kitchen designers, and of course, the local politicians, who knew my father very well, we had a design and permits in hand within six months of purchasing the warehouse. The building was bought for very short money because of its rundown condition and location.

The construction cost, however, was another story. We spent a good two and one-half times more than what we had planned. My father had pledged everything over to the banks including the Caddy. We spent a lot of money, but it was all worth it. The restaurant immediately took off. With little or no advertisement, the restaurant became an overnight success. We all share the same passion for the restaurant and are willing to spend twelve hours a day, six days a week, working our butts off to keep it going. Carl and Frank work in the kitchen. Steve and I take care of operations. I'm the headwaiter, and Steve buses tables. I also lend a hand busing tables, but that's only when we get very busy. I'm also in charge of human resources, which includes the hiring and training of waiters and busboys. We now have seventy-two employees."

Terance comments, "I like the hands-on family-run business approach. I like it very much. It seems to work well no matter what business you're in as long as everyone gets along."

John responds, "We all do get along very well together. The operation is big enough so that we never get in each other's way."

Terance replies, "That's also very good."

Terance glances down at his pad and asks without hesitation, "What do you gross a week?"

John answers, "Our average gross is between $700,000 and $800,000 a week." The number was very close to Terance's earlier computations.

"Our expenses, including finance costs, are around 85 percent of gross."

John leaves it at that. Terance asks, "How much debt are you carrying on your books?"

"This is where things get interesting. At first, the debt was manageable. We were able to pay our overhead and bank loans and still end up with a small profit before taxes. The profit was around 6 percent, and that was OK with us. My father received a small salary for consulting services. We were taking very little salaries, and everything was going fine. We could see paying down the debt within five to ten years, and to do that, we reduced our incomes by about 50 percent. The business was run very frugally, and we could see the light at the end of the tunnel. Things were going along just fine until early 2009 when the bottom fell out of the real-estate market. My father had pledged his portfolios to secure the bank loans, and you probably know the rest of the story. The banks wanted the difference between what my father had pledged in 2005 and what the value of those portfolios are worth in 2009. They are now worth 60 percent of their 2005 values. In order to make up the difference, our father went out and refinanced everything he had and is now very nervous. This is why we wanted to meet you today. We're hoping you can bring us the much-needed cash we need to keep things going. And we will do whatever it takes to keep things going."

Terance looks down at his pad and then looks up at the four men sitting across to him and says without blinking an eye, "I may be able do something. What I'll be looking for is a partnership position. I'm going to want my people to go over your books and your financial liabilities. The amount of money that I will put in will determine my percent of ownership."

Terance is a true businessman. He holds no punches. He is upfront when he says what he needs to make the deal work. He also adds that he likes the culture of the operation, the willingness to give up income for the betterment of the business. He particularly likes the owners' comradery. Terance goes on to say that he likes how the operation is run, the quality of the service, the quality of food, and most importantly, the uniqueness of the decor. Terance adds that he would like them to come back with some dates when his accountants can look over the books. And within a couple of days of that, he would give them an answer on what the deal would be. John seems very impressed with Terance's direct and unemotional approach to his positions. John comments, "Give us a few days, Terance, and we'll have some dates for you, is that OK?"

Terance replies, "It was a pleasure meeting with you four gentlemen, and I will wait to hear from you."

With that, they all shake hands, and Terance leaves the office. As he passes through the restaurant, he hasn't a second thought about the risk he may be taking. He's been in this position many times before and knows the ups and downs of any business deal. This one, however, at face value, is a good opportunity for him. The four owners brought something valuable to the table: their work ethic, their intelligence, their frugality, and their willingness to take chances. Terance believes that John, Steve, Frank, and Carl are what gives the deal its value. Portfolios are filled with assets whose value goes up and down during every economic event. The value of the father's portfolio is the only negative part of their financial crisis, and that is something that Terance could easily fix. Terance feels very good about the meeting. He's optimistic that this is a great opportunity for him and is looking forward to getting into the restaurant business. Terri will be told about his newfound operation once he closes the deal. His meeting with Bobby, Jeremy, and Hank will be a great way to end his day. Terance is on a roll.

Chapter 36

Hank Hunk, Lunch at Poolside with Shirley and Jackie

HANK SPENDS MOST of his morning walking around Las Vegas Boulevard. Being curious about some of the very large construction projects in the immediate area, he wants to get a look at the project signs to see who the contractors, architects, engineers, and owners are. The enormity of the construction is amazing. He wonders what it takes to design and detail a project of that scale. Glancing up at the construction, he couldn't help but notice the banks' names took top billing on all of the projects' signs. From his point of view, it looks like the architects, contractors, and engineers had little or no involvement in the projects, knowing how much imagination and skill it took to design and engineer a building of this magnitude and how much smarts the contractors had to have build it, and yet they somehow weren't worthy of the top billing. The credit went to the people who took somebody else's money and lent it to the developer. Being an architect, Hank is a bit biased; however, he does understand that without the banks' money, there would be no project. Hank doesn't recognize the architect's or the contractor's name but recognizes the developer's name. It is someone whom Hank admired. This guy has what it takes and possesses a great deal of confidence, not to mention a grand vision. Moving from construction site to construction site, he tries to calculate how many months these gigantic projects would be under construction. His best guess is it would take at least two or maybe three years before they are complete. How exciting it would be like to be involved in the design of a hotel like the one he's standing in front off and how wonderful it would be to spend a week as a guest. For now, this kind of involvement would be way out of his league; but someday, with a little bit of luck, he could be a part of something like this.

Checking his watch, he realizes that it's time for him to get back to the hotel and get ready for his lunch date with Jackie and Shirley. Arriving at his room at noon, he immediately begins getting ready; and while doing so, he couldn't help but wonder where his relationship was going with them. Thinking about women was not a priority pastime. Hank is and always was a mama's boy. It was tough going for Hank until he met Kayla. She picked right up on his family values and character. Kayla had the same upbringing as Hank, and like Hank, she loved being with her family. They're a perfect match; Hank's character and personality coincided perfectly with Kayla's. He was the handsome shy guy, and she was the beautiful wholesome woman without the attitude. Kayla is the more dominative figure in their relationship. Hank, being very laid back and a bit naïve, allows Kayla, who is also very street smart, to call most of the shots. With all of this, why is he going through with his lunch date with two sisters that could be ten to twenty years older than him? Presumably, it's lure of Las Vegas, like the old saying: anything that goes on in Las Vegas stays in Las Vegas. Or something like that. Hank is troubled by his thoughts. He wonders if he's reading too much into this arrangement with his lunch date with Shirley and Jackie, which will turn out to be a harmless gesture of friendship. Time will tell. But now it's time to head over to the poolside for lunch.

Hank wants to be prompt but at the same time doesn't want to be early. He doesn't want his new friends to think he is anxious, so he times himself as he heads to the pool so that he would arrive at one minute before 1:00 p.m. As he's approaching the restaurant, he can see Shirley and Jackie sitting at a table under a bright green umbrella. They seem to be talking intensely about something and not paying any attention to anyone around them. Their drinks are already on the table. For a moment, Hank thinks they may have already ordered their food and forgot all about him. How awkward that would be. To save himself from an embarrassing moment, he decides to walk up to their table from their backside and ask if the seat across from them is taken. As he does this, Shirley looks up at Hank and answers, "Yes, it is. It's for a young handsome guy who looks just like you. Please sit down, Hank. We just got here and ordered a couple of iced teas. Why don't you have one? They're the best drinks in the hotel."

With that, Shirley raises her hand and signals the waiter to come to the table. She asks Hank what he wanted to drink. Hank answers, "I'd like an iced tea with lemon."

This prompts Shirley to reply. Shirley asks Hank what he is up to since they last met. Hank explains that he visited a couple of the construction sites along the Las Vegas Boulevard.

Shirley remarks, "What a coincidence. That's what we've been doing."

Hank asks, "Why were you at the construction sites?"

Shirley answers, "Jackie and I worked on the interior design for the guest rooms and public spaces on the sloped glass building that is ready to open. You may have seen our name, Robinson & Robinson, in the little tiny letters on the project's sign. We've been working on this hotel project for almost three years, and now we're so pleased to see it completed."

Hank recognizes the building and is completely overtaken by their involvement in a hotel project. It seems too far-fetched for something like this to be happening. Shirley comments, "So now you know what we do when we are not hanging around the pool. What do you do when you're not fraternizing with all the pretty young women in Las Vegas?"

Hank is ready to respond to her question, but at that moment, his iced tea comes. Looking at Jackie Shirley straight in the eyes, he says, "You're not going to believe this, but I'm an architect. An unemployed architect but an architect nonetheless. Presently, I'm working in the construction end of the business."

With that, Jackie asks, "Which end of the construction business do you mean?"

Hank answers with a chuckle, "I'm a carpet installer in Los Angeles. I've been doing it for about two maybe three years off and on."

Jackie asks, "Who do you work for?"

"West Coast Interiors. We do carpet, floor tile, acoustical tile ceilings, and some drywall and painting."

Jackie responds, "We know all about what you do. You work for Alan Brown and his brother Leon."

"That's right. How do you know them?"

Shirley replies, "We've been working with West Coast for almost eight years now. We renovated the Renaissance Hotel in Los Angeles a couple of years ago and the Bonavista Hotel last year."

Hank says jokingly, "I installed all the carpet in the Bonavista Hotel."

Jackie comments, "What a small world. Who would have thought we had so much in common? It's going to make our topic of conversion so much easier now that we know we can all talk shop together."

The waiter returns to the table to take their orders. Jackie and Shirley order the chicken Caesar salad, and Hank orders the grill chicken sandwich with roasted peppers. They all ask for refills of ice tea. Shirley asks, "So, Hank, what brings you to Las Vegas?"

"I'm here with three friends of mine. We visit Vegas once a year. We have a great time together. I love it here. My friends are quite interesting and very much in the know of what to do while we're here. As a matter of fact, one of the guys found out about this incredible restaurant called Graceland. We had supper there last night, and it was unbelievable. Have you ever been there?"

Jackie and Shirley shake their heads and say no, but they had heard it is something very special.

Hank adds, "I won't tell you what makes it so special, but I will tell you this: the food and service are outstanding, and the inside of the restaurant is beyond description. Even for an architect."

Shirley comments, "I guess Jackie and I will go."

"You will not be disappointed."

Shirley leans back in her chair and gestures to Jackie and says, "What do you think, Jackie, should we ask him now or wait until he finishes lunch?"

Hank looks at them with a puzzled look on his face.

At that moment, the food arrives followed by the iced teas. A kind of a cold sweat comes over Hank. He wonders what on earth is on their mind. Not wanting to prolong his suspicion, he says, "Give it to me slowly."

With that, Shirley looks Hank straight in the eyes and says, "How would you like to be our escort at the grand opening for the Regency Hotel? The opening is for guests only. I promise you we won't embarrass you."

Hank realizes that he'll be meeting with his friends every other day and that they will be going to Reno for a weekend. He's concerned about his commitments, so he asks, "When's the opening?"

"Thursday night, the thirteenth."

Hank quickly recalls his schedule and realizes that he has a meeting with Bobby, Terance, and Jeremy tonight and again on Friday, so Thursday could work. Hank replies, "It may work, except for one thing: what do I need to wear?"

Shirley responds jokingly, "Why don't you come dressed as Elvis?"

Hank imagines, *If only they knew.*

"It's black tie. But don't you worry about a thing. We can take care of all that for you. So what's it going to be, Hank?"

"I think it sounds very exciting."

"Call me at this number after 9:30 p.m."

Shirley writes the telephone number down on a piece of paper and hands it to Hank. Taking the paper, he says, "I'll do it."

When the check comes, Shirley insists on paying. Hank comments that next time, it's going to be his treat. Shirley quickly responds jokingly, "That sounds great. You can take us to Graceland."

"It will be my pleasure."

With that, they embrace each other and say good-bye.

As Hank is walking back to his room, he can't help to think how much he misjudged Shirley and Jackie. I guess it just goes to show you can never judge a book by its cover. It's been a very interesting afternoon for Hank.

Chapter 37

Bobby Shrimp, Supper with Kate and Then a Wonderful Surprise

BOBBY IS ANXIOUS to get back to business. He wants to review his itinerary and make changes as needed. He left Kate in the lobby a few minutes ago and is heading up to his room. He's a bit overwhelmed by all that is going on. Knowing he needs to stay focused on why he's in Las Vegas, he surmises that Kate could become a big distraction for him. It's going to be difficult keeping everything in perspective. Arriving in his room, he looks over the meeting dates and other days outlined in his itinerary that he scheduled with Terance, Jeremy, and Hank. Wondering how he can fit Kate into his tight schedule, along with the meetings scheduled with the guys for tomorrow night, Wednesday, the tenth, and one for the thirteenth, and then the weekend in Reno. With all of these meeting commitments, he only has one night open for Kate. Maybe he could spend some time with her during the day, or maybe he should play it by ear. It may turn out that she's in fact too busy for him.

Bobby receives a flyer for the Reno competition. The competition is scheduled for Saturday and Sunday. The flight he plans to take to Reno is an early-morning flight out of Las Vegas with an arrival time of 12:30 p.m. The competition starts at 5:00 p.m. and continues until 8:00 p.m., so if they decide not to stay overnight, the guys could fly back that evening and be back in Las Vegas before 10:30 p.m. In order to keep things with Kate under control, he'll need to know when she is planning on leaving Las Vegas. He can find that out over dinner tonight. Having more contact with Terance, Jeremy, and Hank would be a big help. Knowing where they are and what they're doing would make things a lot easier for him. Tonight he'll suggest that they try to contact each other at least once a day. Wondering how things were going to go with Kate tonight makes him nervous, in particular about what will happen after supper. Will he and Kate enjoy a nice meal together and leave it at that, or will Kate have something else planned for them? Kate suggesting that he pick her up at her room rather than meeting somewhere in the hotel lobby is comforting, and her lighthearted remark about her mother answering the door and what he should do if that happens was easing his stress, but not enough to justify Kate's comment about him coming in contact with her mother. Maybe her mother would not approve of Kate's activities in Las Vegas because there's someone else in her life? But then again maybe he's reading too much into a harmless joke. But why not? She's a very attractive, intelligent, classy, and witty woman with a whimsical personality, one that Bobby is having a hard time competing with. Knowing his short falls, he wonders how long it's going to take Kate to recognize that he doesn't have the social and intellectual background she has; and when she does, will this be a one-night stand or a vacationer's mentality that anything goes when you're having fun? However, the test for their relationship will be after the vacation. Paranoia is now beginning to set in. Women like Kate don't' stick around that long, and it's making him wonder even more about what she has in store for them after supper, if anything. Tonight he will need to direct their conversation to subjects that won't reveal his commonplace culture or suggest that he's just another low-class vacationer. If only he could talk about why he's in Las Vegas, that could be a very interesting conversation; however, it's much too early for that. She may think he's a nut case.

With the exception of Lynn, Bobby hasn't had a long or fulfilling relationship with any sophisticated woman in his life.

To keep himself from falling off the deep end, he needs to stop thinking about Kate, so he decides to take a walk. During his walk, he realizes that there are a lot fun things they could do together. He makes a mental list of the places they could go after supper. This could be something they could talk about during supper.

It's now 7:00 p.m., and he's back in his room getting ready for tonight. Not wanting to come empty-handed when he arrives at Kate's room, Bobby picked up a bottle of red wine. The wine would be a nice way to break the ice. It's now 7:15 p.m. and time to go. He feels like high-school kid. One last look at himself in the mirror confirms that he looks great in his sport jacket, and the bottle of wine makes him look kind of classy. It isn't quite 7:30 p.m. when he arrives at Kate's room, so he decides to walk past her door and down the hall and back to her room so he would arrive at exactly 7:30 p.m. He knocks on the door and waits for a second for Kate to answer. It's a very long and very stressful second for him. The door opens, and there's Kate looking as beautiful as could be. Her hair is pulled back, revealing a pair of very unique earrings. She is wearing a very sexy skirt and blouse and high-heel shoes that accentuate her slender body. Being overwhelmed by how attractive she looks, he compliments her several times on her appearance.

He gestures, "Kate, you look so beautiful. Are you sure you want to be seen with someone like me?"

Kate looks at him with her whimsical smile and says, "Well, now that you mention it, why don't you just hand me the wine and then hit the road?"

Kate's wisecracking remark makes Bobby very comfortable very quickly. She laughs at her comment and gives Bobby a big friendly hug. Bobby looks around Kate's room and realizes that it's twice as big as his. It's a junior suite with a minibar, a parlor, and a separate bedroom. The view outside her window was spectacular. As Bobby hands her the wine, she says, "Oh how romantic, you know people don't bear gifts on dates anymore. You know what I mean?"

"I sure do."

Kate immediately retrieves two wineglasses from the minibar, opens the bottle, and pours two healthy glasses of wine. The wine helps Bobby improve his mood and relieve some of his tensions. After the first glass, he feels a whole lot better. He notices that Kate is also feeling a bit mellow. He surmises that Kate is intentionally trying to give him a buzz so that he would feel more at ease. Kate gestures that he go over to the couch and sit down. So he does just that. Kate follows him over and sits down very close to him. He isn't expecting that. He takes a quick look around the room and notices that there are piles of files, pads of paper and notebooks, and a computer on the desk. The room looks like a very serious workspace for a woman with witty personality. Feeling somewhat uneasy on how he should start the conversation, he just sits there wondering what to say. Fortunately for him, Kate immediately gets into a riff about bringing too much work on vacation and adds how much she needs this break tonight. Hoping that tonight means more to Kate than just a quick supper, Bobby remarks that he'll do everything he can to make her forget work. Kate thanks him for the encouragement and asks how he likes the hotel, and Bobby goes into an in-detailed description of all the things he thinks are great about the place. He explains that he hasn't dined at any of the restaurants in the hotel, so he can't offer any suggestions where they should go. Kate adds that neither has she, and goes on to say that tonight will be an interesting experience for the both of them. Bobby immediately starts analyzing her response, "interesting experience for the both of them," and wonders if he's in for a fun-filled evening. Bobby doesn't want to mention Graceland restaurant, not yet anyways. He wants to see how things were going to work out tonight. It is now almost 8:00 p.m., and Kate announces, "I made a reservation for the hotel's best restaurant, so let's go. I am starving."

The quirkiness of a beautiful woman saying "I'm starving" intrigues Bobby. It gets him to wonder if she was a tomboy when she was kid or had three older brothers, or maybe she was heavy when she was young and not as beautiful as she is now. Maybe that's it, Bobby hopes so. As they walk down the hallway toward the elevator, Kate walks very closely at his side. She puts her arm around him when she pushes the elevator button. When the elevator arrives at the lobby, Bobby allows Kate to enter first. There are two young couples on the elevator. Kate looks only a few years older than the two young girls; however, she is a lot better looking, so much so that the guys looked her up and down when she walked out of the elevator. It only took a few minutes for Bobby and Kate to arrive at the restaurant. They are greeted by the maître d', who asks if they have a reservation, and Kate replies, "Yes, we do, the name is Shrimp." Bobby is impressed that Kate put the reservation in his name. The maître d' shows them to a wonderful semicircular booth facing the dining room. Bobby wonders if Kate requested this romantic arrangement. He sure hopes so. To start a conversation, Bobby says, "This is a great table."

"I knew you would like it."

"How did you know that?"

"A woman's intuition."

The waiter comes to their table and asks if they would like something to drink before the meal. Kate says, "Yes, that's a good idea. What do you think, Bobby?"

"That sounds great. I'll have a Malibu and pineapple."

"I'll have an imperial martini."

"An excellent choice, madam, I'll be right back with your drinks."

The waiter leaves, and Bobby looks at the menu with delight. There are so many wonderful appetizers, salads, entrées, and desserts to choose from. When the waiter returns with their drinks, he asks if they would like to hear what they have for specials. Bobby acknowledges he would, and with that, the waiter goes through that night's specials; and when he finished, he asks if they needed more time. Kate immediately responds, "I know exactly what I want. How about you, Bobby?"

Bobby answers, "I'm ready to order."

The waiter turns and looks at Kate, and she replies, "I would like the New York sirloin, medium rare, with mushrooms on the side, and a Caesar salad with no anchovies."

The waiter turns to Bobby. "I'll have the exact same thing."

"How would you like your steak cooked?"

"Medium rare, of course."

"Would you like a Caesar salad also?"

"Absolutely with anchovies."

"Well, that makes things easy."

Kate asks Bobby if he would like to have a bottle of wine with dinner.

"Why not? Let's go all out to night."

Kate turns to the waiter and says, "We'll have a bottle of red wine, preferably with a full body. Do you have any suggestions?"

The waiter suggests Chianti. Kate looks over at Bobby.

"How's a Chianti sound to you?"

"It sounds great."

With that, the waiter leaves. Kate turns to Bobby and apologizes for being so quick to answer the waiter's request. Bobby gives Kate a comforting look and assures her that he had absolutely no problem with your taking charge, and he really means it.

There is something about Kate's self-confidence and enterprising personality that is very refreshing and at the same time very seductive to the point that it is turning him on. Her ability to take control of the situation without belittling Bobby is a special trait that Bobby recognizes immediately, and it gets him wondering about what is in store for him tonight.

All through the meal, Bobby and Kate talk about everything under the sun. Bobby never once felt insecure at any time during their conversations. It isn't until Kate asks Bobby if there is anyone back in Boston waiting for him. Bobby doesn't feel threatened by Kate's getting right to the point, and as a matter of fact, he is kind of happy she asked him that question. However, he isn't sure how to answer it. To avoid the details, he dances around the truth by saying that he is single. Fortunately, Kate doesn't ask Bobby to elaborate. To his surprise, she goes into her personal life in great detail. She was married for eight years to a wonderful man; he was a doctor ten years older than she was; he was from Switzerland and that they lived there for four years. Kate becomes very somber when she explains that her precious husband was diagnosed with leukemia and had passed away in Boston two years ago. After that, she decided to stay in New England and ended up living in Portsmouth, New Hampshire, where she got a good job and bought a home. Fortunately, she was left very well off, but very unhappy and lonely. Bobby is humbled by her openness and affection for her late husband. What a lucky guy he was to have someone like Kate. Kate asks Bobby if he had ever been to Europe, and his answer is that he hasn't. Kate comments, "You would really like it, particularly Switzerland. The people are very friendly, just like you."

Kate associating friendly people with him is gratifying. Bobby's confidence is on the rise. Kate and Bobby finish off the wine and food and are ready to leave the restaurant. To keep things going, Bobby asks if she would like to see a show or go to the casino or whatever, and Kate answers, "A show sounds like a great idea. There's a comedy club here in the hotel. It starts at 9:30 p.m. We can make it if we hurry."

Bobby replies enthusiastically, "Great idea, Kate, let's go."

With that, Bobby calls the waiter over to the table to pay the bill. When the waiter arrives at the table, he informs Bobby that the bill was taken care of. Bobby looks over at Kate, and she smiles and replies, "You can pay for the show."

With that, they both get up and leave. Kate thanks the waiter for the great service and tells him how much she enjoyed the evening. Bobby shakes the waiter's hand and also thanks him for a wonderful evening.

At the comedy club, they are greeted by a friendly host, who asks them if they had made reservations, and Bobby answers that they had not. The host looks down at his podium and checks his computer and says, "You're in luck. I have a great table for you, and the show starts in twenty minutes. Please follow me."

They are led to a perfect table six rows back from the stage. To show his gratitude, Bobby hands the host a twenty-dollar bill. Looking around, he notices that almost all the tables have reservation cards on them; thus, he considers himself very lucky. Kate leans toward Bobby and asks how much he tipped the host.

"Two dollars."

"Are you nuts? This is Las Vegas."

"Only kidding. I gave him a twenty."

"That's more like it. I don't like cheap men."

"You won't have to worry about me. I've been known to spend money like a drunken cowboy on payday."

"I'm glad to hear that."

And with that, she puts her hand on Bobby's shoulder and gives it a very sensual squeeze. Bobby asks Kate if she knew what kind of desserts and drinks the club serves. Kate replies, "I'll ask the first person who comes to our table."

Kate no sooner finishes her sentence than a spunky young waitress comes up to the table, lays down a couple of coasters and a small menu, and says, "I'll be right back to take your order."

And so she does. Bobby orders a cappuccino and strawberry cheesecake, and Kate orders a cappuccino and a piece of lemon meringue pie with whipped cream. This prompts Bobby to comment.

"I was thinking of ordering that, but I didn't think it would be chichi enough."

"Who cares about chichi?"

"You're something else." All of Kate's very earthy responses get him to wonder if Kate may have gone through a ton of money on plastic surgery. But then he looks at her real closely and realizes that her beauty is too natural to be cosmetic. Kate looks around the room smiling warmly at all the people sitting at the nearby tables. Her radiance puts smiles on all their faces, particularly Bobby's. The waitress returns with coffees and desserts and asks if they would like something to drink after they finish their coffee. Kate thinks for a moment and replies, "I'll have a Drambuie. What about you, Bobby?"

"I'll have a Malibu with pineapple juice."

"You got it."

And with that, she hands Bobby and Kate the program featuring the comedians that will be performing tonight. Bobby glances over the program and says, "I have to be honest with you, I have never been to a comedy club. I don't recognize any of these comedians."

"The comedians performing toward the end are really funny. I've seen them on television on the comedy station."

Bobby and Kate finish their desserts and cappuccino, and as soon as they are done, the waitress is right back at their table with the drinks just in time for the lights to dim. The first comedian came out and rocked the place, but the third and fourth comedians, just as Kate said, took the walls down. Kate is laughing so hard, tears were coming down her eyes. Bobby is also rolling with laughter. He notices how majestic Kate looks when she is laughing and how catchy her laugh is. Enjoying Kate's company so much, Bobby forgets about all his insecurities. He is constantly looking over at her and wondering who on earth did she inherit her earthy style, uninhibited personality, elegance, and tomboyishness from? He now realizes that his lifestyle has allowed him to miss out on a lot of wonderful relationships, and at the same time, he's afraid that it's all happening too fast. Maybe it's because of the present circumstances: being in Las Vegas, no day-to-day responsibilities, and fun in the sun. Could these circumstances be bringing out only the good in Kate? What's she like when she's back home in Portsmouth? Could she be the blonde bombshell from hell? Bobby tries to get these thoughts out of his mind. At the intermission, the waitress returns to the table and asks if they would like another drink. Kate and Bobby both decline. Kate, however, says, "We can have a drink up in my room when we leave here, if that's OK with you?"

"That sounds like a great idea. If I have one more drink here, I won't make back up to your room."

The show gets over at 11:30 p.m. It's not late nor is it early for Las Vegas, but it was a touch late for Bobby. The waitress returns as the theater lights go on and places the bill on the table. Bobby quickly picks it up, looks at the bill, and hands waitress the payment and tip in cash. Kate takes notice of Bobby's method of payment and says, "Do you always carry that much cash with you?"

"Not always but sometimes."

As they are leaving, Kate grabs Bobby by the arm tightly. It is good that she did because the alcohol is doing a number on him. He is a bit wobbly on the way up from the chair but not enough to be noticed. He actually feels pretty good; he doesn't have a care in the world, and the alcohol is helping him relax, and that's just what he needed.

Bobby and Kate walk down the hall and into the elevator lobby. When the elevator doors open, a group of college kids gets out, and Bobby and Kate get in. Bobby falls back against the wall as the elevator starts to accelerate up to the floors above. Kate takes notice of Bobby's condition, laughs, and comments, "Are you going to make it up to the room?"

"Of course, I'm fine. I just have a slight buzz."

The elevator door slides open on Kate's floor. Bobby is feeling light-headed but not enough to make him feel intoxicated. It is just enough to make them feel real good. When they arrive at Kate's suite, she immediately takes off her high heels and asks Bobby if he minds if she gets into something more comfortable. Having no problem with that at all, Bobby comments, "I don't blame you. I'm not one for being formally dressed up myself."

"Nor am I."

After taking off her shoes, she walks into the bedroom through a small hall adjacent to the parlor. Not wanting to get too comfortable, Bobby remains standing at the minibar just in case he gets the bum's rush, knowing how awkward it would be for him to be sitting there with her looking down at him with her pajamas on. The location offers a perfect view into Kate's bedroom. Bobby tries not to look but couldn't help himself. Kate unzips her black velvet skirt and her silk blouse and then disappears into the closet. When she is back in view, Bobby could see how wonderful a figure she has. Getting overtaken by her beauty, he quickly moves away from the minibar to avoid Kate catching him gawking at her. When she returns to the parlor, she has a pair of loose-fitting shorts and a T-shirt. Being aware that Kate knows he's a bit light-headed from all the drink, he feels that he would be excused if he does or says something stupid. Whimsically, Kate asks Bobby if he would like something to drink, and Bobby replies, "I think I'm done drinking for the night."

Kate then moves over to the sofa and sits down with one leg under the other and gestures to Bobby to come and sit next to her, which he does in a flash. Looking at Bobby straight in the eyes, she says with a warm smile, "I had a fantastic time tonight. I really enjoy your company. You're a great date."

"Kate, you make me feel young again."

"Oh, come on, Bobby, you're not that old."

Bobby gives Kate a huge smile and says, "That's because I'm with you, and you bring a breath of fresh air into my life."

Kate raises her eyebrows and moves closer to Bobby and places a very soft and sensuous kiss on his lower lip. Bobby reaches over to grab Kate by the shoulder, and at the same, she puts both her hands behind his neck and draws him closer to her so that she could kiss him all over his face. He's overwhelmed, and she begins to moan and begins rubbing the back of Bobby's neck and his back. Beginning to get swept off his feet and feeling adventurous at the same time, he rolls down on the sofa and pulls Kate on top of him. Unfortunately, she somehow loses her balance and slides off his chest and onto the floor with a big thump. Bobby tries to stop her from falling but is only able to grab on to her T-shirt, which rips almost in two. As soon as she hits the floor, she begins to laugh hysterically. The situation is comical, and he begins laughing and coughing at the same time. Kate asks if she had scratched him on the way down.

"Just a bit, nothing serious."

"Let me give you something for your injury."

"Forget it. I think it's time for me to leave."

They both look at each other soberly, and Bobby repeats, "I really think it's time I go before I forget how to get back to my room."

"Bobby, the sofa is a convertible bed. You're welcome to sleep here tonight."

"Thank you for the offer, but I think I should go."

"Sure, go right ahead and leave me in time of need."

"Somehow, I don't think that's how it really is."

And with that, they both get up and embrace and gently kiss each other on the cheeks and say good night. As Kate walks Bobby to the door, she looks him straight in the eye and reconfirms, "I meant what I said about tonight. I really had a wonderful time."

Bobby asks Kate when he could see her again.

"Call me anytime, you have my number."

As she opens the door, she says, "I will be waiting to hear from you. Sleep tight tonight."

One last embrace, and he is off. On the way down to his room, he couldn't help but think what might have happened if Kate hadn't fallen on the floor. It really doesn't matter; what matters are the words Kate left him: "I will be waiting to hear from you." That was enough to make his night complete.

Bobby arrives at his hotel room and quickly gets into bed, and as he lies there, he thinks about his beautiful new friend; and with that, he is asleep in less than sixty seconds. Sometimes life is full of wonderful encounters.

Chapter 38

Back to the Voodoo Lounge to Plan the Trip to Reno

JEREMY, TERANCE, AND Bobby all had a busy day prior to the meeting at the Voodoo Lounge. Bobby, arriving early as he always does, waits for the other three guys to show up by 5:30 p.m. Being with Kate last night put him in very good spirits. Today, he is up at around 10:30 a.m., which is unusually late for him, and consequently he almost missed the buffet breakfast. After breakfast, he heads over to the hotel guests' business office and uses the complimentary computers to schedule the flights to Reno. After a quick search, he is able to book four reservations for 10:00 a.m. on Saturday with a weekend special, which offers a round-trip flight for only ninety-five dollars. The return trip back to Las Vegas is going to be at 5:00 p.m. on Sunday. Wanting the option to return on Saturday night, he checks out the flights on Saturday night and finds that there are plenty of empty seats back to Las Vegas. This is good news. It will give the guys the opportunity to return to Las Vegas at 10:00 p.m. on Saturday or Sunday. The up charge to change the flight is only ten dollars. Wanting everything to go as smoothly as possible, he fine-tunes his itinerary for the trip.

When Hank arrives at the lounge, Bobby is talking small talk with the waitress. Bobby introduces Hank to the waitress, Irene. Hank comments, "I was hoping that I would be the first one here, but I guess I'm not."

Irene looks directly at Hank and says, "Well, I'm so glad you're here. Can I get you something?"

Hank is thinking about what he wants to drink when Bobby comments jokingly, "She means something to drink, Hank."

To which Irene replies, "Maybe not?"

While chuckling about her comment, Hank looks at Irene and says, "I'll have a Coors Light."

"One Coors Light coming up."

Bobby and Hank move over to the booth they were at a couple of nights ago with Jeremy and Terance. At close view, Hank notices how tired Bobby looks. Hank comments, "Bobby, my good friend, you look tired. Maybe you should spend more time relaxing and having fun rather than worrying about our activities here in Las Vegas. There are a lot of things to do in Las Vegas that can take your mind off things, if you know what I mean."

Bobby looks over at Hank and thinks to himself, *If Hank only knew what I've been up to, he wouldn't be making these comments.* Rather than explain, Bobby takes a big chug of beer and says, "Well, Hank, as long as you're having fun, that's all I care about. So what's been going on with you, my friend?"

"Well, to start, I met a couple of very nice women with whom I've been spending some time. They asked me to be their escort at an opening ceremony for a new hotel on the strip."

"What makes you think you can handle two women?"

"Oh, it's nothing like that. These women are somewhat older than I am, and they're sisters. They own an interior design firm in Los Angeles, and they just happen to know the guys I work for in LA."

"Hank, I never really understood what you did for work."

Hank replies, "That's a good question. I'm a graduate architect, but unfortunately, I've only worked in architectural firms for about half the time that I have been out of college. I've had a couple of transient jobs that keep me busy when I'm not doing architecture. One of these jobs is working for a flooring company installing carpet. It offers a generous day's pay, and the owners are very good to me. I hope, however, I won't be spending my whole life installing carpet, but until the economy turns around, this work will do just fine."

As soon as Hank finishes his employment history, Terance appears at the booth. The time is 5:50 p.m. Terance sits down next to Hank, and as soon as he does, Irene comes over to the table with Hank's drink.

"Hi there," greets Irene.

"What can I get for you?"

"I'll a have a Coors Light with a twist of lime."

"You got it."

And off she goes to the bar. Terance looks at Bobby and Hank and says, "Well, guys, how have things been going for you?"

Bobby would have liked to go into a full description of his affair last night with Kate but is not sure how Terance would react, so Bobby avoids answering by saying that things are going pretty good, "but not as good as our friend Hank here."

With that, Terance turns and looks at Bobby and says, "I bet a guy with Hank's looks and personality could have a great time here in Las Vegas, if you know what I mean, Bobby."

Bobby looks over at Terance and says, "I know exactly what you mean, and so does Hank."

Bobby looks over at Hank.

"Tell Terance about your date with the two sisters."

Just as Hank is going to repeat his story, Jeremy enters the lounge. Bobby is the first to see him come in and immediately gets up to gives Jeremy a wave to come over to the booth. Hank and Terance turn around to greet Jeremy and immediately notice his new look. Hank comments, "Wow, Jeremy, look at you! What has Las Vegas done to our main man?"

Terance adds, "Jeremy, you look great! Did you have a good night at the casino?"

Bobby then chimes in, "Jeremy, my good friend, you look like a new man. You must be having a great time. What have you been doing?"

Jeremy sits down next to Bobby.

"Guys, I've been pushing the envelope. To start with, I met this wonderful Korean girl."

Hank cuts in, "Let me guess where—a massage parlor?"

With that, all four men break into laughter.

Jeremy grins and says, "Wait, don't laugh. He's exactly right. I did meet her at the massage parlor, but it's not what you think. The place was a first-class operation, and this girl was absolutely out of this world. I'm not one to be doing these kinds of things, and believe me, I wouldn't be telling you about this, but let me tell you, after I left the massage parlor, I was walking on air."

Hank responds, "I just bet you were!"

Terance counters with "I don't know what he's done or with whom he has done it with, but he looks like a new man."

"Thank you very much, Terance. I appreciate all the compliments, but what I need right now to finish an exciting day is one big kick-in-the-ass drink."

With that, Bobby puts his arm around Jeremy.

"You just made my day. I'm glad to see you so happy."

Bobby raises his hand and motions Irene to come over. When she approaches, she looks at Jeremy she says, "You look buff. I'm afraid to ask what you've been up to. But I will ask what you would like to drink?"

"Tequila on the rocks."

Hank continues with his inquiries. "Well, Jeremy, what else have you been doing?"

Becoming very animated, Jeremy shares the details of his trip to the Hoover Dam. He asks if any of them have been to the dam. Their response is they hadn't. Jeremy continues, "Let me tell you how this all came about. After I left the massage parlor, I was feeling adventurous, so I went to the tourist information office to find out what I could do in one day that was exciting and inexpensive. The suggestion was to visit the Hoover Dam. So I got up early this morning and drove to the dam. The ride was exhilarating and didn't take that long. When I arrived, I signed up for the typical tourist's tour. The tour was a wealth of information. I enjoyed it immensely, but my adventure wasn't quite over yet."

The three men listen intently as Jeremy continues, "After the tour of the dam, I took an inflatable boat ride down the Colorado River. It was unbelievable."

Jeremy grows more animated as he describes his adventure. He becomes more articulate as he describes all the details of canyons, the longhorn sheep, the rapids, and the view of the dam from the river. The more Jeremy describes his adventure, the more excited he becomes, which flows over to his engaging friends. They listen emphatically to everything he says and adds, "Wow, that sounds great. It must have been very exciting, and you did this all in one day."

"Absolutely, I did it all in one day."

Jeremy talks for a good half hour about his adventure, and when he finishes, his friend Terance adds, "Jeremy, I wish you had told me you were going to the dam. I would have loved to have gone along. I really enjoy that kind of stuff."

Hank and Bobby also note how much they would have enjoyed taking a trip. The men are genuinely impressed with Jeremy's adventure. Bobby comments, "Jeremy, the next time you think about doing something like this, please let me know."

Jeremy adds that he would have invited them all if this hadn't happened so spontaneously. It was all prompted by his newfound sense of adventure.

"To be honest with you, I really didn't feel all that great when I woke up yesterday morning. I had no ambition to do anything today. It all started with with my decision to go through with the massage with Kie."

"Her name is Kie?" Hank asks.

Jeremy answers, "Yes, and she's Korean."

"Well, Jeremy, I must say it seems you're already on first base."

"First base or no first base, she lifted my spirits and my curiosity and gave me a whole new outlook on life. Immediately after I left the massage parlor, I headed over to the tourist information center and got the information on the dam. It's not just coincidence that all this has happened, and I don't think it's over. I think there's something big on the horizon."

Hank asks, "Like what?"

"I have no idea other than it may have something to do with the competition."

Hank comments, "You think you're going to win?"

"Not in a million years."

"Enough about winning. Tell us about this new look of yours."

"Well, it's like this, Hank: I haven't bought a sport jacket since I don't know when. So I decided to treat myself. And let me tell you, when I got back to my room, I changed into my new clothes, looked in the mirror, and saw a new man. The feeling was uplifting."

"The clothes look great, and the belt is something else. Where did you get it?" Hank adds.

"Oh, the belt, I picked it up at a Native American gift shop on the way back from the dam."

Bobby looks over at Jeremy and says to Hank and Terance, "Let's all toast to the new Jeremy—better yet, let's toast to the new and adventurous Jeremy!"

Bobby, Terance, and Hank have no idea what a wonderful moment this is for the guy who, just two days ago, had nothing to offer them but silence. The enthusiasm that Bobby, Terance, and Hank share with Jeremy over his adventure uplifts his spirits and gives him more confidence than ever before.

Just then, Irene returns to the table and asks if anybody wants another drink, and they all reply, "Absolutely."

Bobby looks over at his three companions and says, "Well, guys, I guess it's time we talk about the trip to Reno. Here's how I see it: we'll leave by plane from the McCarran Airport Saturday at 10:00 a.m. and arrive at 11:00 a.m. in Reno. There we'll pick up the rental car and drive over to Reno Marriott. We should get there by 11:30 a.m. We'll check into the hotel for one night only until we decide what we're going to do. I've confirmed that the hotel is only half full, so we'll have no problem if we decide to stay two nights. If Saturday offers us a confidence builder, we should extend our stay. On the other hand, if we feel that competing on Sunday has no advantages, then we should leave Saturday night or maybe Sunday morning. I booked us to leave on Sunday, but if we decide to leave Saturday night, the up charge is only ten dollars. If the competitors look really good, we may want to stay the next day to watch the rest of the guys compete and leave Sunday night. Whatever we decide, there are flights back to Las Vegas almost every hour. We should at least stay until Sunday morning. That way we can strategize on what we should be doing in Las Vegas. You know the majority of the higher-scoring competitors in Reno return to Las Vegas to compete for the big money. We'll see how things go and make our decision Saturday night. I think it would make sense if we take everything we need to compete so that we're prepared."

Terance chimes in, "It sounds like a good plan to me, Bobby."

Hank adds, "I like it too. If for nothing else, it gives us a chance to socialize with the other guys. You know how we like talking over things with Tony and the rest of the competitors."

Jeremy comments, "I like it too. It would be nice to see the other guys again. I recall that last year we were surprised by the talent of some of the newcomers when they performed in Las Vegas. Maybe this year we'll witness the Elvis we're all looking for. How wonderful that would be."

Bobby answers, "Maybe that's Jeremy's prediction that there's something big on the horizon."

Jeremy mentions that he is worried about the cost since he had been spending more money than he had budgeted for the two-week trip.

"Don't worry, Jeremy," Terance assures him. "I can front you as much money as you need."

Bobby adds, "Absolutely. Don't worry, Jeremy. I'll pay for the flight. You can pay me when you get the money."

Jeremy replies, "Thank you both very much. You don't know how much I appreciate your generosity and friendship. To be honest with you, guys, it goes way beyond that."

Bobby says with a kidding gesture, "Well, Jeremy, I'm glad we have such an impact on you. The plane fare is only ninety-five dollars round trip and an extra ten if we leave Monday morning. The hotel may cost eighty dollars including tax. I booked two rooms so we can bunk up together for forty each. There will be some costs associated with the competition, but that won't be much. I think we can go easy on the food. So I think the whole trip will cost us under $200 each. How's that sound?"

Hank comments, "Sounds good to me."

"Me too," replies Jeremy.

Terance adds jokingly, "I think I can swing it. Maybe we should have an early night tonight."

They all agree. Bobby suggests that they grab a bite to eat and then head back to their hotels unless they had some other ideas. Hank suggests going to his hotel and eating at the Cabana Bar and Grill. "The food is great, and you get a lot for your money, but that's not all—the scenery is the best part of the deal."

Bobby replies, "What do you mean 'the scenery'?"

"You'll see, Bobby. It won't be like Graceland, but you won't be disappointed."

Terance adds, "This all sounds good to me. What do you think, Jeremy?"

Jeremy answers jokingly, "I'm up for anything these days as long as you're paying!"

Bobby glances up at Jeremy with a surprised look. Jeremy quickly replies, "Just kidding!"

Hank adds, "I have my car. I can drive us all to the hotel and then drop everyone off at their hotels after we eat."

Bobby and Terance agree immediately, but Jeremy is hesitant. He does not want Bobby and the guys to know where he is staying, but he accepts Hank's offer. Hank leaves to pick up the car. Bobby, Terance, and Jeremy wait at the entrance to the hotel. The night temperature is perfect, sixty-six degrees and low humidity. Hank drives up to the entrance of the hotel with his mint 1961 white Thunderbird with the top down. As soon as the three guys see the car, they show their excitement. Bobby gets in the front seat, and Jeremy and Terance sit in the backseat. Bobby remarks first, "Jesus, Hank, this car is great! Did you buy it like this, or did you restore it yourself?"

"My father and I did it over a couple of years. My father is a real car buff. He's restored a '53 Caddy just like the one Elvis bought his mother."

Bobby is very interested about the Caddy restoration Hank is describing. He thinks about his restoration project back home and mentions that he would like to meet Hank's father someday. Hank thinks that would be a great idea. Terance comments, "Hank, how did you get such a unique license plate, HND DOG?"

"My father gave it to me as a birthday present. My aunt works at the Registry of Motor Vehicles."

Jeremy adds, "That's one heck of a nice present."

As soon as the three men settle into the car, Hank hits the CD player and plays Elvis singing "Viva Las Vegas." *What a way to travel,* Jeremy thinks. They arrive at Hank's hotel around 8:00 p.m. Hank parks under the canopy at the entry to the hotel and asks the valet if he could keep the car there for about an hour while they eat at the bar and grill. The valet hesitates and says, "We are pretty tight for spaces out front."

The valet then looks away from Hank. Terance overhears the valet's comment and gets out of the car, walks up to the valet, reaches out his hand, and says, "Maybe this will help my friend find a nearby space for his nice car?"

The valet grips Terance's hand, and Terance slips him some cash. The valet yells out to his partner, "Put the T-Bird under the canopy!"

"Thanks, guys. I appreciate it" is Terance's response. The valet looks at the cash in his hand and then at Terance and says, "Yes, sir, anytime."

After the men left the car, Hank turns to Terance and asks, "How much did you slip him?"

"I just gave him a couple of bucks."

Bobby adds, "I bet it was more than a couple of bucks."

Bobby is right—it is more than a couple of bucks; in fact, Terance had slipped the attendant thirty dollars. Terance knows the power of money, especially in a place like Las Vegas. Jeremy is enjoying all the attention the hotel guests are giving them being what was going on with the valet and the beautiful car.

The Cabana Bar and Grill is hopping with people of all ages. As soon as the men arrive at the café, the hostess, who recognizes Hank as a hotel guest, immediately approaches the group. She asks Hank if they would like to sit outside on the patio. Hank says yes, and she asks him to give her a couple of minutes, and she'll have a table for them. Meanwhile, Bobby and Jeremy are busy checking out all of the beautiful women sitting at the bar and at the poolside patio. Bobby looks at Hank and says, "Now I know what you mean by exceptional scenery. Where on earth did all of these beautiful women come from?"

Hank replies jokingly, "I think the hotel has a special vacation deal that allows beautiful women to stay free."

The hostess returns and asks the men to follow her to a poolside table that was right in the middle of a group of fun-loving women. The guys sit down and immediately look over the menu. Bobby quickly sizes up the situation and realizes that all the women sitting around them must be part of a tour group. He turns to the table next to him, where four middle-aged women are sitting, and says, "Excuse me, could you tell me what's good to eat here?"

The women take a long look at him and then respond with a tempting remark, "It depends on what you want to eat."

Bobby gets a little flustered by the remark, but his stature is restored when Jeremy says, "How about if he wants something warm and juicy, what would you recommend?"

Within a split second, both tables break out into laughter, and the introductions begin. The women are with a group from San Diego. They are there in Las Vegas for the show being held at the fashion center.

"All kidding aside," one of them says, "all the food here is great."

One woman asks Hank if he was staying at the hotel to which Hank replies yes. She comments, "I thought so. I've seen you around."

The conversation picks up when they all begin describing how wonderful it is to be in Las Vegas, particularly with the exceptionally warm weather. The women are working on dessert, while the men are waiting for their waitress to bring their meals. Bobby, Hank, Terance, and even Jeremy ate, drank, and carried on with the group for about an hour until they left. Soon after they left, so did the guys. On the way out, Hank compliments Jeremy on his icebreaking remark about the juicy food. Jeremy is feeling really good about himself. The guys are at the hotel entry at 9:45 p.m. Hank walks up to the valet and gives him the parking ticket. The valet drives the Thunderbird up to the front door of the hotel, and the men get in. Hank asks where to, and Bobby immediately replies, "The Bellagio."

Jeremy replies, "I'm staying on E. Sahara Drive."

Terance replies, "The Mandalay Bay."

Hank drops Bobby off first and then drives Terance to the Mandalay Bay. As he got out of the car, he turns to Hank and Jeremy and says, "I'll see you two at the airport tomorrow."

They reply, "See you tomorrow, Terance."

Hank drives off and then turns to Jeremy and says, "Where to?"

Jeremy hesitates and then replies, "The Marriott on East Sahara Drive."

Hank asks for directions, and Jeremy directs him. After a few minutes, Hank is at the hotel and drops Jeremy at the lobby entrance. Before Jeremy gets out of the car, Hank puts his arm on Jeremy's shoulder and says, "You know, my friend, I kid around with you a lot, but I meant everything I said about how great you look tonight and how you're going to the Hoover Dam by yourself really impressed me. I would've loved to have gone with you. I think riding down the Colorado River on an inflatable boat must have been the best."

"At first, I thought you guys would think it was all a bit lame, but now I'm glad I shared my experience with you and wish you could have come. Your interest in my adventure really boosted my spirits. I needed something like that in my life for a long time."

"I'm also impressed with your massage parlor story. You've got some balls doing something like that. I don't think I could muster up the courage to go through with it."

"I'm pleased you mentioned that. Some people wouldn't understand how those kinds of things help your mojo, if you know what I mean."

"I sure do. Sometimes you just have to do what you need to do."

"You're absolutely right, and thanks again for the kind words tonight."

With that, Jeremy says good-bye to Hank and walks toward the hotel lobby. He waits for Hank to drive away before he leaves the Marriott Hotel. He then walks across the street and up one block to his hotel. While he is walking, Jeremy thinks about how great the past couple of days have been for him. He thinks about how much his life is changing. It all started with a very depressing morning, and with just a couple of self-promoted activities, it ended up being two of the best days that he has had in such a long, long time. He wonders about what it takes to change one's life. Is it one big event after another or self-motivating small events? He concludes that he doesn't know the answer to that yet. However, whatever the answer may be, he's happy to be taking charge of life and making things happen. Enjoying the effect he has on the people around him and the positive influence that Bobby, Hank, and Terance have on him elevated his motivation. He concludes that good people attract and influence good people and that provocation can certainly add to the quality of one's life. Because of this, Jeremy is now finally feeling like a lucky man.

Chapter 39

Arriving in Reno

BOBBY, TERANCE, HANK, and Jeremy all arrive at the McCarran International Airport's terminal at 9:00 a.m. with their suit bags, small carry-on cases, makeup kits, and enough clothing for two days. Jeremy and Hank drove to the airport in Hank's car via the Marriot Hotel, and Bobby and Terance took cabs from their hotels. The men gather at the main terminal. Bobby, Hank, and Terance have their boarding passes in hand, which were downloaded at their hotels the night before. Jeremy has to retrieve his boarding pass at the terminal. The electronic flight information screens shows flight L 28 F to Reno, Nevada, departing at 10:00 a.m. on time. Passing through the security checkpoint in just a matter of minutes, they are on their way to the gate with bags in hand. The flight was just under three-quarters of an hour, landing at exactly 10:45 a.m. The plane taxies to the gate, and within ten minutes, the passengers depart through the forward compartment door. They wait patiently for everyone to leave the plane before getting up to gather up their carry-ons and suit bags. The weather looked perfect, the flight was very comfortable, and the time of arrival accommodated their schedule exactly. The men are in very good spirits. Bobby reserved an SUV at Hertz with his gold card membership. The SUV is waiting for them in the parking garage. All Bobby has to do is to read the number next to his name on the reservation board next to the Hertz customer counter, walk into the garage, and look for the number with his name next to it. The SUV is waiting with the trunk open and the keys in the ignition. The men load their apparel in the rear of the vehicle. Bobby gets behind the wheel and starts the SUV, and they head to the exit. The drive to the hotel Atlantis was about three and a half miles. It was a comfortable twenty-minute ride when the SUV arrived at the drop-off area at the main entry to the lobby. Bobby asks the guys to grab a rolling hanger clothes rack and a bellboy. Hank quickly jumps out of the SUV and heads for the lobby. Returning with the rolling rack and a bellboy, the men unload their baggage and place them on the rack and walk into the lobby. Bobby parks the SUV in the rear parking lot of the hotel and joins Hank, Jeremy, and Terance in the lobby of the hotel. Once in the hotel, Bobby confirms their accommodations with the young man at the reservation desk, who welcomes him.

"Sir, your two rooms are ready. They are nonsmoking, twin beds, and have connecting doors."

He then prepares four key access cards and places them in a folded cardholder. He explains that breakfast is served between 6:30 a.m. and 10:30 a.m. in the main dining room. After thanking the young man, they head toward the elevator to the twelfth floor of the atrium tower accompanied by a bellboy. This is going to be the first time they will share rooms together, and it doesn't seem to faze them in the least. The connecting rooms would make it very easy for them to communicate during their stay at the hotel. The idea of doubling up together seems appropriate for the activities in hand. Bobby and Terance enter the first room with the bellboy. They unload their garment bags. Hank and Jeremy wait for the bellboy, who soon takes them to their room. Bobby asks the bellboy to return to his room after he has left Hank and Jeremy's room. He does just that. Bobby slips the bellboy a ten-dollar tip and thanks him for his help. The bellboy thanks Bobby repeatedly and lets Bobby know that if he needed anything, he should call the front desk and ask for Sheik. Bobby confirms that he would do just that. The men immediately get settled in. Bobby notices that the connecting door to Hank and Jeremy's room is already opened. He knocks on the open door and asks, "How's everything going on in here?"

Hank replies, "This place is an outright bargain. The rooms are great, free parking, free breakfast, complimentary bottles of spring water, and it's all for just ninety-five dollars a night. How can you beat that?"

Bobby remarks, "As soon as you guys get settled in, come on over to our room. We need to talk about today."

The competition begins at 5:00 p.m., but nothing really happens until 7:00 p.m., when the performers get onstage. After they settled in, Hank and Jeremy head over to Bobby and Terance's room to discuss the day's schedule. The time is now 11:30 a.m. Hank asks why the change from staying just one day versus staying overnight. Bobby explains that he thought it would be easier for them to relax a bit tonight rather than rush out to grab a late flight. But most importantly, it was because if they decide to compete the next day, they would need a place to get ready for the competition. Terance responds, "I think that was a good decision, Bobby. This will be a lot easier, and the change of tempo for a couple of days won't hurt us."

Bobby adds, "OK, guys, this is what I have in mind for today: we should grab some lunch either in the hotel or take a ride somewhere. I think it makes sense for us to have supper in the hotel, that way we'll be ready for the competition. What do you guys think?"

Terance responds, "I agree."

Jeremy and Hank also agree. Bobby explains that he heard of a restaurant in Reno named Causeways. Hank notes that he had been there the last time he was in Reno, and the food was terrific and inexpensive, and they had a great buffet. Terance responds, "OK then, it's Causeways for us."

Hank and Jeremy head back to their room, and Terance and Bobby push the chairs to one side of the room to make more space, grab their key cards, and head out. Jeremy and Hank are in the hall waiting for them. Watching Bobby put in his key card in his wallet, Hank realizes that he had left his key card in his room and asks the guys if they would wait a minute for him to get his card. Jeremy responds, "Don't worry about it, Hank. I have a key to the room, and we will be arriving back at the same time. We also left the connecting doors to the adjoining room open so that Terance and Bobby could let you in."

"OK," Hank says with a worried look.

"It seems like I could have forgotten my head if it wasn't attached to my body."

Bobby comments, "Pay no attention, Hank. It's all the excitement that's throwing you off guard. Don't worry about forgetting your head. You've got us to carry it."

With that, they laugh and head to the elevator. The hotel's parking lot is a few hundred feet from the lobby door. During the twenty-minute drive to the restaurant, the guys talk about the competition and whom they think would be there. It is going to be like a class reunion with all the regulars, if they in fact show up.

Bobby adds, "I'm actually looking forward to seeing the other guys tonight."

"I'm betting there won't be any surprises this year. I recall that there were a couple of new entries last year, and my recollection is we only get new guys competing every two or three years."

Terance adds, "I wonder if that kid from Texas will be competing this year. You know what I mean—he was really good. I actually think he should have won in Las Vegas."

Bobby adds, "I'm with you, Terance. That kid is really good, and with a little bit of coaching, he could be the next one."

Jeremy immediately picks up on Bobby's comment "the next one" and wonders if finding the next one is the real reason he is there. He wonders if Terance and Bobby think the same. He isn't sure. Even with his perfect voice, he knows he would never have a shot at making it to the top, nor would Terance and Bobby. Bobby has the good moves, but neither of them would have all it would take to win. Hank, on the other hand, is young, looks just like Elvis, and with the right coaching, could make it to the top.

Bobby announces, "Hey, guys, we're here. I'll let you off at the front door so that you can go in and make a reservation while I park the SUV."

Hank says, "That sounds like a plan. Let's go, Jeremy."

Terance replies, "I'll stay with Bobby while you two guys go in."

As Bobby drives, he turns to Terance and asks, "Do you really think the kid from Texas could be the one?"

"I don't know, Bobby. The kid was real good last year, don't you agree?"

"I certainly agree, but do you think he could be the one?"

Terance takes a deep breath and says, "It has to happen soon. I know I'm not the one, and I don't think you think you are the one either, and I truly believe Jeremy knows he could never be the one. Time is ticking away. I'm betting on Hank for our sake, and if it's not him real soon, I hope it's the kid from Texas. We need a main act, someone to unite us. We don't have that someone right now."

Bobby pauses for a moment to take in Terance's words, which hit a nerve. He says soberly, "You know, Terance, your thoughts on this whole thing are exactly how I feel. Our getting together every year for meetings and then going on to compete is somewhat superfluous to my mission. I know as you stated, you and I and Jeremy could never make it to the top. And I also feel as you do—we need to find a main act right away. I want to be present when that happens, and it has to happen soon. This may come as no surprise to you, but my expectations have always been it will have to be Hank. He's young, he looks like Elvis, and in time, with the right kind of coaching, could easily finish in the top five. I don't know if he's aware of how we feel. I'm somewhat worried about his future. He's got a girlfriend back in Los Angeles. I don't want to pressure him into anything. That's why I haven't come right out with my feelings about this before."

"Those are my concerns exactly. I wonder what Jeremy thinks about this. If I had to guess, I think because he likes Hank a lot and Hank respects him, Jeremy would definitely go along with us. I'm betting Jeremy would give anything to see Hank make it to the top. Don't you agree?"

"I certainly agree, and I think we should talk to Jeremy right away."

"Let's do it today."

When Bobby and Terance return to the restaurant, it is packed with people. The hostess approaches Bobby and Terance.

"How may I help you?"

Bobby answers, "There are four of us, and I think the other two guys may already be seated."

"Is one of them a good-looking young man and the other guy somewhat older?"

"That's them."

The hostess asks them to follow her into the dining room and leads them to the booth where Jeremy and Hank are sitting. Bobby asks, "How on earth did you get to sit down so fast? The place is packed with people."

Hank answers, "We were lucky. About a second after we got in the restaurant, a group of about sixty or so people came through the door. They must've been in a bus group from one of the hotels."

Bobby replies, "I guess we were lucky."

Terance asks, without looking at the menu, "What's good to eat here?"

Hank replies, "I think the best deal is the fifteen-dollar buffet. It has everything on the menu and more."

Bobby replies, "I'm going to go for that."

"Same here," responds Terance.

Jeremy replies, "I guess we are all going for the buffet."

When the waitress returns to their table, she asks what they are going to have, and they all answer at once, "The buffet."

The waitress remarks, "Good choice. The salad bar is in the room with the white columns, and the buffet table is just behind that room."

Bobby comments, "Thank you very much. I heard the food was great, and that's why we're here."

"I'm so glad to hear that, gentlemen, and you all enjoy yourselves."

The waitress leaves, and the guys head over to the salad bar and load their plates with everything the restaurant had to offer. Finishing their salads in a matter of minutes, they head over to the buffet table, where there is a line fifty or so people deep. The activity around the buffet tables is intense. The diners are busy going from table to table loading up their plates. The buffet includes three meat carvers, a sushi server, and everything else from pasta to grilled tuna. It is like a cruise ship, which strikes a note with Terance with his meeting with the guys at Graceland. The servers and staff keep the warming trays packed with food and are moving in and out of the kitchen every minute. The men carry their overburdened plates back to the booth, set them down, and head over to drink dispenser. They return, look at the amount of food in front of them, and then look at each other. The silence is broken when Bobby states, "What a restaurant and what a country."

With that, the men dig in.

Chapter 40

Reno Competition and Elevating Hank

THE GUYS SPEND the rest of the afternoon in Bobby and Terance's room discussing the up-and-coming competition. This is the first time they will spend time together in Reno as a group. They used to attend solo prior to forming the pack. Doing most of the talking, Bobby explains how watching the event could help their chances in Las Vegas. Their main focus should be on the young guy from Texas and any other new contenders in the competition. Terance and Jeremy are on the same wavelength as Bobby. They know that this new kid from Texas could sweep the competition. Hank, on the other hand, is not so concerned. He is more interested in picking up some pointers from some of the older competitors who had mastered some of Elvis's choreography and facial expressions. Listening to Bobby, Terance, and Jeremy go on about the guy from Texas, Hank feels they had already conceded defeat, and this new guy is going to be the next Elvis. They got to a point in the conversation when Hank couldn't hold back his feelings and interrupts Bobby's spiel about the talent of the Texas kid. Hank remarks, "Hey, guys, come on. I don't think we came all the way up to Nevada to be cheerleaders for the guy from Texas. I think we can look him over, maybe pick up a few pointers, but as far as I'm concerned, his voice can't hold water to Jeremy's voice, and as for his moves, I think Bobby's choreography makes him look like a broomstick."

Bobby and Terance are broadsided by Hank's remarks. Terance replies, "Well, I'm glad to hear you have the spirit we need to win this competition. As you know or may not know, Bobby and I do this for the love of the event, our friendship with you guys, and the hope that we're here when the 'one and only one' appears, 'the cloned Elvis' walks on the stage and knocks everyone off their feet. I don't know how Jeremy feels, but Bobby and I know it will not be one of us."

Jeremy interrupts, "Terance, I feel the same way. I'm here because of you three guys, and I don't have your kind of friendship, support, or respect back where I'm from. I also know that I don't have what it takes to move up in the competition, and to be honest, I don't really care if I do. I feel exactly like you two do. I want to be here when Elvis comes, or as you say the 'the one and only' who walks onto the stage and knocks everyone off their feet. Over the years and as of right now, I'm very excited by Hank's attitude toward the competition. I believe that the three of us know our shortcomings and that it's Hank who has more of a chance of winning than anyone else I've seen compete. Hank is young, full of life, loaded with energy, and has the looks and passion to be the front man for us. But most importantly, he looks just like Elvis, and with that God-given gift and our help, there is no reason on earth why he shouldn't be the one. He has given me a lot of respect, not that you two haven't, and for that, I will do whatever it takes to make him achieve success in Las Vegas. I admire Hank's passion for the competition. If 'the one' is coming, that one is going to be Hank. So let's forget about this guy from Texas and let's concentrate on our Elvis and make sure he gets the support he needs to win."

Terance and Bobby smile jubilantly now that everyone is on the same page and shares the same mission. Terance comments, "Bobby and I discussed our position this afternoon and came to the same conclusion as you have. We didn't know how you felt nor were we confident that Hank had the desire to become the next Elvis, but after hearing what you just said and Hank's response to the guy from Texas, we are 100 percent behind Hank."

Jeremy is very happy he has the opportunity to express his position, which once again reassures him that he has the ability to analyze the situation and make an enlightening contribution. Hank sits motionless as he looks at his three friends and says, "I don't know what to say other than that I am overwhelmed by your comradery. I don't want to sound like a conceited jerk, but I felt like I had to say something because I saw all of this going down the river, and if that happened, there would be no reason for us to be together anymore."

Bobby interjects, "Hank, none of us really knows each other that well other than the couple of weeks that we spend together here in Las Vegas. Maybe this will all change in time, but for now, the single most important thing I needed to do is to bring closure to our efforts, and in doing so, we needed to resurrect someone, and that someone is you, the cloned Elvis, 'the one.' I only recently learned that Terance had the same expectations, and now I know that Jeremy also shares our mission. I'm extremely excited. I was, however, concerned that our expectations would fall short if we started putting pressure on you and causing you undue stress and consequently pushing you to lose interest in the competition. I was afraid that you would join the ranks of the young and fast, who don't see the need for all of this. I also felt that you may have been the one who wasn't going to show up for this year's competition, but when you arrived at the Voodoo Lounge, my expectations for this year were complete. Now that I know that you have your heart and soul committed to our mission, I have total confidence that it will be you that makes things happen."

Hank is extremely moved by his friend's commitments. He is also touched by their loyalty to one another. Bobby gets up from the table, walks over to the minibar, grabs four beers, opens them, brings them over to the table, and hands each of the guys a bottle. Bobby stands and says, "I propose a toast to the next Elvis."

With that, Terance and Jeremy stand up and toast Hank. Hank has a difficult time holding his emotions back. What Hank doesn't know is that the three humble men that are standing before him possess unimaginable intelligence, accomplishments, and wealth. If he had known their backgrounds, he might have not expected their devotion to his success. Bobby, Terance, and Jeremy sit down around Hank, and Bobby immediately gets into his itinerary. Explaining how their new direction is going to affect the activities that he planned for the remainder of the week, Bobby comments, "I think we should rethink our strategies and start by doing a number of things immediately. First, I think we should pay close attention to tonight's competition and forget about us competing. As you know, the good guys are scheduled first, and the second round of competition is for newcomers and the not-so-good. We don't care about the newcomers because we have the best newcomer sitting among us. We should take exception to anyone that looks new or unique, but other than that, we should make tonight a social event for the four of us. I'm sorry I made you take all your competition stuff to Reno, but it seems like such a minor inconvenience for something that has become such a huge motivation for the four of us. When we get back to Las Vegas, I will implement a plan to get Hank ready for Saturday's competition. We will most definitely have to meet every day to groom our friend for his big début. We'll each have to take on individual responsibilities to ensure that Hank has all he needs to succeed. I don't want to sound too overpowering and too intense about these tasks because we should also be having some fun while we're in Las Vegas. I also don't want Hank to get so uptight over the work ahead of us that it's going to affect his performance. Last but not least, I can't tell you how much of a burden has been lifted off my shoulders from what's aspired at this gathering. I feel much more positive about our future together with Hank as the front man."

Terance follows up with "I feel the same way. This is a big decision we made today, and we need to keep everything in perspective to allow Hank every opportunity to improve his performance. I only wish we had come to this conclusion earlier. We could have had more time to get Hank ready for this weekend's competition. I know for a fact that between the four of us, we can make up for lost time."

The four men discuss the numerous tasks that they need to have in place in order to get Hank ready for the big competition. Each of them now is thinking in a different state of mind from just a few days ago. They all have a very clear vision of what needs to be accomplished. Their friendship has taken on a higher level of compassion. They all now know that they share a common mission. They now have Elvis's protégé. They need to combine their abilities and God-given talents and extend them to Hank. The group's attraction to one another has electrified them to a point where they're all thinking as one. Bobby explains that this was the best thing that has happened to him since they all met years ago. But it is now time for supper, and Bobby announces, "Gentlemen, it's 5:00 p.m. and time for us to get some chow. What do you guys think?"

Hank replies, "I totally agree."

With that, Hank and Jeremy go back into their room, and Bobby and Terance stand, looking at each other with expressions of great contentment. Bobby says, "Well, my friends, I guess we're all on the same page now, so let's go and celebrate."

The four men meet in the hallway outside of Bobby and Terance's room and head down to the dining room in the main building of the Atlantis Hotel. Tonight will be a very special night for Bobby, Terance, Jeremy, and Hank. The four unorthodox friends now share a common mission. What a great day it has been.

Chapter 41

Reno's Elvis Competition

THE GUYS FINISH the meal at the Atlantis Hotel and head over to the hotel's theater. The room is set up for the dinner and a show event and is already filled with people, some of whom they recognized immediately from their previous competitions, some looked somewhat familiar, and the rest looked like curious tourists interested in talking to performers or possibly friends and families of the performers. They take a table up close to the stage so they could have a good look at the competitors. The show tonight is very informal and ranges from very entertaining to not so entertaining. A bubbly waitress comes over to the table and takes the men's drink orders, and when she leaves, a voice a few yards away calls out, "Bobby Shrimp, how the heck are you?"

Bobby looks over to the oncoming greeter and stands up. Offering a big smile and an extended hand, Bobby replies, "Tony B., how are you, my friend? Do you know Terance, Hank, and Jeremy?"

"I sure do. If I had Jeremy's voice and Hank's looks, I would be the King today."

As he laughs over his comment, he puts his hand on Jeremy's shoulder and asks how he was. Terance reaches over and grabs a chair for Tony. Tony sits down and opens the conversation with "What are you guys doing in Reno?"

Bobby answers, "Well, Tony, to be honest, we wanted to check out the talent before it came to Las Vegas."

"Are you guys thinking of competing?"

Bobby answers, "At first we were, but now we're not sure."

"Why is that?"

"We discussed our options when we arrived here, and we've changed our strategy. We feel we can learn more by just watching these guys and comparing notes rather than competing against them."

Tony replies, "It sounds like you're very serious about the competition this year."

"That's absolutely correct, Tony. Terance, Jeremy, and I are not going to compete this year, but our young friend Hank here is going to, and we think he has a good shot at finishing in the top ten if the three of us help him fine-tune his performance."

"I think may you have something good going for you, Bobby. I've been watching Hank for the past couple of years, and I think with his incredible resemblance to Elvis, he sure could go all the way, and with you three guys behind him, what better trainers could he have?"

"The three of us really think so too, Tony."

Tony turns to Jeremy and says, "How are things going with you, Jeremy? I watched your performance last year and noticed a slight tone change in your voice. What was that all about?"

Jeremy answers, "I had some kind of flu virus. It knocked the heck out of me."

Tony asks, "Is your voice OK now?"

"Yes, it feels really good now."

"Jeremy, how did you finish last year?"

Jeremy answers, "I think I ended up in the thirty-second slot."

Tony replies jokingly, "Jeremy, you mean to tell me the Asian woman impersonator came in ahead of you?"

Jeremy replies, "Yes, she did, Tony. I think she had a real good night. She had me convinced she was Elvis." Jeremy rolled his eyes, and the five men roared with laughter.

"Jeremy, you're a great sport. I admire you for that, and you guys bring class to our gig. We would hate to lose you. You know what I mean? It's not about the competition. It's really not even about the late Elvis Presley. It's about friends and comradery and all of us sitting around here having a good laugh and hoping for the best. I have always had a good time with my fellow competitors. It seems we have a very unique niche in life, one that many people would not understand. Some people watch us up there onstage and think that what we're doing is a big joke. Maybe it is, but believe me, the joke is on them. We're all having a great time together. It's almost like a sorority or a cult or whatever you want to call it, but whatever it is keeps us coming to these competitions every year. We try to help each other improve their performances. That's what we're all about. You guys know this kid from Texas is on tonight. I haven't seen him since last year when he walked away with the show. He's real good. Your guy Hank could knock him off the top if he could fine-tune his performance just as Bobby said. Just to keep things in perspective, the kid's name is Ron Brooks. I had a chance to talk to him last year and found him to be a very nice young guy. His attitude and personality fit in very well with the rest of the troop. We're all like a bunch of Boy Scouts trying to become Eagle Scouts. We are constantly trying to help one another out to gain rank."

Bobby responds, "Very well put, Tony. The four of us feel the same way. We're also here for those same reasons, and with Hank as our great young hope, we feel we can bring more to the troop."

"I like your commitment to all of this. Let's hope everyone follows your lead. I'm betting Hank moves up to the top sooner than later."

Tony's remark "sooner than later" strikes a sensitive chord with Bobby, Terance, and Jeremy. Tony stands up and says, "It's going to be show time for me in a half hour or so. I'm going up to my room to get ready."

"OK, Tony, we shall see you after your act."

"You bet."

Tony leaves, and Jeremy asks Bobby, "How long has Tony been doing this?"

"My guess is fifteen years or so. He seems to hold this whole thing together. From what I hear from some of the other guys that know him outside of all of this that he's a very big wheel in the movie business. I think he is with MGM or Warner Bros. I'm not sure which one, but I know it's one of those two."

Jeremy replies, "It seems to me that no matter who you are, the playing field levels out very nicely when we all get together for these events. For some reason, I think these competitions bring out the best in people. We all dress up in Elvis attire, put on wigs, sideburns, and sunglasses, walk up on that stage, and for a moment in time, we completely forget who we are, and we somehow convince ourselves that we're Elvis. I know that's how I feel, and I really enjoy feeling that way."

Hank adds, "I spend a lot of time thinking about how Elvis must have felt when he walked out on that stage, and thousands of people cheered and screamed at the top of their lungs. Those moments must have been indescribable for a young guy who came from nowhere USA. Actually, I believe it was his humble beginnings that gave him his audience appeal and engaging personality."

"And a lot of hard work," adds Terance.

Bobby replies, "You are absolutely right on, Terance. And from this point on, we are going to offer our hard work to Hank."

"Thanks again, guys. You don't know what this means to me."

At that moment, the lights dim, and the master of ceremonies walks onto the stage to announce the first contestant. The first contestant was from Kentucky; the men knew him from the last couple of shows. He was medium built and had some very good moves; his hair was perfect, but his voice was in the middle of the pack. Each contestant sang one song and was on the stage for about three to five minutes. The next fifteen performers fell into the same category as the first guy. They were good but not good enough to hold the audience's attention. It wasn't until Ron Brooks came out. Ron had charisma. He connected with the audience the moment he walked on the stage. It seemed he was able to make eye contact with all the people sitting in front of the stage as far back as six tables. His hair was perfect, his moves were terrific, his looks were close to Elvis's, but not as good as Hank's. His voice was really good but not as good as Jeremy's. All four guys were captivated by his performance. He was real good. However, it looked like he may have put on a few pounds around the gut since last year. Jeremy comments that he must've spent the prize money from last year on food. Nonetheless, he was real good, and his recent weight gain could be reminiscent of the older Las Vegas Elvis. Therefore, it wouldn't diminish his chances of getting a high score. He sang "Viva Las Vegas" and did it unbelievably good. The audience loved him. They gave him a standing ovation when he finished the song. Bobby, Hank, Jeremy, and Terance stood up from the table and cheered him on. The expression on Ronnie's face stuck in Bobby's mind. The kid seemed happier that he was pleasing the audience than winning the contest, and his smiling face and body language seemed very genuine and passionate. He reminded Bobby of Chris Martin of the rock group Coldplay; there was something genuine, down-to-earth, and people-friendly about these two guys. Bobby immediately knew that Ronnie was going to be one of the best. The remainder of the acts fell way short of Ron's performance until a newcomer came to the stage. This kid's name was Ritchie Evans. Ritchie was different. He didn't wear the Elvis emerald-studded jump suit and chrome sunglasses. Ritchie wore black leather pants, a black shirt, and a black leather sport jacket. He had an electric guitar and sat on a stool rather than ranting around stage like everyone else did. The kid's hair was perfect, his height and weight were also perfect, his looks were very close to Elvis's, and his voice was good. But it was his guitar work that was his main attraction. He sang "Treat Me Nice" like no one had ever done it before. He was probably as good as Elvis on guitar without the charisma. He had the song down pat and was able to make eye contact with the audience. This kid was real young, maybe twenty years old. His performance was right up there with Ronnie's. It seemed the audience now had two Elvises to choose from, the young vulnerable one and the older more confident one. Ritchie sang like he was singing to people that he knew and loved dearly. He also received a standing ovation from the audience. Bobby turns to his three friends and says, "I'm glad we came. Watching Ronnie and Ritchie perform tonight has turned my head around. We will need to talk about this at length before we prepare for Hank's performance next week."

Terance looks at Bobby and adds, "I'm not worried about these two great performances. In fact, I'm encouraged. We now know who our competition is and how we should groom Hank. Ritchie sitting in a chair was a very different approach. I don't know how the judges are going to react to it, but I liked it for one reason. And that reason is we may not need to concentrate on Hank's choreography if we come up with something that's similar to Ritchie's."

Jeremy adds, "We should stick around for the judges' decision."

They all agree with Jeremy. The show comes to an end at 10:00 p.m., and as usual, all the competitors come out and mingle with one another and with the people in the audience. This is a very different kind of competition; it is almost like playing golf. Golfers don't try to beat each other; they try to beat the course. These competitors are similar; they are not trying to beat each other but rather they are trying to become Elvis. Tony comes over to the guys' table with a wide grin on his face and says, "How did you like those two guys?"

Bobby, Terance, Jeremy, and Hank know exactly which two guys he is referring to. They all answer at once, "They were great."

Tony is still in costume, as are the rest of the performers. Tony replies, "I have to go somewhere. I'll be right back. Don't go anywhere."

The guys mingle with the performers. All of the performers seem to have one thing in common, and that is that they really enjoy being together. They're like disciples looking for someone to worship. Most of them compete just to be with people who share their joys of life. Nobody cares how affluent, well known, or accomplished one might be. None of that seems to matter when they're together. They all just have a great time doing what they love to do. Bobby glances out over the dining room floor and sees Tony walking toward him with Ronnie and Ritchie. He gestures to Terance, who raises his eyebrows. Tony and his two guests come right over to the waiting men. Tony makes the introductions.

"Boys, I want you to meet my two good friends, Ronnie Brooks and Ritchie Evans." Ronnie and Ritchie reach out to shake the hands of the smiling men, and they all introduce themselves.

"I'm Jeremy Shrinks, and you guys were wonderful."

"I'm Bobby Shrimp, and you guys were the best."

"I'm Terance Best, and I was extremely impressed."

"And I'm Henry Hunk. Everyone calls me Hank, and I could listen to you guys all night."

With that, the men grab chairs from the surrounding tables and all sit down together. Ronnie and Ritchie are still in costume, but somehow they don't look like Tony. Their attire looks understated for this kind of event, particularly Ritchie's. Ritchie is young and shy. He has a Southern drawl in his voice, which makes his costume seem fitting for him. He is very well mannered, as is Ronnie. The two young guys are surprisingly very friendly with one another. Bobby asks, "You guys seem to be friends, is that true?"

Ronnie answers, "We are, Mr. Shrimp."

Bobby interrupts, "Please call me Bobby, all my friends do."

Ronnie replies, "OK, sure enough, Bobby. Ritchie and I attended Providence College in Rhode Island. We played in a band together, and we still get together when we can. Ronnie and I were assigned to the same dorm room. And when we both showed up with guitar cases, we knew immediately that we would be involved in some kind of music. One day, we went for hamburgers for lunch and saw one of those cutout board images of Elvis. It caught my eye, and when Ritchie went into his Elvis voice, I knew what we were going to do next. I'm from Houston, Texas, and Ritchie's from Lexington, Kentucky, and how we ended up in a Catholic college hundreds of miles from where we live is one of life's big mysteries. What is more of a mystery is how we ended up doing this."

Bobby expresses his encouragement and says, "You two guys are the best we have seen since we've been doing this. I hope that you will be able to take your performances to the next level."

Ritchie replies, "Thank you very much for that compliment, Bobby, but this may be the last time for us. I landed a job with the EPA in Boston, and Ronnie is going to be working in his father's investment company. I guess we're going to be busy this upcoming year and won't have time to compete."

Ronnie and Ritchie's words are as sincere as two young guys could possibly be. They are polished, humble, and in a strange way, somewhat pious. Bobby wonders if it is their pious personas that remind him of Elvis. It is a big part of their attraction to him. However, when they announce that their families are in the audience, the whole thing comes to light. It is now very clear to Bobby: these two guys were up there entertaining their families; it was that notion that gave them their tremendous edge. Bobby looks at Hank, and Hank makes an "I know what you're thinking" gesture. Ronnie and Ritchie excuse themselves to be with their parents. The lights in the dining room lower a bit, and the master of ceremonies comes out to the center stage and announces, "Ladies and gentlemen, the judges have made the decision, and for the first time since I don't know when, we have a dead tie. The winners are Ritchie Evans and Ronnie Brooks. Sorry, guys, you'll have to split the winnings. That will be fifty dollars for Ritchie and fifty dollars for Ronnie. Sorry about that, only kidding. Come up onstage and let everybody give you another round of applause."

With that, Ritchie and Ronnie get up on the stage to receive their equal split of the $5,000 prize. The crowd cheers and claps for a good two minutes. The lights get bright, and everyone starts leaving. Tony says good-bye, and the four men head over to the lounge, have a quick drink, and discuss their strategies and what-ifs for about an hour. They all retired to their rooms at the same time. They agreed to meet at 8:00 a.m.

in the lobby. They planned on taking the 11:00 a.m. flight back to Las Vegas.

The next day, they have an early breakfast and are in the lobby checking out by 9:30 a.m. As they are leaving the hotel, they run into Ritchie and Ronnie and their parents. The boys introduced their parents to Bobby, Jeremy, Hank, and Terance. They talked about Reno and Las Vegas for a few minutes and then left to go to Las Vegas. Out of costume, the two young guys look like a couple of wholesome, clean-cut college students who are on vacation with their mothers and fathers. Bobby notices the attitude both boys had toward their parents, which reminds him of Elvis's admiration for his parents. He knows that this is what gave these two guys the confidence and persona when they were up on the stage. He wonders if Hank's family ties are similar. From what he knows about Hank so far, he feels very optimistic.

Chapter 42

Back in Las Vegas

THE GUYS ARRIVE back in Las Vegas on Sunday at around 12:30 p.m. On the trip back, Bobby and Terance talk about the new direction for Hank. They both agree that the number-one priority should be how they are going to groom Hank into becoming the young Elvis. The look should be somewhat similar to Ritchie's act but with a different hook. Bobby also discusses probing into Hank's home life to see if there are some similarities between Elvis and him. Terance cautions Bobby that that should be done very delicately. Bobby agrees.

When the four men disembark from the plane, they regroup in the main terminal, and then all agree to meet Monday night to start gearing up for the big show on Saturday night. They know that they are going to have to make a lot of changes to their schedules in order to accommodate Hank's preparation. Time is of the essence. Hank offers to drive each of the guys back to their hotels. They all accept gratefully. Jeremy is dropped off first and then Terance, and now Bobby is alone in the car with Hank. Realizing that this would be a good time for him to do some probing into Hank's background, Bobby starts the conversation by mentioning that he is going to call home to see how things are going. He isn't going to come right out and mention Lynn's name. Rather, he would hint about how he missed some of his close friends and his brother, Jesse. Bobby starts the conversation with "It's been a week since I've been home, and I sure would like to know if everyone and everything is OK back there. When I was younger, I didn't miss home as much as I do now. It seems I can't stay away too long without feeling that something is missing."

Hank doesn't respond. Realizing he needs to push the envelope, Bobby jests, "Hank, I bet a guy like you has a boatload of good-looking young women waiting for you back home?" Bobby ushers a slight laugh after that comment.

Hank replies, "No, that's not it at all. I'm a one girl kind of guy."

"Well, Hank, that is very refreshing to hear."

Bobby is impressed that Hank is very conservative about his relationships. Hank begins talking about Kayla and how much they have in common. He also explains how much he enjoys her family and how much she enjoys his family.

"As soon as I get back to my hotel, I am going to call Kayla. I told her I was going to when I returned from Reno, and then I'm going to call my mother and father. They worry about me as if I was a fifteen-year-old kid."

Bobby is getting even more inspired hearing Hank talk about his family and his girlfriend's family. Hank turns the table around a bit on Bobby and asks him if he had a special someone back home, and Bobby explains that he is involved with a very nice woman who keeps him out of trouble. Being glad to hear that, Hank asks in a very serious tone, "What do you know about Terance and Jeremy?"

"I think probably as much as you do. As a matter of fact, you and I probably know more about each other, because of this conversation, than I know about them. For that matter, I don't know what they know about us. I'm not sure I would want to pry into their lives. I think they may be more complicated, in very different ways, than yours and mine."

Hank agrees and adds, "There's something about Jeremy I like. I was very moved by his sincere appreciation of our comments on his new clothes and his experience at the Hoover Dam. If I had to guess, I would say that Jeremy has not been living a very happy life. I feel that our taking an interest in what he says and does builds up his confidence. He seems to be more relaxed around us now more than any other time we've been together. I also think that he is a very smart guy just by the way he's able to describe the things that happened to him and how he tends to remember everything that's said or happens around him. I don't know if you have noticed how he is able to pick up on things very quickly. The one thing that stands out the most about him is the way he protects his vulnerability. He and I talked a lot last night about Ronnie and Ritchie. It seems that Jeremy was very quick to detect that they were not very passionate about the competition. He somehow knew that they probably would not be competing next year, and then when Ritchie and Ronnie announced that this was their last year competing, I realized that Jeremy had incredible perception. Jeremy said that he could see it in their eyes when they came over to talk to us with Tony last night. Jeremy explained that they seemed appreciative of the compliments but not in a way that somebody who is passionate about the competition. He went on to say that he felt that Ritchie and Ronnie were performing exclusively for their mothers and fathers. He felt that these two guys were doing this as a gesture of appreciation to their families. He explained that he surmised by their attitudes that they live a very good life, a direct result of their upbringing. Their fifteen minutes of fame was for their mothers and fathers only. The audience didn't matter that much to either of them. Jeremy could tell, by the way their fathers and mothers were looking at them, that they had a sense of pride for what their boys were doing. Their inspiration would not be felt by run-of-the-mill parents. Jeremy explained that having your family supporting you can get you anywhere you want to go in life, even, as crazy as it sounds, to being the top dog at an Elvis competition. He ended by saying that not many of us have or had that kind of support and encouragement in our lives, and that's why I think that Ritchie and Ronnie don't need this Elvis acclaim as much as the rest of the performers do."

Bobby is silent for few seconds. He realizes that Jeremy is able to see what he had seen in Ritchie and Ronnie but more clearly and much more in depth. Bobby comments, "Hank, I think Jeremy's right. I also think you're right about Jeremy's incredible perception of people. I too realized some of these things that Jeremy was describing to you about Ritchie and Ronnie but fell short of why they didn't need to compete. I feel very good about our conversation. I also feel good that Ritchie and Ronnie will be competing in Las Vegas because it will give us something to measure up to. If we decide to use some of the stuff from their acts, we will need to use a lot of subtleties to pull it off. But we can go over that this week. I think Terance has some good ideas, and I think Jeremy can have something to add."

Hank responds, "I'm sure that Jeremy's newfound confidence will bring a lot to the table for me, as will Terance and you. Where will we be meeting next?"

Bobby answers, "I think it will be either at Terance's hotel or mine. I will call Terance and see where he wants to meet."

"I will do whatever you guys want me to do."

The two men arrive at the main entrance to the Bellagio hotel and say good-bye. Bobby repeats, "I'll call you before 5:00 p.m. tomorrow."

Hank says OK and drives off. Now that Bobby is alone, he couldn't help but feel guilty toward his actions. He knows deep down inside that it is Kate he is anxious to call, not home. To relieve some of his guilt, he decides to call Lynn. Unfortunately, she isn't home, so he leaves a message on the answering machine. His message is "Hi there, it's me, Bobby. I miss you. I'll call again."

He then immediately calls Kate on her cell phone. She picks up on the first ring and answers with "Hi, this is Kate."

"Hey, Kate, this is Bobby. How are you?"

"I'm just fine. Where are you right now, Bobby?"

"I'm here in my room. Where are you?"

"I'm at the poolside getting some sun. Why don't you come down and join me?"

Bobby couldn't resist Kate's invitation, so he says, "I'll be there in a few minutes."

"I'll be waiting for you."

Bobby places his suit in the closet, takes off his pants and shirt, throws on a pair of shorts and a T-shirt, and heads down to the pool feeling like a young kid heading to a party. When he arrives at the poolside, it is mobbed with people; he has to use his cell phone to locate Kate. Kate gives Bobby a couple of landmarks, and Bobby is at her side in under a minute. Kate is lying down on a chaise lounge reading a book. She has a black two-piece bathing suit on that complements her body to a T. Her hair is pulled back, but this time, it is in a ponytail, giving her a youthful look. Bobby walks up beside her, and she turns to him, slides her sunglasses down to the tip of her nose, and smiles as she looks up to the obviously gawking man in the funky shorts and T-shirt. Kate's first words are "Bobby, don't you have a bathing suit?"

"You're not going to believe this, Kate, but I forgot it."

"Well, then I guess we'll have to go and get you one real soon so that you don't look like you just arrived from the seventies."

Hearing that, Bobby looks around and notices that in fact he is the only one wearing shorts; everyone else is wearing bathing suits with the exception of the hotel staff. Now Bobby is feeling a little bit self-conscious. Bobby is comforted by Kate's comment about getting him a bathing suit real soon. Bobby reads into her comment, "We will have to get you one real soon," as a suggestion that they would be spending some time together today or tomorrow. Bobby asks Kate what she's reading.

"It's a book on tax incentives and government regulations on investment opportunities."

"That sounds a bit over my head."

"It's really not that complicated. I will give you a twenty-minute summary, but not right now. Now I want to know how Reno was?"

"It was kind of interesting. It's not quite Las Vegas, but I enjoyed it there. Unfortunately, I was only there for one night to visit with a couple of guys whom I met on a previous trip to Las Vegas. We stayed at the Atlantis Hotel. It was really nice."

"That's a coincidence. I was watching TV last night, and they had these guys impersonating Elvis Presley in the main ballroom of the Atlantis Hotel. It was a great hoot. Some of the performers were kind of strange, but there were these two young guys, Ritchie something and Ronnie something, that were really good. I don't know that much about Elvis, but these two guys were very convincing. They had something the other guys didn't."

Bobby wants to cut in and tell her the whole story but holds off and only comments that he and his friends watched a few of the acts and were lucky enough to catch Ritchie's act toward the end of the show. Kate asks, "Bobby, what makes grown men dress up like Elvis Presley, go out on a stage, and try to imitate him?"

"I don't really know, but I would guess it's like acting out a fantasy with other people who share the same fantasy. You know what I mean?"

"You could be right. People do strange things to keep themselves from going over the edge."

Bobby goes on, "Maybe it's because they're hoping for something. I guess some people do it for fun, the social contacts, the money, eluding loneliness, comradely, or maybe they have a mission."

"I can understand all that except for the mission part."

"Let's say you have a desire to bring someone back to life. Let's say, for a number of good reasons, that someone is Elvis Presley. Your reasons are you thought he was great, he had a huge influence on your life, he made a huge impact on music, you feel he died too young, and if he was alive today, he would be still be a big impact on your life. You feel that you have a kinship toward him. Maybe you look somewhat like him or have a voice like his or something else that ties his life to yours. Then one day you somehow meet up with a group of guys who share the same thoughts and feelings toward Elvis as you do. And with this, you become drawn together. As you become more involved in this thing, you realize you all share the same mission, and it's not about the competition or a show. It's more than that. You wish that during one of these competitions, somewhere, somehow, someone would rise up as the cloned

Elvis. I would guess that it would be the greatest moment in one's life to be there when that time comes."

"Bobby, that's really deep. How do you know so much about these competitors?"

Bobby answers, "I don't think I really have to know them to understand what draws them together. I may not be quite like them. But who knows? Everybody needs something in his or her life to look forward to, as do I, and so must you, Kate."

"I know all about that. But right now, I'm starving. How would you like to grab something at the cabana?"

"That sounds like a great idea."

Fearing that maybe he said a little bit too much about the Elvis Presley mission, he is now hoping she would forget about the whole thing. If she should find out why he's really in Las Vegas, how would he explain it? He could say that he and his friends were in Las Vegas to help Hank with his preparations for the competition. That would work.

Kate gets up off the lounge chair and grabs Bobby's hands and pulls him up.

"What are you doing?"

"I'm starving, so let's go to the cabana and get something to eat and then let's go down to the hotel mall and get you a bathing suit."

Bobby replies, "OK, whatever you say."

Bobby and Kate briskly walk over to the cabana restaurant, grab a couple of salads, iced teas, and are off to the mall within forty-five minutes. Bobby feels a little uncomfortable with Kate helping him pick out his bathing suit. Not really wanting one, he has to look interested, although he isn't. After a few "what do you thinks" and "how does this looks," Bobby purchases a nondescript bathing suit, and off they go back to the hotel pool. Kate insists that Bobby put the new bathing suit on so they could go in the pool together. Bobby obliges and changes into the bathing suit in the men's room and quickly returns. As soon as Kate sees Bobby, she replies, "Now you look like you're part of the scene. Let's take a dip."

Bobby isn't much of a pool person, but he goes along with Kate's wishes. Walking out in front of him, he could see how attractive she was and wondered why this sexy, young, good-looking, and intelligent woman is attracted to him. Maybe there's something wrong. But he doesn't want to dwell on that notion. Now he's going to enjoy every minute he can with Kate. Kate dives into the water and beckons Bobby to jump in. Taking the pool stairs, he walks into the warm pool water. Kate swims over to him and grabs him by the hand and leads him off to deeper water. The pool is packed with mostly young people; this gives Bobby an uncomfortable sense of being out of place. Entering the deep water, Kate gets behind him and slowly pushes him forward into the water and swims up on his back so that they are layered one on top of the other. Bobby begins to swim slowly toward the other end of the pool. With arms wrapped around his upper body, she presses her chest into his back, which excites him to a point of embarrassment. Knowing that he is caught between the devil and the deep blue sea, he knows that Kate has to be aware that he couldn't get out of the pool without being embarrassed. He surmises that she is doing this on purpose just to tease him. She is succeeding. Kate squeezes Bobby real tight and rolls him on the side, which is not a good position for him to be in. Bobby turns to Kate and says quietly and kiddingly, "Are you trying to embarrass me in front of all these people?"

"What on earth do you mean?"

She giggles and presses up really tight to his back and then pushes him off to swim to the edge of the pool. Taking a deep breath, he looks around, hoping no one is looking at him, and swims over to the edge of the pool just in time to see Kate push up and out of the pool. Her agility is extremely impressive. He unfortunately has to walk over to the steps to get out of pool. However, for him, his moment of embarrassment had passed.

Kate is toweling off when Bobby returns to the lounge chairs. He grabs his towel and wipes himself down. Kate positions the two lounge chairs so that she would be facing the sun and sits down with the back of the lounge chair in the upright position. Bobby does the same. For a moment, Bobby feels a bit awkward sitting there with nothing to say, but it passes when Kate says, "Bobby, in the very short period of the time since I've known you, it's made a big difference in my stay here. I wanted to get away so I could work a bit and relax, but it seems that the thing I enjoy doing the most is being with you."

Bobby replies, "I got to tell you, Kate, I feel the same way. You're a very different kind of person, and to be perfectly honest, I've never been with such a good-natured, witty, and thoughtful woman as you. I don't want to sound like I'm overanxious, but I couldn't wait to get back from Reno so I could be with you again."

Kate replies, "That's very inspirational. I haven't been myself since I lost my husband, Walter. He was everything to me. My life has been empty for the past couple of years. I felt I had to get away and have a change of scenery to rejuvenate my spirits. And by some good fortune, I end up sitting next to you in an airplane. Your pleasant disposition is such a comfort for me, and the other night, when you decided it was time for you to leave my room, was a true account of the kind of gentleman you are. I don't know what other guy would have left a woman's room in Las Vegas without trying to put the moves on her, particularly when they were both a bit tipsy."

Bobby doesn't know how to answer. The truth of the matter is he is afraid to put the moves on her for fear that she would turn him down and bring the whole relationship to an end. So Bobby just shrugs his shoulders and says, "I'm happy just to be hanging around the pool with you. I live a very frugal and simple life. I work a lot and look forward to times when I don't have to think about all of my responsibilities. That's one of the reasons I came to Las Vegas—to visit with friends and take in the city. However, now that I'm with you, you're the only thing on my mind."

Kate reaches over, grabs Bobby's hand, squeezes it tightly, pulls him close to her, kisses him on the cheek, and says, "I want to be with you tonight."

"My thoughts exactly. What do you want to do tonight?"

"Well, now that you mention it, I was thinking of about going to this restaurant that everyone is talking about. It's in the industrial area of the city. The restaurant's name is Graceland."

Bobby doesn't want to let on that he had already been there. Fearing that she might ask questions, he doesn't want to answer. So he goes along with the notion that it would be a new experience for the both of them.

"I made reservations for us at 8:30 p.m. So we'll meet in my room at 7:30 p.m. and take a cab over to the restaurant?"

"I think that'll work out just great."

Bobby and Kate hang around the pool for a couple of hours, which gives Kate time to explain the book she is reading. Outlining the contents of the book in very clear and simple language allows Bobby to understand most everything she is explaining to him. By 5:00 p.m., they are on their way back to their rooms, and Bobby is again walking on cloud nine. He would have never imagined that his relationship with Kate would be so engaging in such a short period of time. He wonders again that maybe it's the lure of the Las Vegas life, and under other circumstances, Kate would have been just another beautiful woman Bobby couldn't impress.

Returning to his room, Bobby immediately calls home, hoping Lynn wouldn't answer. She doesn't. Bobby leaves another message on the answering machine and sits down at the desk next to the window and begins to jot down some notes he feels would require immediate action by the group in order to groom Hank. Thinking about what they needed to do, he remembers all the videos he had back in his office. A library of movies, concerts, biographies, and all kinds of things stashed back at his office. It would be a good for Hank to see Elvis performing at different stages of his life. He immediately calls his brother, Jesse. Jesse is always available and picks up on the first ring and answers, "Hey, Bobby, how are you? Is everything OK in Las Vegas?"

"I'm just fine, Jesse. How are things going at the shop?"

"We're busy as hell, brother, and we need you back ASAP."

"I'll be in Boston next Sunday at 8:00 p.m. I'll call you when I land."

"I can pick you up at the airport if you want me to."

"That won't be necessary, Jesse, but I do need a favor."

"Anything you want, brother. What is it?"

"I want you to go into my file cabinet that I keep in the closet in my office. In the bottom drawer, I have a bunch of old videos. I want you to take them to J & R Electronics Sales and Repairs. Do you know where that is, Jesse?"

"Yes, I do. It's over on Highland Avenue in Salem."

"Good, then this is what I want you to do. I want you to have all the videotapes transferred onto CD-ROMs first thing Monday morning and tell them you want it done rush and make sure you tell them it's for me. Have Irene write a check for the cost of the transfer and then immediately take them to the UPS store and overnight them to me in Las Vegas. Here's the address."

"Hold on a second, Bobby. I need to get a pencil and paper to write all this down." Jesse grabs a pencil and paper and asks Bobby to give him the address.

"Send them to me at Robert Shrimp, the Bellagio Hotel and Casino, room 1215, Las Vegas, Nevada, 01370. Give UPS my cell phone number as a telephone number and send it overnight with arrival before noon the next day, OK?"

"I got it. By the way, what's this all about?"

"I'll explain everything when I get home."

"Bobby, I got the price to replace all the upholstery in the Caddy from L & L this week."

"That's good. How much is it?"

"The number they quoted was $6,800 for everything."

"What do you mean by everything?"

"Everything means the dashboard, the side panels, rear window deck, seats, and all miscellaneous trim."

"How are they going to do it? Are they going to replace everything or restore it?"

Jesse answers, "They're going to need to replace everything because the interior of the car is far too gone. They will need to pull everything out and replace it to the exact detail of that year car."

"That's a great price for them. They're usually high."

"I think they quoted a low price for two reasons: one, they wanted the publicity if the car goes to show, and second and more important, they like you, and that's about it."

"Well, then tell them to get started right away, and oh by the way, how long did they say it's going to take?"

"They guessed it would be one to one and a half weeks from when they receive the parts."

"Good work, Jesse. I can always depend on you."

"Thanks. Is there anything else you need?"

"No, Jesse, that's it. Oh, Jesse, there is one thing. I've been calling Lynn on her cell phone and on the house phone and haven't been able to reach her. Has she contacted you?"

"I haven't heard anything from her this past week. She could be at her mother's or her sister's house."

"I'll check there. I'll see you when I get back."

Bobby turns off his cell phone and begins to think about his vintage car for a moment and then about Lynn then about Hank and finally about Kate and begins to wonder if things are getting a little bit complicated in his life.

Chapter 43

Jeremy Shrinks Back in Las Vegas

JEREMY IS VERY relieved that Hank agreed to be the main attraction. There would be no more disappointments and no ridicules aimed at his performance; now he will be the man behind the scenes and loving every minute of it. His objective is now to groom Hank. Feeling very good about his recent turn of events, he now had a purpose in life, and it includes Bobby and Terance. The three of them working together to elevate Hank to stardom is just what Jeremy needs. Things seem to be coming together very nicely for him, so he decides to give his daughter, Marie, a call at the college. He punches in her speed dial number, and Marie answers on the second ring, "Hi, Dad."

"Hi, sweetheart, how is everything going with you?"

"Everything is going great, Dad. You know Isaiah will be in Florida in March, and he's going to want to see you."

"That sounds very good to me. I'll be happy to make the trip down to the Coral Gables. Just let me know what dates will be good?"

"I will, Dad. I'll call you a couple of weeks before he arrives. By the way, where are you now?"

Jeremy answers, "I'm in Las Vegas, Nevada."

"What on earth are you doing in Las Vegas?"

"I'm with two good friends of mine, and we are working with this young guy on a very special project."

"What very special project?"

"I'll tell you all about when I get down to Coral Gables."

"OK, Dad. What else have you been doing up there? I hope you're not gambling away the little money you have?"

Jeremy answers, "No, I haven't been doing any like that. As a matter of fact, I took a trip to the Hoover Dam all by myself. I went on a group tour through the dam, which turned out to be very interesting. But the most exciting thing I did was taking an inflatable boat ride down the Colorado River's Black Canyon. The boat ride was breathtaking. There were eight of us on the boat along with the tour guide. The guide explained everything about river, the canyons, and the species of wildlife that inhabited the canyons. You wouldn't believe these canyons. They jetted straight up out of the water hundreds of feet in the air. The river had these intense rapids, and in a matter of seconds, the boat was floating in crystal-clear calm open pools. It was all beyond explanation. The only way I can describe it is that it was indescribable."

Marie interjects, "Dad, you sound so enlightened. Is it because you're away from that useless girlfriend of yours, Evelyn, or are you just having a good time with somebody else?"

"I'm not with anyone else right now."

"What do you mean not right now?"

"I mean just what I said—not right now, but maybe in the near future, I may be with somebody else." Jeremy is afraid to explain too much about Kie for fear that he may be reading too much into their relationship, so he changes the subject.

"I was feeling kind of down out the other day, so I decided to go out and buy myself some new clothes. I bought a really nice sport jacket, a great pair of pants, a nice shirt, and a pair of shoes. It was all so very inexpensive, and when I met up with my friends that night, they all thought I looked great."

Marie inquisitively replies, "What on earth has gotten into you? Are you trying to impress somebody?"

"No, I wanted to do this for myself. It took just a few little self-motivated activities, and now I feel like a new person, and it feels great."

"Dad, I really and truly like the way you sound. I am so, so happy for you. I just hope you don't have some over-the-hill Las Vegas babes hanging around you."

"No no, it's far from that."

"Well, then can you tell me what is closer to your present situation?"

"I'll tell you all about it in due time, but as of right now, I'm not sure what I want to do next." Jeremy, however, knew exactly what he wanted to do next. He wanted to go over to the parlor and get a massage from Kie.

"Well, Dad, whatever makes you happy and keeps you in the state of mind that you're in right now is certainly OK by me even if by some crazy chance that something else is an Asian girl at a massage parlor."

Jeremy almost drops the phone on the floor.

"OK, sweetheart, I'll call you again real soon."

"One more thing, Dad, have you talked to Mom?"

"I was thinking of giving her a call today."

"That sounds like a good idea. Why don't you do that? Well, then good-bye for now. Love you, Dad."

Marie and Jeremy end their conversation with him not being 100 percent convinced that he should give his ex-wife Karla a call. He is pondering what to do: should he call Karla, take a nap, or call to see if Kie is working; and if she was, would she have time to give him a massage? Jeremy thinks about the three options and immediately calls Kie. To his great fortune, she is working and could fit him in at 5:00 p.m. Jeremy is now feeling both anxious and vulnerable at the same time, being concerned about how it is going to play out with Kie; will she be as caring and friendly as the first time she worked on him, or would she be all business now that he's a captured client?

To dismiss his anxiety, Jeremy decides to call Karla. She picks up the phone on the second ring and answers hello.

"Karla, it's me, Jeremy. How are you?"

"I'm doing great. I just got off the phone with Marie, and she informed me that Isaiah was going to be in Coral Gables in March."

"I know all about that. Are you planning to go down to visit?"

Jeremy tells Karla that he is planning on being there in March, and Karla is too.

"That's great. We'll all be together. I'm going to look forward to that."

"Jeremy, you sound so upbeat. What's been going on in your life?"

"A lot of things have happened to me in a very short period of time, and I have been feeling very positive lately."

"By the way, Jeremy, where are you?"

"I'm in Las Vegas with some very good friends of mine, and we're having a great time. I'm going to be here one more week, and then I'm heading back home."

"Well, Jeremy, you have a good time in Vegas, and don't let the casinos or the hookers take what little money you have."

"I won't."

Jeremy is not surprised that Karla doesn't show any enthusiasm toward his new state of mind. Jeremy knows that Karla is still very disappointed in him, and the fact that he is shacking up with some lowlifes doesn't help matters. Karla had big plans for him, but he let her down along with himself; and since then, his life has been heading to nowheresville until now. Now Jeremy had a reason to push himself. He feels that he's gained the respect of his friends, and this gives him a feeling of belonging—something he needed all his life. A meaningful relationship with Kie would be the icing on the cake. He hopes that this isn't some fantasy that he fabricated in his mind. He knows he'll have to work things out with Kie. He is now getting very rambunctious and doesn't know what to do it himself, so he lies down on the bed and looks up at the ceiling and thinks about what he is going to say when he sees her again. He tries to come up with something unique but couldn't seem to gather anything creative, so he decides to let it go. He'd play it by ear. One thing that he does know is that he's going to wear his new clothes to the parlor. Counting the minutes and trying to kill time, he decides to call Evelyn. The phone rings five times before Evelyn picks up.

"Hello, who is it?"

"It's me, Jeremy. Where have you been? I tried calling you a couple of times this week."

"I was at my sister's house."

"Where the hell are you?"

"I'm in Vegas with some friends."

"Oh, that's just great. How long are you going to be there?"

"I'll be here one more week."

"Great. I'll be either here in the trailer or at my sister's house."

Jeremy wants to say he wishes she would stay at her sister's house; they deserve one another. Evelyn's sister is a leech and a good for nothing. Jeremy's been having second thoughts about Evelyn for some time now and feels that this would be a good time for him to end their relationship. Not being absolutely sure that he has anything solid with Kie and not wanting to be alone, he doesn't want to put Evelyn out just yet. Evelyn's been his only company, bad as it is, for a number of years. So Jeremy ends his conversation with "Well, whatever, good-bye."

Jeremy is a bit upset with himself for even calling Karla and Evelyn. They are not very supportive and always leave him feeling depressed and disappointed about his past life. Being with Kie today is going to be a very critical moment for him. Wondering if he might have made a mistake seeing her so soon, he ponders his options and decides, *What the hell, I have to do this, or I will keep on second-guessing what could have happened if I don't.* It is now time for Jeremy to leave for his appointment at the parlor. He gets himself all decked out in his new clothes, takes one last look at himself in the mirror, and is off. Jeremy arrives at the parlor ten minutes early just to make sure he'd be on time. Everything inside is exactly how it was a couple of days ago. The owner notices him as he walks in and immediately approaches him with a warm smile and a friendly embrace, which makes him feel like they are long-lost friends. Being very smart, he knows that the owner is very entrepreneurial, and Jeremy is the customer. But it still feels real good to be greeted so warmly. With nerves still on end, he takes a seat and is offered some spring water from the young girl behind the desk, which he accepts. He confirms that he would be seeing Kie, and the girl obliges, "Oh yes, Mr. Shrinks, she's been waiting for you."

Her comment about "she's been waiting for you" makes Jeremy feel more relaxed, but he is still skeptical. Jeremy is waiting anxiously for Kie to arrive, and when she walks through the door, he immediately is on pins and needles, wondering if she would even recognize him, considering she must see dozens of clients over the period of a couple of days.

Kie walks over to Jeremy with extended arms and gives him a big hug and says, "Mr. Shrinks, you look wonderful. I must have done something very good for you for you to come back so soon and looking so good."

Jeremy doesn't know what to say other than "Kie, you don't know the half of it."

"You can tell me all about it inside." Taking his arm, she walks him into the massage area and hands him his bathrobe and says, "You know the routine, and when you're done, I'll be in room 7."

Jeremy wonders, *Seven, that means seventh heaven*. After a quick steam shower and toweling off, he throws a bathrobe on and heads over to room 7, where Kie is waiting. She looks even better than what he had remembered, dressed all in white made her look even more seductive. Her face looks radiant, and Jeremy becomes very excited; thus, he has to take off the bathrobe discreetly and lie down on the table quickly so as not to be embarrassed. Kie remembers the lotion Jeremy requested last time and starts right in on his treatment.

"So," Kie said, "what have you been doing?"

Jeremy describes his trip to Reno and Hoover Dam. Kie interrupts when Jeremy mentioned the Hoover Dam.

"How did you like the dam?"

Jeremy explains how much he loved it. He describes the tour of the dam, the Colorado River, the canyons, and Lake Meade. She asks if he had taken the boat ride down the river and if he got to see the longhorn deer. Jeremy asks how she knew about the deer. She explains that she had taken her brother to the Hoover Dam last fall. Jeremy is very impressed and wonders if she experienced the same enjoyment that he did when she took the inflatable boat ride down the river. For the entire time Kie is giving Jeremy his massage, they talked about the Hoover Dam and Colorado River. Jeremy is taken in by her enthusiasm. One very interesting thing that comes out of the conversation is that Kie mentions that she had never been to Reno and wants to go there to experience the city. She asks him whom he went with. He explains that he went with three friends. Kie dives deeply into Jeremy's personal life when she asks, "You didn't come with your wife?"

Jeremy quickly answers, "No, I'm divorced."

"Oh, I'm very sorry to hear that, Mr. Shrinks."

"Don't be. It was a long time ago."

Kie is being very forthcoming with their conversation, and she makes Jeremy's day when she says very seriously, "I would really like to go to Reno. Are you going again?" Jeremy feels this is a direct invitation for a follow-up for something, but he doesn't know what that something could be. Kie is applying more physical contact than the last time she worked on Jeremy. Jeremy is floating on air. Kie just keeps on saying very encouraging things to him. She asks him about her note and confirms that she meant every word she wrote.

Jeremy laughs and says, "I bet you write that same note to everyone."

"Yeah, that's right. How did you know? I have hundreds of them written with the same message. I just have to write in a different name."

With that, she then gives Jeremy a big push with her midsection, which almost knocks him off the table. They both laugh together, which builds up Jeremy's courage to say, "I'm not going back to Reno for a while, but I know a place in Las Vegas where the food and the atmosphere is like nothing you have ever seen. Would you be interested in going?"

Kie looks down at him and says, "I will have to let you know." Her remark is a big letdown for Jeremy. Was everything just part of an act to appear friendly to the customers? The massage ends as it did before. Kie leaves the room, and Jeremy dresses himself feeling a bit rejected, contemplating that maybe he was fantasizing a little bit too much. However, he knows he had to give it a shot, and Kie seemed so anxious to do something with him. But it all ended so abruptly. Kie is waiting at the end of the hall with a small envelope and folded paper. Feeling rejected, he couldn't look her straight in the eye, so he takes the envelope and leaves. He pays his bill and walks to his car. He throws Kie's envelope on the dashboard and drives back to the hotel.

He is completely disenchanted by what had happened. So when he arrives back at the parking lot, he angrily grabs the envelope and throws it in the trash can. He feels a little uneasy about what he has done, so he retrieves it. He knows he would have to live up to his disappointments and try to put everything out of his mind. When he arrives in his room, he changes into his street clothes. He retrieves Kie's envelope and angrily rips it open. Expecting the worst, he slowly opens the small plain piece of paper and reads: "Dear Jeremy, I would really like to go to that special restaurant with you. Please call me at 1-661-710-6988 after 7:00 p.m. Kie." At the bottom of the note was written, "PS I only have fifty of these kinds of notes, so please return it when we get together."

Jeremy is elated. He reads the note three times and yells out, "Thank you, God!"

Chapter 44

Terance Calls Home

TERANCE IS VERY pleased with the latest developments. Things have worked out much better than he could have ever expected. Having a clear and sound game plan with Hank as the front man for the competition was very motivating. He also has the possibility of closing a very exciting deal with the owners of Graceland. The restaurant deal is a very special opportunity that could offer a direct involvement for his wife, Terri.

While attending business school, she worked part time at a high-end restaurant and then went on to work full time with the management staff after she graduated. She and Terance saw each other off and on for around four years. Terri was very busy moving up the corporate ladder at the restaurant, and Terance was working night and day getting his development company off the ground. It wasn't until they were in the late twenties that they decided to get married. It was a wonderful time for them. They were both ready to begin a family, and they had the financial wherewithal to live a quality life together.

Terri quit her job after their first child. That was a hard thing for her to do because she loved the restaurant business, but it was now time for a family. She always reminisced about her time at the restaurant and constantly reminded Terance how she would love to return to work when the kids were older.

Terance would make sure that there was language in the contract that would allow someone of his choice to participate in an upper level management position, and Terri would be the one to fill that role. He knew the second Terri experienced the culture of Graceland, she would welcome the opportunity to be part of the business. The other partners would have no problem with her joining the team, knowing that the day-to-day operation was too much for them to handle alone. Terance wanted to tell Terri about the deal immediately but decided to wait until the contract was signed and sealed. He wouldn't want Terri to get her hopes up and then have to be disappointed if the deal fell through. Wanting to reassure himself that Terri would be up for this new challenge, he decided that he would hint around about her returning to work. So he dials the home phone number, which is answered on the second ring with "Hi, Terance, I've been waiting for you to call. How are you doing?"

"I'm doing fine, and things are moving along here very nicely."

"When are you going to tell me about this secret deal?"

"As soon as I close it."

"OK, Mr. Secret Man. I guess I can wait a little longer."

With that, Terri lets out a subtle laugh. Terance moves quickly to change the subject and then goes into a riff about all the restaurants on the strip and how many more were being built in the new hotels. He describes the grandeur, the variety, and the quality of each of the restaurants he visited but doesn't mention Graceland. He comments, "I think if you were here, you would probably get an urge to get back into the restaurant business, particularly if you were to see the sophisticated way these places are being run and the amount of money that can be made. All the big-name restaurants are here in the strip, and they're all very busy and making a lot of money. It's such a pleasure to see all the busyness. I think it would be nice to be a part of that."

Terri replies, "I don't know if I want to relocate to Las Vegas, but I certainly would welcome the opportunity to get back in it sooner rather than later now that the kids don't need their mommy eight hours a day. I'm just not sure I would like to relocate. I kind of love it here in Coral Gables, and so do the children."

"If you didn't have to relocate, would you jump back in?"

Terri answers, "Oh, in a New York minute, but the restaurant would have to be something special."

"I wouldn't want anything but the best for my precious wife."

"What are you planning on doing, buying a restaurant?"

"Yes, I'm planning on buying one so you can have a job."

"OK, big boy, I'm ready to go. When do we start?"

Both of them laughed together over Terri's comment.

"You know we miss you a lot when you're out of town. The kids and I need you around. So you'd better get home right away."

"I know how you feel. I miss you and the kids and can't wait to get home."

Terance asks Terri how things are going around the house, and she explains that things were going as well as could be expected.

"It's only going to be one more week, and I am going to be back home, hopefully with some very exciting news."

"I miss you very much. You take care of yourself."

"And I miss you too. I'll call you back tomorrow." Terance now feels more anxious to close the deal with the owners of Graceland. He would call his accountant to check on the progress with the review of the books tomorrow. Terance is hoping for the best.

Chapter 45

Hank and Shirley

HANK IS LOOKING forward to working with Terance, Bobby, and Jeremy. This would be the first time that they would work as a group with a common cause, and Hank is now that cause. Never would he have dreamed it would have come out this way, but it did, and so he's going to make the best of it. The most important thing for him is not to let his friends down, so he knows he needs to get very serious about his performance. He couldn't help thinking about how good the two guys from Providence College did in Reno, and this worries him. What will Bobby, Terance, and Jeremy come up with to overcome their great performances? If only Jeremy could somehow give him his voice, he could be way ahead of the pack. But that's not possible. He'll just have to wait and see what Jeremy has in store for him. Hank's attention now turns to Terance, who's always been a big question mark. Maybe he'll be the manager or the go-to person? The all-around coach will be Bobby, and the assistant coach will be Jeremy. All these expectations are making him nervous. Everything needs to come together in such a short period of time. A couple of days ago, the only thing Hank had on his mind were Kayla, Shirley, and Jackie. Now he has all this. A break from his anxieties was in order, so he decides to give Shirley a call just to chat a bit. He dials up her number and gets Shirley's telephone message: "Hi, this is Shirley. Please leave your phone number, and I will be sure to get back to you." Hank leaves a short message and decides to sit it out for a few minutes before coming up with the second option to relieve his anxiety. His next call will be to Kayla. But before he does, he wants to think through how much he should tell her about Bobby, Terance, and Jeremy. Up to now, he's been keeping all the goings-on in Las Vegas to himself. However, if the competition goes well Saturday night, Hank feels, what better time for him to explain his trips to Kayla and his family? If he finishes first, it would be a joyous moment for him, and then he could explain everything about his special friends and the competition to everyone back home, particularly his grandmother. Kayla's reaction to all this Elvis stuff would still be somewhat unpredictable, but the more he thinks it through, the more he knows she would be very supportive and understanding and would be very excited about him winning the contest. Kayla picks up the phone after two rings and answers, "Hey, Hank, how's everything going?"

"Much better than expected. I don't want to explain anything right now for fear that I might be putting a jinx on what is happening or what could happen."

"Don't worry, Hank. I'm not going to tell a soul."

Hank is tempted to tell her everything, but instead he says, "I'll give you a hint. I may not be spending the rest of my life installing carpet."

"That's all you are going to tell me?"

"That's it," Hank replies with a chuckle.

"OK, I guess I can wait until you get back home. Are you keeping out of trouble? Las Vegas is a very tempting city."

"Yes, of course, I am. I haven't even been inside a casino."

"So what have you been doing in your spare time?" Hank doesn't want to mention Shirley and Jackie, so he decides to talk about his new friends. He explains who they are in very abstract details but articulates the experiences he had with them at the Graceland restaurant. The trip to Reno is discussed along with the great hotel they stayed in and how inexpensive it was. But he doesn't mention why they went. Hank's involvement with his new friends is good news for Kayla. His description of them leads Kayla to believe that they are somewhat geekish. This is also comforting. Kayla replies, "I'm happy to hear that you are in good company."

"They are very thoughtful guys, and they've given me some suggestions on how to get ahead."

"Everything is very quiet around here since you've been gone, and I'm beginning to feel very lonely. I can't wait for you to return home. As a matter of fact, I got so lonely, I thought about driving out to Las Vegas so I could be with you for a couple of days, but all of a sudden, things got a little crazy, so I guess I'll have to wait for you to come home."

Hank feels a chill go through his skin just thinking about Kayla showing up in Las Vegas unexpectedly. What a problem that would have been for him.

"What I think we should do is plan a trip just the two of us and spend three or four days here. I think this time would have been a little bit difficult for us to enjoy our stay together because of all the running around I'm doing."

"You're right. We should plan the trip together, but right now, I need to cut this conversation short so I can take my mother to the mall, and I'm running a bit late."

"Not to worry. I'll call you back in a couple of days."

With that, they say good-bye.

Hank's cell phone rings the second he signs off; it is Shirley on the phone. She is glad that he called because they need to talk about Thursday night. The event will be black tie, which means they'll have to rent him a tuxedo.

"What are you doing later today, let's say, around 6:30 p.m. to 7:30 p.m.?"

"Not that much."

"Good. How about coming down to the hotel lobby so that we can take a ride and get you a tuxedo today?"

"I can be there at 6:30 p.m. or earlier if you want me to. I have absolutely no plans for tonight."

"OK, then let's meet in the lobby in one hour. The whole thing shouldn't take any more than forty-five minutes, and don't worry about the cost of the rental. Jackie and I will take care of that."

"I really appreciate that. I'm running a little low on cash."

Shirley responds, "OK. I'll see you in the lobby at 6:30 p.m."

Their conversation ends, and now with an hour to kill, Hank decides to stay put in his room, take a shower, and get ready for his rendezvous with Shirley. At 6:20 p.m., he is ready to go. Arriving in the lobby at exactly 6:30 p.m., he notices Shirley talking with a distinguished-looking guy with gray hair. Hank walks over to them, and Shirley immediately introduces them to one another.

"Hank, I would like you to meet David Anderson. David is the senior partner at the design firm that remodeled the hotel."

Hank offers his hand, smiles, and says, "Hello, David, I am Henry Hunk."

"Nice to meet you."

"Nice to meet you too, Henry." David looks back at Shirley and says, "I have to go take care of some business. I will see you later on. It was nice to meet you, Henry. Will I be seeing you on Thursday night?"

"You bet. Jackie, Hank, and I will be there."

David leaves in a hurry, and Hank and Shirley head out. Shirley suggests they have the doorman get them a cab. Hank offers to use his car. Shirley agrees, and soon she is in full view of the mint Thunderbird convertible with the license plate HND DOG. She responds, "What have we here? Hound Dog. Who do you think you are—Elvis? I absolutely love your car. My father had one just like this when I was a teenager. Jackie and I used to drive is up and down Sunset Strip like a couple of movie stars."

Shirley asks Hank if he restored the car himself.

"My father and I worked on it together. My father is a real car buff."

"I guess he is."

Shirley gives Hank directions to the tuxedo shop. The ride took them only fifteen minutes. The place is located in a big mall with hundreds of stores. Shirley directs Hank where to park the car and then accompanies him into the shop. As soon as they walk in, a young man immediately comes over to them and says, "I'm Fred. Can I help you?"

"Fred, we need a tux for my friend, and we need it right away."

"What's right away?"

"This Thursday night."

"That's not a problem. Why don't you look around and see what you like."

"I know exactly what we need."

Shirley immediately walks over to a mannequin wearing a traditional black tux, white shirt, and black bowtie, and says, "This is exactly what we want."

"Good choice. Now if I can take some measurements, we can get your friend fitted."

The measurements are taken, and Fred goes to the back of the shop and returns with the tux. Fred asks Hank to try the tux on. Hank takes the tux over to the dressing room and tries it on. He returns to show Shirley and Fred how it fits. Shirley looks Hank up and down and comments, "It's a perfect fit, except the pants may be a tad long, but we should be able to get you a pair that will fit you perfectly, isn't that right, Fred?"

"That won't be a problem. Will there be anything else?"

"He needs a pair of shoes and cufflinks for the shirt."

"What size of shoes do you wear?"

"I wear a size 11 shoe and a size 17 collar shirt."

"I have those sizes available for you now. Would you like to take them with you?"

"We don't need them now. We'll pick them up when we pick up the tux."

Shirley heads over to the display counter and picks out a pair of black onyx cufflinks.

"I think these will do. What do you think, Hank?"

"Looks good to me."

Hank wonders what Fred must be thinking about all of this. The way Shirley takes over makes it look like Hank is a kept man and Shirley's the cougar or the overpowering mother with the young son. But then again, Shirley is much too young to be his mother. Maybe she's the rich older wife getting her young stud ready for a night on the town. Hank loses his train of thought when he sees Shirley hand Fred her American Express card and announces that they would be back to pick up the suit on Thursday around 5:00 p.m. Fred assures them that it would be ready and thanks them for their business. As they are walking to the car, Hank is concerned about how much control Shirley has over him. It is both comforting and maybe suggestive of things to come. Hank doesn't know what is coming, but he knows it would be interesting. As they are driving back to the hotel, Shirley comments, "You looked so handsome in that tuxedo."

Hank thanks her for the compliment and asks, "Where to now?"

Shirley thinks a minute and says, "Let's get something to eat. It will be my treat. I know a little Italian restaurant just off the strip. What do you think, Hank?"

"I love Italian food."

"OK, then let's go. I'll give you directions."

Hank drives about fifteen minutes, and they arrive at the restaurant at 7:45 p.m. The restaurant is very crowded, but somehow Shirley is able to get a table right away. Hank doesn't want to ask how she was able to pull that off. They sat down and had a couple of glasses of wine and the best veal Parmesan Hank ever had. They talk at length about the hotel opening, and Shirley explains about how hard and long Jackie, the staff, and she had to work to get the job out to bid. Hank knows all about charetting. He and Shirley have a lot to say about the long and stressful hours design firms encounter in order to meet the client's deadlines. They both, however, admit they love doing it, particularly when it resulted in something like what was in store for Shirley and Jackie on Thursday night. Shirley is very businesslike through the entire dinner. She and Hank have an engaging conversation, which Hank enjoys very much. Thus, he doesn't want to push employment opportunities. He is hoping Shirley would come up with something for him.

After supper, they drive back to the hotel, and Shirley suggests a drink at the cabana. Hank obliges, and they spend another hour talking shop. It is now 9:30 p.m., and Shirley announces that she has to turn in early for an early morning meeting at the hotel. Hank insists on paying for the drinks.

Shirley obliges, and he puts the tab on his hotel room charge. Hank and Shirley walk into the hotel and over to the elevator lobby. As they get in the elevator, Shirley gets in first and pushes the elevator button and asks Hank for his floor number.

"Twelve."

Shirley pushes 12 and then 18. The elevator door closes, and the elevator starts to climb. Shirley turns to Hank and says, "Would you do me a favor? I want you to check out some of the display boards we have for the hotel opening. You may need to help Jackie and me take them to the hotel an hour before things get started."

"Sure, I would love to see the boards."

They get off at the eighteenth floor. When Shirley opens the door to the room, Hank is surprised to see Jackie wearing blue jeans and a T-shirt working away on one of the display boards. Shirley calls out, "Look whom I brought along to help us carry the boards to the hotel tomorrow."

Jackie immediately puts her arms around Hank and gives him a warm and ladylike embrace. Jackie asks, "Is he all set with the tux?"

"We can pick it up on Thursday."

"That's great."

Shirley explains that she brought Hank along so that he can have a look at the boards before they brought them over to the hotel. The boards are spread out all over the hotel suite. Hank takes the time to look at each and every board and is extremely impressed with how much work Shirley and Jackie put into this presentation. Hank compliments them on their work and expresses how happy he is that they asked him to be their guest at the hotel opening.

"Don't mention it, Hank. We're all going to have a lot of fun on Thursday night. I'll call you tomorrow on your cell phone to let you know what's going on."

Hank says good night. As he walks to the elevator, he couldn't help but think how many other doors Shirley could open for him.

Chapter 46

Bobby Shrimp, Conceiving Hank's New Look

THE DVDS ARRIVED two days after Bobby instructed his brother, Jesse, to convert the videotapes and overnight them to the Bellagio Hotel. Bobby had received a phone message earlier that day from the front desk at the hotel informing him that he had an overnight package, and it was waiting for him at the mail center. He immediately picks up the package and brings it up to his room. Fortunately, the room has a wide-screen LCD television with a built-in DVD player. It is 3:00 p.m. on Tuesday when he places the first disc in the DVD player. The disc is titled "Elvis on *The Ed Sullivan Show.*" The recording is black and white, but it is extremely clear. It started off with Ed Sullivan introducing Elvis. The TV cameras panned the theater to show an audience of screaming and cheering young men and women. The date of the broadcast was 1956; a very young Elvis was appearing with the Jordanaires. His hair was jet black and was combed back on the side with a striking pompadour above his forehead. The look was very popular back then. Elvis was wearing a perfectly tailored sport jacket that was a tad long. The extra length gave Presley a long lean look. His skin was shiny, and his eyes were crystal clear. The TV camera framed his face. Sullivan did not want the TV viewers to see Presley's body gyrations while he was performing. The close-ups give Bobby the opportunity to study Elvis's facial expressions and eye movement. He is astonished from looking at the close-ups of Elvis's face how much Hank looked like the young Elvis Presley. Closely studying Elvis's flashy clothing and his striking hairstyle, facial expressions, eye contact with the audience, and powerful voice is what made him stand out. He was definitely the main attraction. The audience's reaction to him was overwhelming. Rock and roll was born. A new king was crowned, at a very young age, to bring in the new sound that would revolutionize music. Realizing that Hank would need a major overhaul to pick up where Elvis left off, he decides to approach this transformation in the stages. First, he would do the easy things. The clothing would be first and would be exactly how he saw it on *The Ed Sullivan Show*. Finding a tailor quickly would be the first order of business, and it has to be a tailor who could make the sport jacket exactly like the one Elvis wore on *The Ed Sullivan Show*. He has photos to show the tailors but also remembers a particular prop that was displayed in a hamburger restaurant. The display was a cardboard cutout of the young Elvis Presley. He'd photograph it and take it with him. The second order of business would be to find the slacks, shirt, and shoes. The slacks and shirt would be easy. The shoes would be more difficult. Elvis was wearing snap jacks in the photos. Bobby outlines what needs to be done to accomplish all of this in four days. He writes down the procedures. Jeremy would be in charge of finding the shirt, slacks, and shoes. They would seek out the tailor to make the jacket and a stylist to recreate Elvis's hairstyle. None of this is hard; it is just going to take time. Elvis had a particular guitar that Hank would need for his performance. Terance would be the most likely one to take on that task. Fortunately, Hank has a lot of things going for him. His hair color is similar to Elvis's, his height and weight are very similar, and his looks are extremely similar. All he needed are Elvis's charisma and voice. The look Bobby has in mind is different from Ronnie's and Ritchie's. It would also be completely different from the other performers wearing the white emerald Las Vegas jumpsuits.

Recalling one of Elvis's performances that he recorded after he just gotten out of the army, he thinks about that look for Hank. An early meeting would be a must, so he decides to call the guys and suggest a meeting at 3:00 p.m. on Tuesday in his room. Or maybe not his room for fear that Kate may come by unexpectedly. He calls Terance.

"Hey, Terance, it's Bobby. I've been working out some of the details for Hank's performance on Saturday night. I want to pass on some of my thoughts by you, Jeremy, and Hank. I think we need to meet earlier on Tuesday to go over what needs to be done."

"That sounds like what we should do. I've been thinking of some ways to improve Hank's performance, and I would like to discuss my ideas with you, Jeremy, and Hank."

"I like your enthusiasm, Terance. I've been sitting in my room watching some DVDs that I made of some of Presley's early stuff."

"It's funny you should say his early stuff because that's where I'm going with my thoughts."

Bobby replies, "No kidding, Terance. That's great, but I have a favor to ask of you."

"Whatever you want."

Bobby asks, "How big is your hotel room?"

"I have a three-room suite."

"Do you have a DVD player in your suite?"

"I honestly don't know. But I can tell you one thing: I have a large flat-screen TV in every room. One of them must have a DVD player. I'll check. Hold on one minute"—Terance returns—"As a matter of fact, Bobby, I have three DVD players in my suite."

"That's good. Would it be possible for us to meet in your hotel suite to view my DVDs and talk about grooming Hank for Saturday night?"

"That's exactly what I had in mind, Bobby."

"That's wonderful. I'll call Hank and Jeremy and see if I can get them there at 3:00 p.m. on Tuesday. Will that date and time work for you?"

"The date and time are perfect."

"I'll call you back once I confirm the meeting with Jeremy and Hank."

"I'll be waiting for your call."

As soon as Bobby ends his conversation with Terance, he immediately calls Hank. Hank is 100 percent ready to go. The afternoon meeting fits perfectly into his schedule. Hank explains to Bobby that he would need Thursday night off to be with some special friends. Bobby thinks about his commitment to see Kate and explains to Hank that having Thursday night off would also work for him. Jeremy is also good to go for Tuesday at 3:00 p.m. Bobby gives Jeremy a heads-up about the voice improvements. Jeremy relieves some of Bobby's anxieties when he says that he had some ideas.

Everyone seems to be on the same page and working toward Hank's success. This is a great moment for Bobby. He sits down at his desk and starts to write out his work plan for the next four days. Everybody is ready to go. As he writes, he wonders how good Hank is at playing the guitar and how much of a change from his routine he would actually go along with. Bobby sits back and thinks about all this. While watching the DVDs of Elvis on *The Ed Sullivan Show*, he wonders, *If we could get Hank to look and sound like this, we would surely resurrect Elvis Presley.*

Bobby now turns his thoughts to Kate, longing to see her again; but knowing he is going to be very busy except for Thursday night, Thursday night would be perfect for a rendezvous. This, however, needed to be confirmed, so he picks up his cell phone and punches in Kate's number. Kate answers the on the first ring with "Hey, Bobby, how are you?"

Bobby thinks to himself she already has his number on speed dial. Bobby doesn't know if that is good or bad. Good, however, is more like it.

"I'm fine, Kate. I've been thinking of you, and I'd like to have lunch with you this Tuesday afternoon."

"That's tomorrow."

"I know."

"What time and place, or should we do something compulsive?"

"Let's do something compulsive."

"Call me at 11:00 a.m."

"I will."

With that, they say good-bye. Bobby feels it would be a good idea to have a face-to-face talk with Kate so that he could explain his busy schedule and plan to meet with her on Thursday night. Maybe they could go to Graceland. It would be a great thing to do for their last few days together. Bobby has no idea what was going to happen when the vacation was over. The fact Kate lives only one hour from him makes it even more difficult. How is he going to explain Lynn to Kate, and vice versa? Not having much luck with sophisticated women is haunting Bobby. He could be headed for a big letdown. He doesn't want to hurt Lynn over an infatuation. Either way, he could end up alone. With all this going through Bobby's mind, he decides he should be spending more time thinking about where he was going to get a custom-tailored sport jacket for Hank in two days. Bobby realizes that he's over his head in many ways. He's made a lot of commitments to people that are close to him. He hopes he can pull it off. He's been over his head before and came out just fine. This trip to Las Vegas is a major pressure cooker for Bobby, but he wouldn't have it any other way. He enjoys the action. It's so much better than having an empty plate.

Chapter 47

Jeremy Has Lunch with Kie

JEREMY IS AWAKENED by his cell phone. He reaches over and picks up the phone and hears Bobby's voice greeting him.

"Hey, Jeremy, I hope I didn't wake you?"

"No, not at all. I'm used to getting up early. What's up, Bobby?"

"Today is going to be a big day for the four of us. We're going to be working on the new look for Hank, which I think I have under control. We're also going to need to work on his choreography and most importantly on his voice, and that, my friend, is where you come in. I had all my tapes of Elvis converted to DVDs and shipped to me overnight. They'll be arriving this morning. We can use them to pick up some pointers on Elvis, particularly his clothing. My DVDs have some songs but not as much as I had hoped to have."

Jeremy interrupts, "You're in luck, *amigo*. I always bring all my Elvis DVDs when I travel to Vegas."

Bobby responds joyfully, "That's great news, Jeremy. That's a huge weight off my shoulders. The plan is to meet at 5:00 p.m. at Terance's suite at the Mandalay Bay Hotel. Do you know where it is?"

"How can I miss it? It dominates the upper end of Las Vegas Boulevard."

"His room number is 1621."

"It all sounds good to me. Should I bring my DVD player along with the DVDs?"

Bobby replies, "You don't need it. Terance has one in his room, or should I say in every room."

"I guess one should surmise that Terance has a suite. I bet he's a high roller."

"I don't know if he is high roller. He may have gotten some kind of a package deal. Getting back to Hank, what I would like you to focus in on, Jeremy, is Hank's voice. You unquestionably have the best Elvis voice since Elvis himself. Hank's voice is almost good but not good enough. I think it's been holding him back from finishing higher in the competition."

"I agree. I have some ideas about improving his voice performance."

"Do Terance and Hank know about tonight's meeting and the work ahead of us?"

"I talked to Terance last night, and he's up to date on everything. I need to call Hank and let him know about the meeting time and the location. I also gave Hank a heads-up about the amount of time he will need to set aside to buy clothes, get himself groomed, and rehearse. He's my next phone call."

"I'll be looking forward to seeing you tonight."

"I'll see you then."

With that, the two men hang up their phones, and Jeremy gets out of bed and gets ready for the day. He is very anxious to call Kie to arrange for Wednesday.

A leisurely breakfast in the hotel lobby is his choice today, and then he would call Kie at 9:30 a.m.; that seems like an appropriate time. What if she says she's busy this week and couldn't see him, or worse what if she brushed him off? Knowing he needs to clear his mind of these pessimistic assumptions, he starts thinking about all the positive things that he has recently experienced. After a very leisurely breakfast, he spends the morning breakfast reading *USA Today* at the poolside with the guests. Most of them are couples his age, which makes him wish he has someone to spend his time with. It is now time to call Kie. Rather than being alone in his room, he'd call her at the poolside. He feels that bad news is always better heard with distractions, and where he sits offers a lot of distractions. Nervously removing the piece of paper with Kie's phone number from his pocket, he gives her a call. The phone rings five or six times before her voice message comes on: "Hi, this is Kie. Please leave your name and phone number, and I will call you right back."

Being disappointed she didn't answer the phone, he leaves a message: "This is Jeremy. I want to talk you. I can call you back in a half hour, or if you're available before that, you can call me at 781-245-2721." Within seconds, his cell phone rings, thinking it is Bobby with some last-minute plans. He is extremely surprised to hear Kie's voice.

"Hey, Jeremy, it's Kie. I missed your phone call by a second. How are you?"

"I'm doing great."

"Well, I'm just so glad to hear from you."

"I hope you're doing fine too. I called to see if you have some time this week to meet me for lunch?"

"It depends on what time, Jeremy. I work 2:00 p.m. to 10:00 p.m. on Sundays, Mondays, and Tuesdays, and 10:00 a.m. to 6:00 p.m. on Thursdays and Fridays. I have all Saturdays as day off."

"Well, I can do any one of those days. I'm hoping the sooner the better."

"The sooner the better is good for me. How does this afternoon sound?"

"This afternoon sounds great. What should we do? Do you want to meet somewhere, or do you want me to come pick you up?"

Jerry is hoping she doesn't want him to pick her up in his junk car, and to his good fortune, Kie suggests that they meet at Harrah's restaurant at 12:30 p.m.

"That's a great idea. I'll be looking forward to seeing you."

He needs to get himself ready but realizes he doesn't want to wear the same clothes he had on Sunday, so he decides to take a fast trip to the mall and buy some leisure clothing. At the mall, he buys a colorful shirt, shorts, a pair of New Balance sneakers, and a pair of fashionable sunglasses. Returning at the hotel, he quickly changes into his new attire and heads over to

Harrah's. It is walking distance from his hotel, which he does briskly so he could arrive before Kie did. Arriving at Harrah's at 12:15 p.m., he takes a chair in the lobby facing the entry and waits for Kie to arrive. Ten minutes later, Kie arrives. At first, Jeremy doesn't recognize her because the outfit she is wearing makes her look like the quintessential tourist. Jeremy stands up from his chair and waves his hand to attract her attention. As soon as she sees him, she smiles and walks over with open arms.

"So good to see you again, Jeremy," she says with enthusiasm.

"So good to see you too, Kie."

Kie asks, "Have you been here before?"

"No, I haven't. This is one heck of a place."

"I like it here a lot. I'm sure you will too. Let's head over to the poolside cafe and grab a table."

On their way to their table, Jeremy allows Kie to walk in front of him until he reaches the table, where he pulls out a chair from under the table and gestures to Kie to sit down.

"What a gentleman."

Jeremy smiles and sits down across from her. Kie takes off her sunglasses and reaches over the table and grabs Jeremy's hand and says, "I'm so happy you called. I'm sorry if I did not respond right away in the parlor. We're not supposed to fraternize with the clients while we're working. After work, however, we can do whatever we want. I saw the look on your face when you left. I wanted you to know why I had to be so curt, but you didn't give me a chance to do that."

"Thank you very much for telling me that, Kie. We're here together now, and that's all that matters."

The waitress approaches the table and asks if they would like something to drink. Kie suggests iced tea with lemon, and Jeremy requests the same. Jeremy asks what she would recommend for lunch, and Kie suggests the grilled sirloin over Caesar salad is their specialty. Jeremy confesses that he never had a grilled sirloin over Caesar salad but would like to try it. The waitress returns with the drinks. Kie orders two grilled sirloins over Caesar salad. Jeremy is uncertain about what he should talk about, so he decides to have Kie do all the talking. To encourage this, he asks Kie how she got started in the massage business. She is happy to oblige and explains that she first had to go to school to earn a certification, and when she was certified, it was very easy for her to get a job. Jeremy asks where she went to school. Kie tells him she attended the University of Las Vegas, where her brother graduated with an accounting degree, and he is now in Vancouver, Canada. She goes on to explain that her father came to the USA in the seventies, and she attended elementary school in Costa Mesa, California. Jeremy does some quick math and comes to the conclusion that Kie could be in her late thirties or early forties. However, she doesn't look older than late twenties. Jeremy asks how she ended up in Las Vegas. She tells him her mother died when she was in high school, and her father packed up everything and moved the family to Las Vegas, where there were more opportunities for him, and he's still working as a staff accountant at the Mandalay Bay Hotel. She goes on to explain that her brother is following in her father's footsteps.

"How come you didn't want to become an accountant?"

"I wanted to be a teacher, but unfortunately, I got married when I was twenty-one and had a couple of kids, and by the time I was finished raising the family, it was a little too late for me to be a teacher, so I decided to pursue physical therapy. I ended up at the parlor four years ago, and thank goodness I did. We make three times as much money as teachers."

"Where are your husband and kids?"

"The kids are at home with me. They're both at the university, and my ex-husband is in California. He visits us every other month. We still get along very well even though he can't understand my desire to work as a massage therapist. How about you, Jeremy?"

"I have a daughter, Marie. She's in her last year at the University of Miami, and I've been divorced for a long time. I live in Yukon, Oklahoma. I work in retail."

"What are you doing in Las Vegas?"

"I am working with three friends on a competition that's happening in town this weekend."

COMPETING FOR ELVIS

"What kind of competition?"

Jeremy answers cautiously, "Well, it's kind of a talent show. You know, singing, dancing, that kind of thing."

Just at the moment, the food comes, and Jeremy takes that opportunity to change the subject. He explains that he is also going to be in town until Sunday and would very much like to see her again before he left. "It's too bad you're leaving so soon. We've had hardly had time to get to know each other."

"Maybe we can see each other later on this week, possibly Thursday night after work. We can go to that special restaurant I was telling you about."

"I would like that."

Jeremy proposes a toast. They touch glasses and smile at one another. Jeremy is very impressed with what he could piece together about his new friend. It is very different from what he had expected. She's not as young as he thought she was; thus, Marie couldn't bug him about robbing the cradle. Second, she has an air of intelligence he liked very much; but most importantly, she seems to be a wholesome family-oriented woman. Her children are old enough to be on their own like Marie, she is divorced like him, and she is working at a job below her abilities but making a lot of money doing it.

Jeremy and Kie carried on for an hour and a half, and Kie announces that she has to leave for work. When the bill came, Kie insists they split the check. Her gesture hits a positive note with Jeremy. He walks Kie to her car and is impressed to see that Kie is driving a 525 BMW convertible. Her fashionable look and the car go very well together. He hasn't been this happy since Marie was born. He wonders, it's never too late to turn your life around; you just have to push yourself a bit, think positive, and when good things happen, it's because you make them happen. It's been a very long time since so many positive things have come to him.

Chapter 48

Bobby Shrimp Making Arrangements with Terance Best

TERANCE RECEIVES BOBBY'S phone call at 10:30 a.m. Bobby wants to give Terance a heads-up on his conversation with Jeremy and to describe what kinds of challenges lay in the future for the four men. He explains that he has outlined what he thinks need to be in place to accomplish a winning performance for Hank. Terance is in agreement with everything Bobby said but is very concerned about the time frame. To resolve his concerns, Terance suggests meeting every night for the rest of the week and spending the majority of the time rehearsing with Hank. However, he would need a part of one of those days to finish up a business matter he had in town. Bobby understands Terance's schedule and notes that he also needs a little time for himself. Terance asks Bobby if Hank is up to date with everything. Bobby explains he hasn't called Hank yet but is going to call him right after he finishes his call with him. The good news is that Bobby has talked to Jeremy, and he has DVDs, videotapes, and audios of Elvis with him in Las Vegas, and a lot of Hank's new look could be inspired by viewing his DVDs. He also informs Terance that Jeremy is very much on board with all of this and that he has some ideas about improving Hank's voice. Terance is very happy to hear that. Terance comments that he had the room ready for tonight for as long as it would take to get things going. Bobby explains they needed to get Hank's new clothes, hairstyle, and the right guitar for his new act. Terance is quick to add that the guitar would not be a problem. The clothes, however, would be something else, depending on the look Bobby wanted for Hank. Bobby explains that it would be the young Elvis that he would be trying to clone, not the Las Vegas Elvis. Terance is all for the new direction. Bobby ends the conversation with "Well, Terance, it'll only take a lot of hard work and a bit of money to make all this work."

Terance replies, "I know all about hard work. And don't worry about the money."

The conversation ends, and Bobby is ready to call Hank.

Chapter 49

Hank Hunk Receives Bobby's Phone Call

HANK IS HANGING out around the pool when he receives Bobby's phone call. The time is 11:00 a.m. Just finishing a late breakfast, he is relaxing in order to build up his energy to go full force with the prep work for the competition. He is wondering when Bobby is going to call him, and when he does, the tone of Bobby's voice confirms that he is in good spirits. Bobby explains the new schedule, noting that he had previously talked to Terance and Jeremy about his vision for Hank's performance and that they were in total agreement; it is a big boost for Hank's moral. After listening to Bobby's strategy about overcoming the kids from Providence's Elvis in leather look, Hank agrees that he needs something new, something fresh, and something very special. He is very enthusiastic about Bobby's new direction for him. Bobby expresses his appreciation for Hank's willingness to make the change. He, however, warns Hank that there would be a lot to do to make the changes. Clothes would have to be purchased, a new hairstyle would need to be in place, and most importantly, his voice would need to come full circle. The guitar would also be a big part of the act. Hank confesses that he could actually play the guitar very well and would be looking forward to showing them how good he was. Bobby asks Hank if he could commit to meeting every day for at least four hours per day, starting on Wednesday. Hank is fine with the schedule and the changes that need to be made but explains to Bobby that he has a commitment for Thursday night. Bobby doesn't have a problem with that. Bobby asks if he could make the meeting at 3:00 p.m. in Terance's room at the Mandalay Bay Hotel. Hank is agreeable to the time and lets Bobby know that he is willing to do anything Terance, Jeremy, and he had planned for him. Bobby explains that he would outline in detail what needed to be done and by whom at the 3:00 p.m. meeting. Hank again praises Bobby for taking such an interest in him. Being very appreciative of Hank's sincerity, he goes on to say that the kind words should also be extended to Terance and Jeremy. No matter what happens, win or lose, the important thing is that they all came together for single cause, which would bring their friendship to a new level. Upon ending the conversation with Hank, he immediately calls Terance and Jeremy back to let them know that Hank is 100 percent committed. Things are looking up for the four amigos.

Chapter 50

The Four Men Plan for the Resurrection of Elvis

IN ORDER TO get things ready for the meeting, Bobby arrives at Terance's suite at 2:50 p.m., ten minutes early; Terance is waiting for Bobby. He somehow knows he would be first to arrive and welcomes his friend with open arms.

"I'm glad you arrived early. I may need a little help with the DVD and moving some furniture around to make room for Hank's rehearsals."

"I'm ready to do that."

Entering the room, he gets a full view of Terance's suite and is overwhelmed by its size and decor.

"My god, what an incredible pad you have, my friend. This place is bigger than my house. I can't wait to see the expressions on Hank and Jeremy's face when they get a load of all this."

Terance smiles and then shows Bobby around. As he is doing so, he comments, "I think the parlor area would be the best location for us to set up. It's flanked by two bedrooms and has a good-sized TV console with a DVD player. What do you think?"

"I'm with you."

"In order to save time, how about having the meals delivered to the room so that we can eat and converse about Hank's up-and-coming performance?" Bobby agrees.

Terance has all kinds of treats placed around the suite. There are beers of all kinds, soft drinks, fruit drinks, coffee, hard liquor, finger food, and trail mix placed everywhere. Bobby helps himself to the bowl of trail mix the moment he saw it.

"I can eat this stuff all day."

"I am the same way. I got five pounds of it."

Bobby walks over to the window and looks out to see the Las Vegas strip and the mountains in the distance. While Terance is checking out the DVD player, he hears a knock on the door; it is Jeremy, and it is exactly 3:00 p.m. Looking at Jeremy's facial expressions, Bobby could tell that Jeremy couldn't believe his friend Terance is such a high roller. Jeremy comments, "This looks like a high-roller pad. Are you a big gambler?"

"I certainly am, but I don't do any gambling in the casinos."

Terance notices that Jeremy is carrying a gym bag similar to the one Bobby brought. Terance asks Jeremy and Bobby if they have the DVDs, and with that, Bobby and Jeremy open the bags and lay the DVDs on the coffee table in the parlor.

Being dressed very casually, it is a good indication that they aren't planning on dining out at a fancy restaurant. The time is now 3:15 p.m., and suddenly there is a knock on the door. All feels a sigh of relief. Hopefully the person on the other side of the door is Hank, and it was. Terance jumps up briskly and opens the door. Hank is also very impressed with Terance's accommodations. He asks Terance, "Do you have other people staying with you?"

"No, I am here alone."

"I was just kidding. How about if I move in with you?"

"I want to move in with you too," replies Jeremy.

"That won't be a problem, however, one of you is going to have to sleep on the pullout sofa in the parlor, or you can bunk up together in a queen-size bed in the second bedroom."

Jeremy replies, "I don't know about sleeping together in the queen-size bed."

Terance replies, "Only kidding."

Bobby interjects, "Now that we have all the sleeping arrangements behind us, let us decide on how we can make all this work."

Jeremy responds, "I think we can make it all work."

Terance adds, "Absolutely."

Hank replies, "I will do anything you guys want me to do, anything."

"That's great, Hank, then you can sleep with Jeremy tonight in the queen bed while I bunk up on the pullout."

With Bobby's remark, all four men chuckle and settle in for a night of planning and viewing DVDs.

It is now time to get down to business. Bobby hands each of them an outline of what needs to be accomplished within a very short week and remarks that the outline should be viewed as suggestions, more or less; the actual itinerary would come out of tonight's meeting. They all agree, however, after quickly reading through Bobby's outline; they all agree that Bobby has all the bases covered. Bobby immediately begins explaining the crucial issues. First, they need to get clothing for Hank. Bobby passes around the photo of Elvis that he feels should be the look for Hank. The photo shows the young Elvis wearing a light blue sport jacket, black trousers, an open shirt, a skinny belt, and what looked like to be snap jack shoes or loafers. Bobby reiterates that since they all agreed on the look, the challenge would be finding the clothes that matched the photo and, more importantly, having them ready for Saturday or preferably by Friday night. Terance notes that they only had three days to accomplish this, and time is of the essence. Agreeing with Terance, Bobby asks if anyone has any ideas. Terance notes that the only possibility of having the clothes ready by Friday is to find a tailor who specializes in custom-made clothing and get him going ASAP. This means they would have to find him/her by tomorrow morning and arrange for Hank to be fitted on the same day. Terance notes, "Finding that tailor is not going to be the problem. The problem will be locating the exact fabric for the jacket, trousers, and shirt and meeting the deadline."

Bobby asks, "Who wants to take charge of the clothes?" Jeremy volunteers and notes that he knows someone in Las Vegas that could hook him up with the right tailor.

"I'll call them first thing in the morning and get some names, and then Hank and I will hopefully be in a tailor's shop by midmorning."

Bobby explains that there would be a couple of other things that need to be taken care of. One will be the guitar, the other one will be getting Hank a haircut like the one in the photo. Bobby volunteers for the haircut and plans to have Hank ready for the stylist by Thursday morning.

Accomplishing these three things would put the most critical objectives behind them, and now it is time to start looking at the DVDs. Suggesting that they wouldn't have time to watch all the DVDs at normal speed, Bobby explains that he would fast forward over parts that would not be beneficial to Hank's act. He pulls out a bunch DVDs and explains that it's the earlier performances that they should be concentrating on. The first DVD is titled "Elvis on Sullivan 1957." The image of Ed Sullivan came on the TV screen as he announced, "And now, ladies and gentlemen, boys and girls, let's hear it for Elvis Presley." The camera scans the audience, and the audio picks up the screaming and applauding that rock the theater. The camera then turns on to Elvis with a full-length view of the young, bigger-than-life idol of millions. Bobby pointed out that Elvis was wearing the exact clothing that was in the photo he passed out earlier. His looks, his posture, his facial expressions, his voice, and his body movements had the crowd going out of control, and with the Jordanaires backing him up, it all was perfect. The group was very basic but extremely effective. The sound equipment was much less sophisticated than the rock bands that followed him. With Elvis's presence, there was no need for modern-day electronics. Elvis was all that was needed for the excitement. While viewing the DVDs, Bobby wonders, *How could one young kid from nowheresville, USA, get up onstage in New York City and rock the people into hysteria?* Bringing back this moment in time is Bobby's mission, and for all the millions of baby boomers who want Elvis back in their lives. In the DVD, Elvis sang "Treat Me Nice," one of Bobby's favorites but not one of Elvis's biggest hits. Elvis sang the song so perfectly, his voice resonated throughout the theater and elevated above the screams and cries of the mesmerized audience. Bobby would have given anything to be there. Jeremy replies, "I remember watching this show with my mother on a black-and-white television. I can still remember the chills that ran through my body."

Bobby adds, "I was under ten years old when I saw this video, and I can still remember my excitement. Somehow we have to create this image. Do we all agree?"

They all agree wholeheartedly. Terance explains that it is going to take some doing to get their friend Hank to this level, but they need to try. And they need to begin immediately. Jeremy adds in a serious tone, "The coaching, grooming, and perfecting Elvis's voice will all come in good time. More importantly, we need to realize our mission is much more than winning the competition. We are in fact competing for Elvis. We're not here to copy, imitate, or impersonate him but rather to resurrect him through our young friend Hank."

Bobby adds, "We may need a little help from above to accomplish our mission, but nonetheless, it all starts tonight with the four of us."

The four men look at each other somberly. Bobby and Jeremy's words strike a very vital nerve within their souls. They viewed a couple of hours of Elvis's documentaries and stage performances. The footage showed different levels of Elvis's ability as a front man. The later videos taken around the time Elvis was fully in throne in Las Vegas were much more produced. Hank's present age would have been very close to Elvis's age, and his height, body weight, hair, and looks were dead ringers for the young Elvis. The time is now 5:30 p.m., and Terance asks if supper is in order. They all agree. The plan is to order takeout from the fast-food restaurant across the street. After ordering the food, Terance volunteers to pick it up, and then he heads for the door.

"I'll be back in fifteen minutes."

Bobby offers to help pay for the meal, but Terance refuses to take any money. Jeremy reaches into his somewhat-tattered gym bag and pulls out his audios on DVDs. He places them on the coffee table and suggests that they wait until Terance returns before moving on with songs. Within fifteen minutes, Terance is back with the meals. He places the takeouts on the minibar at the rear of the parlor and brings out a generous assortment of beers, sparkling water, soft drinks, and bottles of Pellegrino. The four men sit around the bar, eating, drinking, and contemplating Hank's new image. When they finished eating, they bring their drinks over to the coffee table, and Jeremy pushes in the first DVD. Jeremy explains that this is the song he remembers when he was young. At the time, it sent shock waves through his body. He explained that when he was younger, his voice sounded almost close to Elvis. However, as he grew older, his voice matured. He began listening very closely to how Elvis emphasized the words in the songs. He paid particular attention to Elvis's rhythm techniques, and soon after, his voice began to change, and he was able to sound exactly like him. Jeremy is convinced that when Elvis died, he inherited Elvis's voice. It was a miracle. Jeremy assures the guys that in a short period of time, he could drastically improve Hank's voice, and with the right song, it will almost be perfect. The choice of songs will be of utmost importance. The guys want to know what song he had in mind. Jeremy is not sure, but he knows it needs to be a short and a very recognizable song, and it shouldn't challenge Hank's octaves. He needs background to help cover up some of the imperfections that may occur in Hank's voice. This could be accomplished with some good guitar work as part of the act. Jeremy adds, "At this point in time, there are a bunch of songs that I'm thinking about. The ones that stand out are 'I'm All Shook Up,' 'Treat Me Nice,' or 'Blue Suede Shoes.'"

He asks the three other guys what they think. Bobby thinks that they should leave it up to Jeremy and Hank. Terance agrees. Jeremy and Hank would have to work it out. The time is now almost 10:30 p.m. Bobby suggests a heads-up call at 2:00 p.m. tomorrow to check on how things are proceeding with getting Hank's clothes, haircut, and guitar. They all agree, and Bobby adds, "Hopefully by the time we meet tomorrow at 3:00 p.m., we should have the song selected, Hank's clothing being made, his haircut scheduled, and the guitar in hand. Well, what do you think, guys, can we handle it?"

Terance replies, "You bet we can."

Jeremy adds, "We will definitely try our best."

Bobby turns to Hank and says, "I couldn't be happier for you, Hank. You have a couple of good friends pushing for you."

Terance interjects, "And don't leave yourself out on the group of good friends, Bobby. Without you, none of us could have happened. We wouldn't be here today trying to resurrect Elvis if it wasn't for your devotion and passion for our mission."

With that, Hank stands up and looks down at the three men and says, "You three guys are somewhat strangers to me. We have been meeting for a number of years in Las Vegas and then returning home to our personal lives without a trace of what or who we are. It now seems I have a clear understanding of the kind of men you are, and I am overwhelmed by your generosity, your trust in me, and your unselfish devotion to my success. I don't know how to thank you for all of this other than to say what my grandmother repeated when I was growing up. 'Good people attract to good people' is what she told me. And you three guys exemplify her teachings. I will do everything I possibly can not to let you down."

Bobby thanks Hank for his sincere compliment and adds, "Don't worry, Hank, you won't let us down."

Bobby turns to Terance and offers his thanks again for the use of his suite and then adds, "Oh, by the way, Terance, how much was the meal?"

Terance comments, "Bobby, my good friend, please don't worry about the cost of the meal."

Bobby understands none too clearly what Terance is alluding to.

Chapter 51

Jeremy and Hank Find a Tailor

JEREMY IS UP early. After showering, shaving, and getting dressed, he follows his breakfast routine and is back in the room by 7:30 a.m. He wants to call Kie to see if she could help him find a tailor for Hank's jacket by Friday but is concerned about how early it was. Not wanting to wake Kie, he spends the next hour and a half looking through the Las Vegas telephone directory for tailors. Writing down a few phone numbers and making a few phone calls, he realizes he was getting a lot of answering machines telling him the time of day the shops opened and what time they closed. After a few calls, he realizes that the majority of the tailors open at 8:00 a.m. He did, however, reach one tailor who answered the phone himself. The man has a very heavy accent, and Jeremy has a difficult time understanding him, and vice versa. Jeremy repeats the need to have the sport jacket custom-tailored by Friday evening. The tailor responds, "Not this Friday. That would be impossible." Jeremy thanks him and quickly hangs up and decides to call Hank. Together they could plan the morning. Getting his voice recording on his cell phone, he leaves a message to call him back. Returning to the phone book, he begins writing down more phone numbers to call before he calls Kie. He is about to make his second call when his phone rings; it is Hank. Jeremy asks if he had gone out for breakfast, and Hank replies that he hadn't.

Hank explains that he is going to make some phone calls to local tailors this morning. Jeremy says as soon as he connects with someone who can do the work, he would call Hank back and let him know what the plan is. That is agreeable to Hank.

Jeremy reiterates that he would call Hank as soon as he makes a connection. As soon as they hang up, Jeremy begins making calls to tailors. He got a lot of "Sorry, we can't help you." He asks one tailor if he knows anyone who could take on the work in such a short period of time. His reply is no.

The tailor abruptly hangs up. Jeremy is beginning to get a sinking feeling. Maybe the custom-made jacket and trousers are out of the question. Thinking about other alternatives, he goes back to the telephone book and looks for costumes for rent. His first call is to a costume rental shop that advertised that they had everything back to the Roman Empire. It is worth a shot. So he calls. A very pleasant-sounding young woman answers the phone. She wishes him good morning and welcomes him.

"How can I help you, sir?"

While explaining what he needed, the young woman listens patiently. Then she explains that the rental shop has racks of Elvis costumes, but they are mostly the Las Vegas jumpsuit types. Jeremy explains that he is looking for something that Elvis would have worn in his early years. What Jeremy is looking for is not something they had, but he may want to take a look at some of their period costumes that may be similar. Confused by the term "period costumes," he asks for a description. The young woman describes how the shop has clothing from each decade.

"For instance," she said, "we have the forties look, fifties look, zoot suits, the seventies look, the disco look, bell-bottom pants of all kinds, big collar shirts of all kinds, leisure suits, even the grunge look, you name it, we have it."

This could work for Jeremy, so he asks, "What about the sizes?"

The young girl confirms that the critical thing is the sizes, although they have a lot of sixes available. Getting one to fit perfectly could be a problem. Jeremy asks, "Do you have shoes from each decade?"

"Yes, we do. What size are you looking for?"

Jeremy answers, "I'm not sure, I would guess around size 10 to 11."

"That wouldn't be a problem."

"What about snap jacks?"

"We have racks of them of all sizes."

"I don't believe you have all this stuff!"

"It's because of all of the live-show performances in Las Vegas. There is a big demand for costumes."

"I'm staying at the Western Hotel. How long will it take me to drive to your shop?"

"The ride should take no more than twenty minutes."

It is now 8:15 a.m., which is early enough for him to take a quick ride over to the shop and check it out; and if things look good, he would call Hank; if not, he would call Kie to see if she could help. Jeremy informs the young woman that he would be there within the half hour.

He arrives at the shop in just under fifteen minutes. The storefront window displays elaborate costumes, one of them featuring Elvis in a white jumpsuit as the centerpiece. Entering the shop, he is impressed at how big it is and how many racks of costumes are lined up in rows in every direction. A middle-aged man greets him and asks if he could help him. Jeremy explains that he'd just gotten off the phone with a young woman who knows what he is looking for. He confirms that he must have been talking to his daughter, Karen.

"It could be. I never did ask her name."

"It has to be her. She's the only other person here this morning. I will get her for you."

Excusing himself, he walks to the back of the store; and in a few seconds, he and his daughter walk over to Jeremy. The young woman is full of smiles and introduces herself.

"You must be the person who is trying to locate the early Elvis-look costume."

Jeremy explains that he was that person.

"Well, then let me show you what we have here."

With that, Karen escorts Jeremy to a section of the floor that has racks of clothing with display tags with only numerical descriptions. The descriptions read fifties, sixties, seventies, eighties, and nineties. There are racks upon racks of sport jackets from which Karen pulls out one from the fifties that is real close to the style pictured in Bobby's photo. Unfortunately, in haste, Jeremy left the photo in his room. He wanted to show it to Karen so she would have a better idea of what he was looking for. Karen pulls out jacket after jacket, each of them looking close to what he thought the look should be. Rather than continue trying to find the jacket without the photo, he asks to see the shirt selections. The shirts that Karen shows Jeremy seem to be right on the mark from what he remembered in the photo. The next thing he wants to see is the shoes. The shoe selection is unbelievable. As Jeremy looks over the hundreds of pairs of shoes, he couldn't believe how many ridiculous styles of shoes there were and how quickly he had forgotten them. The styles that were in vogue in the fifties, sixties, and seventies were never to be seen again. Karen asks Jeremy if he would like to try on any of the costumes. Jeremy apologizes for not telling her that the costume is not for him but for a friend and that his friend and he would be coming back to the shop today to get fitted.

"We're open until 9:00 p.m."

"I'll be back with my friend before 9:00 p.m."

Jeremy left feeling that he had half of his task accomplished; however, the biggest piece is still unresolved, and that was a sport jacket and pants.

It is now 9:30 a.m. and a good time to call Kie. Kie answers the phone immediately. From the sound of Kie's voice, she seems like she was very happy to hear from him. Opening the conversation with how great a time he had at lunch with her yesterday, he asks if she had Thursday night open for supper. She answers with a very encouraging yes, which uplifts Jeremy. Kie asks Jeremy where he is.

"Well, it's funny that you should ask because I'm just leaving a costume shop on the east side."

"What on earth are you doing there?"

"It's a long story, but I'll explain it all to you tomorrow night."

"OK, I can wait. Where are we going tomorrow night with you dressed up as Elvis Presley?"

Jeremy is a bit surprised by her remarks but counters with "I was thinking of coming as Jimi Hendrix."

Kie laughs and says, "That's fine. I'll wear my Janis Joplin costume."

"I need to get serious. I need your help with something important."

"And what would that be?"

"I need a very special tailor who can make a custom sport jacket for my friend for a very special event on this Saturday night."

"You can find anything you want in Las Vegas."

"The clothing that I am looking for is not something you can find on a rack."

"I think I can help you."

Jeremy is relieved to hear this.

"I have a client who's a tailor. He used to work in a men's custom suit shop in Hong Kong, and he once told me that he could measure a customer in the morning and have the suit ready for that night and did it regularly."

"That's just what I need."

"The shop is located about six blocks from the strip heading west on W. Tropicana Drive. The name of the place is Lee's Custom Tailors. I don't have his number, but I'm sure that you could get it from the telephone directory or call information."

"I'll call immediately after I get off the phone. I'll be looking forward to seeing you tomorrow at 7:00 p.m."

"That's great. Let's talk again tomorrow in the afternoon."

"I'll call."

Jeremy immediately calls information and gets Lee's Custom Tailor's phone number. The phone rings; he asks for Mr. Lee. Mr. Lee comes to the phone, and Jeremy describes what he needs and who recommended him to call him. Hearing it was Kie, he tells Jeremy to come in the immediately. Jeremy confirms he would be there within the hour. Mr. Lee replies,

"That would be fine. When you come in, I'll be able see what I can do."

Jeremy immediately calls Hank and tells him what he has planned and where they need to go. Hank offers to pick Jeremy up in ten minutes. Needing more time to relocate to the other hotel lobby, he asks Hank to make it more like fifteen minutes. Arriving in exactly fifteen minutes, he and Jeremy head over to Lee's Custom Tailor. As they enter the shop, they are greeted by an older Chinese gentleman who spoke perfect English. Jeremy introduces himself as the person he spoke to on the phone earlier this morning and then introduces Hank. Mr. Lee seems very pleased and accommodating. He is a very distinguished-looking man who wears a cloth measuring tape around his neck. He asks Hank and Jeremy to come around to the rear of the shop.

The rear the shop is populated with people on sewing machines. Clothes are lying everywhere. Remembering to bring the picture of the young Elvis, Jeremy hands it to Mr. Lee and says, "This is the jacket and trousers we need."

"The pants are not a problem—it's the color of the jacket. I can't be sure I can get the exact color. I'll make a few calls around town. I won't be able to tell you for sure. I think I know where I can get this material—it's the color that's the problem. If I can get it, I can tailor the jacket exactly as you see it in this photo. I'll need to measure your friend and to get things going."

Mr. Lee asks Hank to stand on the raised platform. He begins taking measurements and dictates them to his assistant. Jeremy asks how long it would be before he knew if he could get the color. Mr. Lee answers, "If you can wait thirty-plus minutes or if you want to come back in forty-five minutes, I will have an answer for you."

Spending the next forty-five minutes in a small coffee shop up the street from the shop, Jeremy explains about his good fortune at the costume shop and the luck he had with finding the shirt and shoes. After forty-five minutes, they head back to Mr. Lee's shop. Jeremy is feeling somewhat nervous. If

Mr. Lee couldn't come up with the color match, then they are back to square one. To say the least, Jeremy is more nervous than Hank. Mr. Lee greets them with a big smile. Jeremy's nervousness disappears immediately. He announces that he has pulled off a miracle and tracked down the exact color match with a fabric supplier in North Las Vegas. He would send one of his people over to pick up the fabric this afternoon, and by 4:00 p.m. tomorrow, they could come in for Hank's final fitting. By Friday at 2:00 p.m., he should have exactly what Hank needs. He ends with "Will that be all, gentlemen?"

Jeremy could not help but ask how much it was all going to cost. Mr. Lee replies that he couldn't tell them the exact amount because he doesn't have the cost of the material for the jacket but added that he would have the cost for Jeremy that afternoon. Asking Mr. Lee if he could give him a high to low cost for the work, Mr. Lee hesitates and then asks Jeremy to give him a couple of minutes. He goes over to the cashier counter, takes out a pad of paper, and begins jotting down numbers.

"You know there's a premium for making clothing within twenty-four hours, and the material and color of the fabric is also a premium."

"I understand that very clearly."

"It's going to be around $700 plus or minus."

The cost is twice as much as much as Jeremy would have guessed, but he has no other options.

"I'll need a $200 deposit before I can get started."

Hank immediately reaches into his wallet and pulls out his credit card. Now it is time to head over to the costume shop, and by 2:00 p.m., Hank has his shoes and shirt in hand, and his jacket and pants are being made.

Jeremy immediately calls Bobby with the good news. Bobby is overwhelmed by how much Jeremy and Hank have accomplished in such a short period of time. Complimenting Jeremy over and over again for his exceptional achievement makes Jeremy feel great.

Chapter 52

Bobby Finds the Barber

BOBBY IS DELIGHTED with Jeremy's positive news about finding someone who could tailor Hank's jacket and pants by Friday. Bobby also has good news for Jeremy and Hank. He explains that he had spent the morning looking for a hairstylist and found one that could give Hank the exact haircut Elvis had in the photo.

Starting with the telephone directory, he realizes after just a couple of calls, he isn't getting anywhere. So he decides to go down to the hotel's concierge desk. He shows the photo to the concierge to see what he could come up with, and as luck would have it, the concierge knows of four hair salons that he thinks could do it. He hands Bobby a piece of paper with the names and addresses of the four locations that specialized in theatrical grooming. He leaves the hotel at exactly 9:00 a.m. and heads to first salon on the list, Felicia M. Hairstylist at CT Rose Salon on E. Sunset Road. Bobby takes a cab to the salon. The driver is asked to wait ten minutes while he goes in to talk to the stylists. The salon is bustling with stylists, manicurists, pedicurists, and people washing hair and coloring hair. Noticing a young girl sitting behind a desk, he asks if it is possible to talk to a stylist about a special haircut. She asks Bobby what style he has in mind, and Bobby shows the picture he had of Elvis. The girl looks closely at the picture and then at Bobby and looks puzzled. Bobby explains that haircut would not be for him but rather for a friend that had a similar hairstyle. The girl asks Bobby to wait a minute while she shows the picture around. Bobby agrees, and the young girl walks into a room where an older, distinguished-looking gentleman is working on something on a table. Watching as she shows the photo to the man, Bobby notices that the he is looking very closely at the picture and then looks up through the window at Bobby. He comes through the door of the room and waves for him to come over to him. The young girl introduces Bobby to the older gentleman whose name is Mr. Diego. Bobby introduces himself, and then he and Mr. Diego look at the photo. Mr. Diego asks Bobby, "How old is your friend?"

"He's early to midtwenties."

"What condition is your friend's hair in now? Is it long, thick, thin, curly, etc.?"

"His hair is kind of long, somewhat thick, but not too thick."

Mr. Diego looks at Bobby and comments, "I know this picture of Elvis. It's all over the country at the fast-food restaurants."

"That's where I took the picture of the photo."

Mr. Diego invites Bobby into the room where he is working. When Bobby looks down at the table where Diego is working, he could also see about twenty to thirty photos of celebrities. He recognizes most of them immediately. Everyone was there, from Tom Cruise to Jerry Garcia. Mr. Diego looks at Bobby and then at the table and says, "We get all kinds of requests here. Most of the time, they're for performers working in the theater acts along the strip. And sometimes it's the up-and-coming in the music business. But most of the time, it's the average everyday guy who decides he needs to reinvent himself. This early photo you have of Elvis with the pompadour was how he looked some fifty years ago. You don't see this hairstyle anymore. Is your friend a performer?"

"Yes, he's somewhat of a performer."

"He wouldn't be one of the performers in the Elvis event at the Tropicana, would he?"

"That's exactly why we need the haircut."

"You could actually pass for Presley with the proper haircut and a little bit of makeup."

"I've tried over the years, but I can't come close to the guy who needs this haircut."

"How much does your friend look like Elvis?"

"He looks a lot like Elvis."

"I'm a huge fan of Elvis, always have been, always will be. The young generation has no idea what he had. He was the first and the last to make a lasting impression on me. When do you want to come in with your young friend? What's his name?"

"Hank."

"By the way, my good friend, I usually book out three weeks, however, in this case, I'm very anxious to see this young guy who looks just like Elvis."

"You won't be disappointed."

"Good, then I'll see you tomorrow at 10:00 a.m. with your young friend."

On the way out of the salon, Bobby asked the young girl how much a haircut with Mr. Diego would cost.

"The cost should be between $200 and $250, depending on what condition your friend's hair is in."

Bobby rushes out to the waiting cab and requests the driver to take him back to the hotel. On the way back, he dials up Terance's cell phone and lets him know of his and Jeremy's success. Terance is thrilled with the good news and mentions he is heading out to pick up the guitar. Bobby comments that he is very excited that everything seems to be going so smoothly. Terance mentions that he would be looking forward to seeing Bobby tonight.

Being very pleased with the outcome of the day, he decides to call Kate. He dials up her number, and when she answers, he says in one sentence, "Hi, Kate, how are you—I can't wait to see you again."

"You must have ESP. I was just going to call you."

"How about we get together tomorrow night?"

"That sounds great. I can't wait to see you again."

Bobby was now in high gear.

Chapter 53

Terance and the Guitar

TERANCE IS VERY pleased to hear that Hank, Jeremy, and Bobby had great success with their assignments. He is also able to give Bobby some good news about the guitar. Earlier that morning, Terance began his expedition to find a guitar for Hank. He began his search by visiting the concierge in the hotel lobby at the Mandalay Bay at 8:00 a.m. The concierge was in his early sixties or late fifties, and Terance's request was taken very seriously once Terance explained why he needed to purchase the guitar that day. The concierge immediately responded with phone numbers of musical instrument dealers but hesitated to give Terance his standard issue list. He carefully went over each of the dealers that he felt would be able to accommodate him. He described the pros and cons of each of his recommendations. When it was all said and done, Terance was given three guitar shops to visit. Each shop had a special niche in the world of musical instruments. Having no idea why purchasing a guitar would have so many reasons why you should choose one dealer over the other, he was nonetheless very grateful to the concierge. Terance was back up in his room at around 8:30 a.m. He tried to reach Terri by phone but got her voice greeting on the answering machine. He left a message that he would call her back. His first stop would be Ed Roman's Guitars, which was located on Dean Martin Drive. It was almost walking distance, but Terance decided to take a taxi. When he arrived at Ed Roman's, he was amazed at the number of guitars that were on display. The guitars were grouped by the makers' names, such as Gibson, Fender, Les Paul, etc.

Prior to making a trip out to this music shop, Terance download Ed Roman's web page on his laptop. He was very impressed with the information the web page had to offer. The culture of Ed Roman's shop went way beyond knowing about the guitars. It described the musicians' lives that played these special instruments. There was a beautiful testament to Elvis on Ed's web page. The testimonial read, "His talent, good looks, sensuality, charisma, and good humor endeared him to millions, as did the humanity and human kindness he demonstrated throughout his life." These words stuck in Terance's mind and reminded him why he had to resurrect Elvis. Elvis's persona struck a strong likeness to Terance's outlook on life. He lacked Elvis's looks, talent, and charisma, but not his passion and human kindness. Terance always believed that he was not only blessed but was also extremely lucky. Now he was going to offer his good fortunes to his young friend Hank.

Terance walked around the shop for just a few seconds when Ed Roman himself approached him and asked if he could help. After informing Ed that the concierge at the Mandalay Bay Hotel gave him his name, Ed asked Terance if he had something in mind. Terance reached into his pocket and pulled out the picture of Elvis holding the acoustic guitar he wanted. Terance says, "This is what I'm looking for, Ed," pointing to the guitar in the picture that Bobby had given him.

Ed asked if he could view the picture closely, and Terance handed it over to him. Ed studies the photograph and says, "This is a Gibson Elvis Presley Dove."

"I guess that's the one I'm looking for."

He brought Terance into a room full of Gibson acoustic guitars that were hanging on the walls and mounted on racks on the floor. He was very impressed to say the least. Ed walks over to a dark-colored guitar, removes it from the rack, and brings it over to Terance and says, "This is the guitar you're looking for, and it's a legend."

Terance took the guitar from Ed, put the strap around his neck, and held it in his hands; and within a second, a chill went through his body. The guitar in the picture was now in his hands, and it was very moving. Ed noticed that Terance was obviously delighted and asked if it was for him or a gift for somebody. Terance replied that it was a gift for a very special friend for a very special occasion.

"Would that special occasion be the Elvis competition being held this week?"

"That could be it."

"Well, this will certainly help. Can your friend play?"

"He can."

Ed noticed the passion in Terance's expressions and immediately knew that this wasn't just a guitar for a friend. This was much more special than that. Ed explained to Terance how little people knew about Elvis's guitar ability. Most people's image of Elvis is in his looks, voice, and him strumming a few strings every now and then. Ed was quick to point out that Elvis was the virtuoso on the guitar and that he could play as good as anyone. His voice and his looks were so captivating that his talent on the guitar was overlooked. Terance wanted Ed to meet Hank and asked what his schedule was. Ed said that he was in the shop every day from 8:00 a.m. to 5:00 p.m., five days a week.

"Can I pay for the guitar and take it with me now?"

"Absolutely, but before you do, I want to string it up and tune it so that your friend Hank can play it immediately. Oh, by the way, don't you want to know how much this is going to cost you before you to walk out the door with this guitar?"

"Yes, of course, whatever it costs." Ed somehow knew that Terance would have no problem with the cost.

Ed then reached for the tag hanging from the neck of the guitar and said, "This baby is going to run you $8,300."

Terance didn't bat an eye.

Ed remarked, "Somehow I didn't think the price was going to be a problem."

Terance just shrugged his shoulders and smiled. Ed walked to the back of the shop and within ten minutes was back with the guitar. He wrapped the guitar strap around his neck and played the chords to "I'm All Shook Up," which shook Terance right down to his shoes. The sound that came out of the guitar was captivating. Terance thought, *Wait until the guys get a load of this.*

Ed placed the guitar into a black case and then reached behind the counter and added a second guitar strap and happily noted that both guitar straps were on the house. Terance handed Ed his American Express card, and Ed processed the transaction. They shook hands, and Ed wished him good luck and said good-bye. Ed adds, "I want to see your friend."

Terance agreed that he would bring him by this week. Terance left Ed Roman's feeling jubilant, lucky, and ready to go. He had what he wanted in his hands. He couldn't wait to see Hank holding the guitar.

Chapter 54

Terance is Back in His Hotel Suite with the Guys

TERANCE RETURNS TO his hotel with the prized guitar. After carefully removing it from the guitar case, he stares at it for a few moments and then starts to play. Terance could play as good as any amateur. The beautiful sound resonating from guitar inspires Terance to play a group of chords and some melody. To extend his delight for the instrument, he places it upright on the sofa in the parlor. This way, it would be the first thing the guys saw when they enter the room. More finger food is needed for the 5:00 p.m. meeting, so he goes out before the guys arrived. He returns at 4:30 p.m. and begins arranging the room for Hank's rehearsal. At 4:45 p.m., Bobby arrives. After greeting him, he points to the sofa. Bobby immediately sees the guitar and rushes over to the sofa. He is ice-cold quiet for at least thirty seconds before he spoke. He says with excitement, "My god! Terance, that's it. That's the guitar! It's the one in the photo."

Bobby removes the photo from his pocket and gestures to Terance to come over and take a look, but Terance just smiles and remains at the opposite end of the room.

"I know, Bobby. I have the copy of the photo. You gave it to me the other night."

"Where on earth did you get the guitar, and how much was it?"

"Ed Roman's Guitars on Dean Martin Drive. Let's say it was north of $500."

"How much north?"

Terance shrugs his shoulders, smiles, and raises his eyebrows a couple of times.

"I still can't believe you got it. Wait until Hank and Jeremy see this." Bobby reaches over the sofa and picks up the guitar like it is a spiritual relic. He plays a few chords and lets the sound resonate through his head. Terance comments that he had the same reaction when he first saw the guitar. He couldn't believe that he actually pulled this off in such a short period of time.

"I congratulate you, Terance. You simply know how to get things done."

Terance is a person who didn't need compliments but accepts Bobby's graciously.

"I was very lucky today. Very lucky."

The two men are interrupted by a knock on the door. It was Jeremy and Hank. They drove over in Hank's car. Terance opens the door, and the two men enter, greet Terance, and then look over at Bobby holding the Elvis Presley's Gibson. Jeremy's jaw drops, and Hank's eyes flashes wide open. They rush over to Bobby and stare at the instrument as if it is a newborn infant.

"What do you think, guys? Did Terance come through for us?"

"This is too good to be true. Where did you get it?"

Bobby answers for Terance, "Less than a mile from the hotel on Dean Martin Drive."

Jeremy asks if he could hold a guitar, and Bobby hands over to him with care. Jeremy takes the guitar and starts playing. The sound is perfect. Jeremy hands the guitar to Hank.

"I need to see what you look like holding it."

Hank carefully takes the guitar from Jeremy, wraps the strap around his neck, looks at Terance, and says, "I just don't know what to say, guys."

Terance replies with a smile, "Don't say anything, just play something for us."

Hank looks over at Terance, Bobby, and Jeremy, takes three steps backward, looks down at the guitar, and belts out

"Blue Suede Shoes" like they never heard it before. Hank's guitar-playing ability is far superior to his three friends. Sitting on the sofa, they watch Hank in awe. When Hank finishes the song, he smiles at the three men who were in shock and asks, "How was that?"

Bobby asks, "Where on earth did you learn how to play the guitar like that?"

"My mother was a music teacher, and she taught me how to play, and my father also played. I started playing when I was six years old. My father and my father's two brothers would come over to the house on the weekends, and the three brothers and my mother would play for hours while I danced around the floor."

Hank adds that his father and mother could not only play the guitar but also sing and had terrific voices. His father told him that the four of them played together in college at local bars to earn spending money. He explained that his father and mother got married a year after they graduated from college. He was born a year later. At this point in his life, his father knew he had to get a day job; and with that, the band broke up. They still play together at least once a month at his house.

"I wanted to follow in their footsteps but felt I couldn't make a go of it. What I do in Las Vegas is the closest I came to in the music business. It's architecture for me now."

Jeremy comments, "I think from what I just witnessed, you surely can make a go of it now. What do you think, guys?"

Terance and Bobby agree wholeheartedly. Hank unstraps the guitar and places it back in the case next to the sofa, and the four men sit down to go over the tasks for the evening. Bobby explains that they don't have much time with Saturday only three days away. They need to move quickly. Tonight is the night they should concentrate on Hank's voice. Jeremy would need to be the main guy to help Hank with voice improvements. Bobby replies, "Terance and I will sit back and watch and will play any tapes or videos that you need to fine-tune your voice."

Jeremy adds, "To help matters, we should get a mic and an amplifier as soon as possible. We don't need them right now. Tomorrow or Friday would be good."

Terance volunteers to pick them up. Jeremy asks for Bobby's DVD that had the song "Treat Me Nice." Bobby just happens to have one handy. While the DVD plays, Jeremy asks Hank to carefully listen to how Elvis embellishes the words to the song. He repeatedly asks Hank to concentrate on how the words were sung for six other songs. After the last song, he looks at Hank straight in the eyes and says, "The objective is not to imitate Elvis but rather to become Elvis. You need to get into his karma, his passion for music, and his ability to mix gospel with rhythm and blues. You have to push the envelope. Most importantly, you have to stop thinking that you're Hank. You now must convince yourself that you're Elvis Presley. The secret to my ability to sound like Presley is predicated by the fact that I'm able to close out the world around me and hear only his voice in my mind. I hear it perfectly, and when the words leave my mouth, they are his, not mine. To be honest with you, to this day, I can't believe it's me singing. It's a God-given gift. Unfortunately, I was never able to do anything with it. I have the voice but not the charisma. You, however, have the talent, the looks, and the charisma, and with the help from Bobby, Terance, and me, you will succeed. So the minute you place that guitar strap around your neck, move up to the mic and make eye contact with the audience. You must believe that you are no longer Hank Hunk from LA, but rather you're Elvis. You have to believe that deep down inside. Let Elvis's spirit guide you through the performance, and remember, he now *exists through you*. You are now the King."

Hank steps back, takes a deep breath, smiles at his three companions, and says in a perfect Elvis voice, "Thank you very much, Jeremy."

The three men enjoy Hank's innuendo and begin cheering and clapping and asking for more. Hank goes right into "I'm All Shook Up." He sounds very good but not good enough for Jeremy. Jeremy applauds enthusiastically and comments, "I have an idea. You play, and I'll sing."

As Hank plays and Jeremy sings, Bobby and Terance look on in awe. The sound and the look are riveting with Hank playing the guitar and Jeremy singing the words. The resemblance to Elvis is perfect. When they finish, Jeremy asks Hank if he heard the words he was singing, and Hank answers, "Not really. It sounded like I was singing, not you."

"That's exactly it, Hank. It's you singing. Now all you need to do is to master Elvis's way of singing the words in your mind. Keep going over it and over it and over it. Let's now try something else. Let's take just one line from one of Elvis's songs. I want you to listen to the words."

Jeremy plays a DVD and turns it off just after one line. Jeremy asks Hank to repeat that one verse by saying it, not singing it, and make it come from within as if he was trying to convince them that these were his words and this is how he feels. Jeremy adds, "You must become compassionate, convincing, and genuine. Now give me the words as Elvis would."

Hank begins the verse and slowly says the words to Jeremy. The sound comes out of Hank very differently. His voice becomes passionate and convincing. He begins to transform himself. It is somewhat hypnotic. There is a person within Hank that is taking over Hank's state of mind. Jeremy compliments Hank on the great improvement, and they go on with the same routine for the remaining verses; and with every new verse, Hank becomes more and more convincing. Terance interrupts to suggest that it's now a good time to take a break and have a bite to eat. Bobby immediately replies, "It's my treat. I'm going down to the deli around the corner to pick up some food for us. Give me your orders."

Terance asks, "How do you know how good the food is there?"

Bobby answers, "I don't. The place just looks good."

They all give Bobby a puzzled look. Terance feels it would be a better idea if they all go down to the deli for a needed break. Some fresh air would help relieve some stress. They may be pushing Hank a little too hard. All agree. Bobby is right about the place; the food is very good. They quickly eat, and Bobby picks up the tab, and they return to Terance's suite. Bobby reminds Hank that tomorrow, he is scheduled for his haircut with Mr. Diego at 10:00 a.m. Jeremy adds that tomorrow at 2:00 p.m., he and Hank are scheduled to pick up Hank's clothes. Terance asks what time would they be finished. Jeremy answers that they would be finished no later than 2:30 p.m. Terance is very comfortable with that time and confirms that 2:30 p.m. would give him ample time to pick up the amp and mic.

"We can all meet back here at 2:45 p.m. for dry run and practice for couple of hours."

Bobby comments that he knows that Hank has plans for Thursday night and admits that he also has plans. However, they all should commit to being back at Terance's hotel at 2:30 p.m. to make a big push. They pray that Hank could endure all the pressure.

Hank adds that he needed to pick up his tux on Thursday for the hotel gala that night. He assures them that it wouldn't be a problem if they could be finished by 5:30 p.m. They all agree that 5:30 p.m. would be the cutoff time. Thursday night is going to be a make-it-or-break-it night for Bobby and Kate. Jeremy is counting the hours to being with Kie. Hank is unsure what is in store for him with Jackie and Shirley. Terance had his meeting scheduled with the boys from the restaurant that night, and his offer would be presented to them in person. Thursday evening is going to be a very big night for the guys.

Chapter 55

Thursday Is a Very Busy Day for the Boys

BOBBY CALLS HANK at 8:00 a.m. on Thursday to remind him that he has a haircut scheduled with Mr. Diego at 9:00 a.m. Hank is barely awake when Bobby called. He offers to pick Bobby up at 8:30 a.m. so they could drive to the salon together. Accepting Hank's offer, Bobby says he'd be waiting at the hotel entry. They hang up, and Bobby immediately calls Terance to let him know about the day's activities. Terance informs Bobby that he would be at the hotel most of the day, and maybe they could meet after Hank had his haircut. This is agreeable for Bobby. He would confirm with Jeremy and Hank on a time and give Terance a call back. Everyone agree with the plan, and they confirm that after Hank had his haircut, they would get together at Terance's hotel at 10:45 a.m., and then they would all leave together for the fitting. The timing is good for Jeremy and Hank. It gives them about one-half hour before they have to leave for the fitting. The fitting should take no longer than one-half hour, which gives them ample time to make the 1:30 p.m. rehearsal meeting at Terance's hotel. Immediately after ending their conversation with Jeremy, Bobby calls Terance to inform him that everyone confirmed the 10:45 a.m. and 1:30 p.m. meeting times. The next call is to Kate. Kate answers the phone on the second ring, and Bobby joyfully announces that he would be over to pick her up at 7:00 p.m. Kate replies, "I will be looking forward to seeing you."

Bobby knows he has his day cut out for him, as do Hank and Jeremy. He goes down to the lobby to grab a quick breakfast and returns to the room to get ready for Hank's arrival at 8:30 a.m. At 8:25 a.m., Bobby is waiting outside the hotel lobby for Hank. At 8:40 a.m., Hank finally arrives. Hank apologizes for being late, and Bobby assures him that they had nothing to worry about. They have ample time to make the appointment. They arrive at the salon at 8:50 a.m. The salon is already in high gear. Bobby introduces Hank and himself to the receptionist and informs the young girl that Hank has a 10:00 a.m. appointment with Mr. Diego. The girl asks Hank and Bobby to take a seat. Within five minutes, Mr. Diego appears and escorts Hank and Bobby into the salon area where he has his chair. Looking Hank up and down, Mr. Diego smiles and says to Hank in serious tone, "Your friend wasn't kidding when he said you looked a lot like Elvis. However, when I am finished with you, you'll look exactly like Elvis. To begin, I think we should touch up your hair a couple of shades darker before I style it. I'll have Cary, my color expert, start on you right away."

Mr. Diego heads over to the other side of the studio and returns with a middle-aged woman wearing a smock and a big smile. Cary tells Hank that she would be coloring his hair. Mr. Diego has given her the exact color, and she is ready when he is. Hank asks, "What color are you going to make my hair?"

Cary replies, "Just a couple of shades darker than it is now. It will be a very subtle change, even your friends won't notice the difference."

Bobby asks, "How long is the coloring going to take?"

"No more than forty-five minutes."

"Well, then let's get started."

Cary asks Bobby if he wants to wait or come back in an hour and a half when the haircut is finished. This sounds like a good idea to Bobby. He would return forty-five minutes when Mr. Diego starts the haircut.

"I'll be back in forty-five minutes."

"That's good. I will see you when you return."

Bobby leaves, and Cary brings Hank over to a small room where she does the coloring. A few minutes later, Mr. Diego enters the room to check on her progress and makes a few suggestions. The coloring took just forty-five minutes, and now it is time to wash Hank's hair. The wash was performed by a young girl who worked part time at the salon. She seems to take a keen interest in Hank and talks his ear off for the whole time she washed his hair. Three shampoos and three rinses later, Hank asks jokingly if she is afraid she is going to wash the color out.

"Not at all, not the way Cary colors hair."

Mr. Diego comes by to the wash area and looks intensely at the young girl, and without saying a word, she immediately towel-dries Hank's hair vigorously. As Hank sits down in Mr. Diego's chair, he notices Bobby looking into the studio area. Smiling at Hank, Bobby then retreats to the waiting area. Mr. Diego looks at Hank's hair and comments on the perfect coloring job Cary had done. Diego starts right in with his scissors and comb. Hank asks if he is aware of the haircut he is looking for, and Diego points to his side table at an eight-by-ten photo of Elvis in his early twenties.

"That's it," Hank comments.

"I know," says Mr. Diego. "Your friend Bobby has a similar photo. I'm sure you must've seen it."

Diego moves around Hank's scalp like an artist contemplating on his next masterpiece. Two young interns gather around him to watch their master at work. As Diego works, he explains in detail each technique he is using to the interns. Diego's passion for his work impressed Hank. Diego moves around the chair and looks at Hank from the front then to the side and then to the back. He moves his scissors quickly and precisely up and down the sides and clips and combs and clips and changes his scissors four times and sprays Hank's hair with a mist of water before using the razor to layer his hair so that the styling would look natural. Hair spray would not be necessary. Nearing completion, Diego asks one of the young interns to fetch Bobby so he could have a look at his friend. When Bobby arrives, Diego is blow-drying Hank's hair, combing up the pompadour, and combing the sides back. Diego is blocking his view of Hank's head, so he doesn't have a full look at Hank. Diego reaches over and picks up his mirror and hands it over to Hank so that he could view the style from all sides. Holding the mirror at different angles, Hank looks in wonder at the haircut. He is delighted. He compliments Diego for his mastery. Diego turns Hank around in the chair to face Bobby. Bobby looks at Hank in total amazement and replies, "Mr. Diego, I can't believe what you have done. Everything is perfect—the color, the side burns, the pompadour, and the slick backsides and the length. It's all so perfect. You turned him into Elvis."

Diego smiles and thanks both Bobby and Hank for the generous compliments. Bobby couldn't take his eyes of Hank. He says over and over again, "It's unbelievable what you've done for us, Mr. Diego."

Diego instructs Hank how to blow-dry and comb his hair and then wishes Hank good luck with the competition. The bill came to $300. Hank walks over to the young girl who washed his hair and slips her a ten-dollar tip. The two men leave the salon with a feeling of accomplishment. Bobby turns to Hank and says, "Wait until Terance and Jeremy get a look at you."

The two men immediately drive to Terance's hotel. As Hank and Bobby walk through the lobby, Bobby notices a number of odd looks by people walking by Hank. It seems that Hank's haircut is getting mixed reviews. When Terance opens the door, he is amazed at Hank's new look. He calls over to Jeremy, who is looking through DVDs, and says, "Look who's here."

Moving quickly over to the door, Jeremy looks at Hank up and down and says, "My god, it's Elvis."

The four men leave together in Hank's car to Lee's Custom Tailor. When they arrive at the shop, Mr. Lee is waiting on a customer. Jeremy goes over to the cashier's table to announce that they are here for Hank Hunk's fitting. Mr. Lee approaches the four men with an extended hand. Jeremy introduces Bobby and Terance to Mr. Lee, and Mr. Lee leads the four men to the back of the shop. He asks Hank to go into the fitting room to try on the trousers and then come out with his shoes and shirt on. Hank steps up on the platform with Mr. Lee by his side. Mr. Lee removes the jacket from the suit bag hanging on the wall and helps Hank put on the jacket. He slides his hands across the shoulders of the jacket and pulls down the bottom so that the garment hangs perfectly. He buttons one button and stands back so that Jeremy, Bobby, and Terance could see Hank in full view. The men are speechless. They say nothing for thirty seconds. They just walk around Hank, glancing at him up and down. Bobby finally speaks up and says, "Guys, we have exactly what want. We got it because of Mr. Lee. He created the exact look for Hank."

Mr. Lee responds soberly, "He looks exactly how I remember Elvis. I'm very happy you got me involved in this. I am going to want a picture of him."

Bobby replies, "We'll be having a photo shoot of Hank on Saturday, and we will be sure to get you a print."

The four men congratulate Mr. Lee on his excellent work. The jacket and pants required no alterations. They fit Hank perfectly. Bobby takes the photo of Elvis out of his pocket and compares the style and color of the jacket and finds it to be a perfect match. They pay the bill and head back to Terance's hotel room.

All that had happened in such a very short period of time is way beyond Bobby's expectations. The passion and generosity they received from all the people who helped them achieve Hank's transformation were more than he could have hoped for. The good fortune the four men have been experiencing ever since they decided it would be Hank that they would elevate to Elvis came as a blessing. Their success could be attributed to the admiration that they had for the late Elvis Presley.

Hank drops Terance and Bobby off at Terance's hotel and then drives Jeremy back to the decoy. It is now 4:30 p.m., and Hank needs to pick up his tux for his big night with Shirley and Jackie. Bobby has to get back to his hotel and get ready for his date with Kate. Jeremy has to get ready for his rendezvous with Kie, and Terance has to get ready for his meeting with the restaurant people. Thursday evening is going to be very interesting night for the four happy guys.

Chapter 56

Thursday Night is a Big Night for Jeremy Shrinks

JEREMY RUSHES OVER to his hotel after Hank drops him off at the decoy. He needs to make a critical decision tonight. He has to decide if he should tell Kie that he's a lonely store clerk from Yukon, Oklahoma, with little to offer other than a broken-down trailer. His true identity may need to be revealed to his friends Bobby, Hank, and Terance at some point in time. But now is not the time. Kie, however, needs to be told sooner than later just in case she accepts an offer to come visit him in Yukon. He enjoys Kie's company too much to jeopardize his relationship with her. This being his last weekend in Las Vegas doesn't give him much time to take the relationship to another level, but before he does that, he needs to come up with something to explain why he leads such a humble lifestyle. Trying to think things out, he realizes there's no easy way to get him out of his predicament other than just telling the truth. However, the truth could be the end of their relationship. What's she going to think of him if he has to pick her up in his beat-up old Ford Falcon? Pondering his situation, he realizes he can't let her see his car. He needs an excuse why he can't pick her up. Hoping that she will volunteer to pick him up, he comes up with the idea of taking a cab to the restaurant with the hope that she will volunteer to pick him up. He calls her, and she picks up immediately. Jeremy mentions that he will be picking her up by taxicab, which she has no problem with. She suggests that he come to the Parlor rather than to her apartment. He agrees, and she explains that to save time and cab fares, they could go right from the Parlor to East Las Vegas where she lives. This all sounds very good to Jeremy, but what if she wants to go back to his room after supper? That would also be a problem for him. His shabby hotel accommodations are all part of his austerity program. If a future with Kie was meant to be, then the truth should be a part of it. The cab ride to the parlor is the plan, and when he arrives, the two of them can decide where to go for supper; and if for some reason they end up at his hotel, then so be it.

Getting ready to go in record-breaking time, he calls down to the front desk and asks the desk clerk how he should make arrangements for a taxicab. She explains that she would take care of it, and all she needs to know is what time he was leaving. He arrives in the lobby within five minutes and sees the cab waiting for him. He thanks the receptionist, tells the cabdriver the address and heads off to the parlor. Arriving at the parlor, Jeremy asks the cabdriver to wait until he returns. He quickly runs into the building and finds Kie talking to a couple of patrons in the reception area. As soon as she sees Jeremy, she smiles and says good-bye to the patrons. As she walks toward Jeremy, he looks her up and down and notices that she looks even more gorgeous tonight than she did at the hotel. Giving Jeremy a warm hug, she asks where they are off to. Having no plans, he suggests it would be better if they planned the evening together. Kie thinks that is very considerate of him. Jeremy explains that he has a taxicab waiting outside with the meter running. Kie tells Jeremy to go pay the cabdriver for the fare and send him on his way. They will use her car tonight. Jeremy asks, "Are you sure?"

"I'm absolutely sure."

Jeremy pays the fare and gives the driver a generous tip. As soon as they are in the car, Jeremy asks, "What do you suggest?"

"What kind of food are you in for tonight, or how about that restaurant you and your friends went to last week? Do you want to go there again, or do you want to try something different?"

Jeremy answers, "I could go there again, but I wouldn't mind trying something different if you have someplace that you think I would like."

"I don't know anything that would be better than the restaurant you described to me when you were with your friends."

"Then it's off to Graceland for us."

Arriving at Graceland at 7:30 p.m. is good timing for early dinner. As they approach the entrance, Kie doesn't seem that impressed by the building's industrial look from the exterior. As soon as they enter the waiting area, the hostess greets them and asks if they had a reservation. Jeremy explains that they don't. Looking down at the computer screen, the hostess confirms that she could seat them in five minutes. Together they say five minutes would be fine. The hostess gives Jeremy an electronic calling device and asks him to take his seat. They do, and in exactly five minutes, Jeremy's buzzer sounds. They are escorted to their table, and as soon as Kie enters the dining room and witnesses all the activity, she immediately gets excited. When she is in full view of the replica of Graceland, she is overwhelmed. She asks Jeremy how he found out about the place. He explains that his friend Bobby knew about it. Her excitement for the restaurant makes Jeremy's night.

While enjoying a wonderful meal together, they talk about everything under the sun. The complimentary bottle of wine and Kie's excitement help Jeremy overcome the anxieties he was feeling earlier in the evening. When it is time to leave, Jeremy looks over at Kie and says, "These last few days have been the best days I have had in a very long time, and it's all because of you."

Kie responds, "I'm so glad to be such an influence on you. I'm so grateful to you because you have been so very generous with your time. I'm not used to that."

When the bill came, Kie insists they split it. Jeremy thankfully obliges. They leave the restaurant around 9:30 p.m. It is still early, so Kie asks if he would be interested in doing a little gambling, and Jeremy answers that he would but adds that he isn't much of a gambler. Kie notes that she isn't much of a gambler either but explains when she does gamble, she follows a rule; a sixty-dollar limit for the night is her rule. If she loses sixty dollars or wins sixty dollars, she quits. Jeremy likes her approach to gambling, and with that, they are off to Circus Circus for a night at the roulette wheel.

They had a great time at the casino and left with more money than they started with. Noticing how Kie's influence got him to do things that he may have not done on his own is something he enjoys very much. As they are leaving the casino, Kie asks Jeremy where he is staying. Jeremy is ready to give her directions to the decoy hotel but changes his mind and gives her directions to his hotel. As they are driving to Jeremy's hotel, he explains that he is on a limited budget and doesn't plan on spending much time at the hotel, so she shouldn't expect something too special. He is very encouraged when Kie agrees with him and goes on to say that if you're not going to take advantage of the hotel's amenities, it doesn't make sense to pay the extra money. Being very relieved by her point of view, Jeremy adds, "Now I won't feel like a low roller."

Kie replies with an inquisitive laugh, "Is this an invitation?"

Jeremy is taken off guard by her comment. Not knowing what to say, he explains that he doesn't know how to answer her question without sounding presumptuous. She smiles and says, "I'm a big girl. I can handle most any situation, and I would enjoy seeing a hotel as lower-budget kind as it may be."

Jeremy notes that low budget is a kind description. With that, they both look at each other and enjoy a laugh. They park the car and head into the lobby and proceed up to his room. Kie removes her shoes immediately upon entering the room and sits down on the chair across from the bed. She glances over at the fifteen-year-old TV sitting on the shabby-looking bureau and says with a slightly sarcastic grin, "It's not that bad."

Jeremy rolls his eyes and walks over to the end of his bed and sits down in front of Kie. Kie gets up from her chair and sits beside him on the bed. Jeremy picks up the remote for the TV and hits the button. The late show comes on, and Kie slides to the back on the bed, her back resting up against the headboard. Jeremy follows suit, and they watch TV for about fifteen minutes. Kie grabs the remote and clicks off the TV, reaches around Jeremy's back, and pulls him closer to her. She begins rubbing his back, his neck, and his shoulders. Jeremy reaches around her back and rolls her over on top of him. Jeremy fears a premature event. That didn't happen, and they shared a very passionate evening together. The next day, Jeremy is awakened by Kie, who is fully dressed by 7:00 a.m. Before she left, she said that she had a wonderful time and that she will call him later on in the day. With Kie gone, Jeremy is left staring up at the ceiling, thinking about his experience, and recalling how long it's been since a woman made him feel so complete. It is apparent how much he needs Kie to be in his life and what he would need to do to make that possible. He dwells on this over and over again and concludes that it all materialized from his reinventing himself. You just need to make the effort to take some chances, and for that, his life was going to change for forever.

Chapter 57

Terance Closes the Deal

TERANCE ARRIVES AT Graceland at 6:30 p.m. to meet with John, Carl, Frank, and Steve to discuss his offer for the restaurant. Luckily, he doesn't come in contact with Jeremy and Kie. The offer was Federal Expressed to the restaurant. It arrived on Tuesday. Terance had the offer drawn up by his attorneys after a thorough review by his CPAs. They meticulously went over the restaurant's books and tax returns. The offer spelled out Terance's ownership position and his purchase offer for 50 percent of the stock. Terance would pay for all arrearages the restaurant had on the books, plus John's father for his share in the corporation, which amounted to 50 percent of the stock and real estate. The offer gave Terance half ownership of the corporation and the real estate and gave him final say on future locations for Graceland restaurants. His accountants will have the right to go over the books at the end of each quarter. Terance had one other stipulation in the agreement that made the deal perfect for him, and that was he would have the right to add his wife, Terri, to the management team and one other person to the restaurant staff. The offer was $8 million in cash. The cash offer relieved all outstanding debts and contributed $1 million toward present and future capital needs. The brothers and cousins would remain in control of the restaurant's operations. They would keep their present positions for a minimum of ten years or whenever the partnership decided to sell the business. A buy-sell agreement was in the offer, which had to be signed by each shareholder. Terance believed his offer was fair and equitable to all parties. Having signed all kinds of ownership agreements, buy-sell agreements, and limited partnerships for his real estate development corporations, this agreement was nothing out of the ordinary except that he would hold this deal personally. The $8 million cash would be out of his personal accounts, with net assets and cash on hand in excess of $280 million. Thus, the $8 million offer for the restaurant wasn't that big a deal for him. The loss of interest on his cash investments was no problem for him. His real-estate appraiser valued the building to be in excess of a $2.5 million. The buy down of outstanding debts, from Terance's cash contribution, would add approximately $250,000 a year for five years to the restaurant's gross profits. Terance's downside in five years would be a mere $125,000, a very acceptable risk for someone who was getting into a deal for something other than financial gains.

Being a little concerned that he hadn't heard anything from the partners, he calls his attorneys earlier that morning and is informed that no one had called and that FedEx had confirmed the delivery of the offer. Terance is hoping for some sign of acceptance from the restaurant owners by now.

The taxi ride to the restaurant took around twenty minutes, making Terance's arrival ten minutes early. As he enters the restaurant, a hostess greets him, and he explains that he is there to meet with John, Carl, Frank, and Steve. A call is made to the office, and Terance is asked if he knew where they were going to meet. He does, and then he walks alone through the restaurant to the office. The door to the office is closed, so he knocks once and waits. Hearing people talking inside, he waits a moment longer until John opens the door and invites him in. He immediately recognizes everyone in the office, except for an older gentleman who is sitting at John's desk. He has to be John's father. John introduces Terance to an older gentleman, who in fact is his father. Terance is offered a seat, and for a very long minute, no one says a word. This kind of reception of poker-faced participants is not unusual for Terance. However, to Terance's advantage, he knows he has the upper hand because they need him a lot more than he needs them. So he plays along. He sits down, slowly opens his manila envelope, and removes his copy of the offer. He looks up at the five men sitting across from him and explains why he doesn't want any attorneys at this point in the negotiations, and that is because he wants to explain everything to them in layman's terms. Terance comments, "I'm sure you all read the agreement and may or may not have any questions."

John's father responds, "Mr. Best, I have a question: do you have any restaurant experience?"

Terance answers, "None at all."

"Why are you interested in our restaurant?"

"I'm glad you asked that question. I would have been surprised if you didn't. I have three reasons why I'm interested in your restaurant. First, I think your restaurant has a very good potential for making a good profit. Second, I think my financial strength and my wife's restaurant experience would be a major contributor to the success of our partnership."

Terance looks at each of the five men sitting across from him straight in the eye and says, "And last but not least, I have this thing for Elvis Presley, which is probably the biggest motivator for me being here."

John's father turns and looks at his sons and nephews and says, "I have nothing else to say."

With that, John's father immediately gets up from his chair, walks over to Terance, holds out his hand, and says, "In principle, Mr. Best, we have a deal."

Terance immediately grins and says, "I am so very happy for all of us."

John's father puts his arm around Terance's shoulder and thanks him for his candid responses to his questions and his very equitable offer. With that, John Jr. breaks open a bottle of champagne, and they all toast to the new partnership. John's father thanks Terance again and begins explaining in detail his financial dilemma. His candidness impresses Terance. He surmises that John and his family are down-to-earth, hardworking, and trustworthy people. This is a very good start for someone who makes a point of surrounding himself with people whom he could trust.

John's father is very interested in Terance's reply about "I have this thing about Elvis Presley." Terance explains how much he admires Elvis and how impressed he is that the motif is based on Elvis's life. Terance wants to tell him what he is doing in Las Vegas but decides to keep that for a future get-together. He explains that any changes to the offer should be worked out within thirty days as stipulated in the offer and that he would be wiring $50,000 into their account as soon as his attorney draws up the paperwork. With that, the men shake hands again, and Terance leaves. Terance has closed a lot of deals in his life but not one quite as rewarding as this one. He is going to treat himself to a lavish dinner after he calls Terri.

Returning to his room around 8:00 p.m., he pours himself a large glass of cranberry juice, sits down, removes his cell phone from his pocket, and presses his speed dial number for home. Terri answers the phone immediately and is so surprised to hear from Terance so soon; he had called earlier that day. She asks him if there is anything wrong. Terance answers, "No, just the opposite."

"What do you mean just the opposite?"

Terance cheerfully explains, "We now are 50 percent owners of one of the most incredible restaurants in the country."

"Get out. Are you serious?"

"I'm very serious."

Terance explains that the deal is not signed and sealed, but it looks like it's a done deal.

"The best part is that you can participate in a management level at any point in time we choose."

"Are you kidding me? This sounds too good to be true."

"I'm not kidding, and when you see this restaurant, you're going to think I'm a genius."

"I already know you're a genius. I just don't know when you're kidding."

"I'm not kidding. The five partners have a great thing going, except that they are undercapitalized and in debt up to their ears. It all had to with the state of the economy. I'm going to be their sugar daddy and bring some cash to the table."

Terri asks, "How much is my sugar daddy bringing to the table?"

"A mere $8 million in cash."

Terri asks when she could see the restaurant, and Terance explains that it shouldn't take more than a month before they close the deal. Terri asks Terance if this is the big secret deal that has everyone buzzing about in the office. Terance replies, "You could say that."

"Is there something else you're doing in Las Vegas other than the restaurant deal?"

"No, that's it."

"Well, then, Terance, we will have a lot to talk about when you get home."

"We sure will."

With that, they say good-bye. Terance sits back in his sofa, looks out the window of his hotel suite, takes another drink of cranberry juice, and thinks about what Terri had said about them having a lot to talk about. Terance knows that Terri is much more savvy than she lets on to be. He ponders Terri's remark about there being something else he's doing while he has been in Las Vegas. In the very near future, he'll have to explain everything to Terri, and a lot of that will depend on his good friend Hank's performance this weekend. A lot of intense changes are in the future for Terance.

Chapter 58

Hank Hunk, Tonight Is the Big Night Out for Hank

HANK IS BACK in his room checking out his tuxedo for the big night out with Shirley and Jackie. Shirley calls him earlier to confirm that they would be waiting in the hotel lobby at 6:30 p.m. and that the three of them would be taking a cab to the party. Hank removes the tux and goes over to the closet where he has his Elvis jacket hanging. He tries the jacket on one more time and stands in front of the mirror; he feels like the King himself. It is now 6:15 p.m., and Hank is ready to go. He knows he is going to get a lot of flack about the haircut from the two sisters, but he has a good answer for them. He is getting a lot of attention from people as he is passing through the lobby, particularly middle-aged women. A small group of Japanese tourists pass in front of him, and one of them takes a picture. Just as the flash goes off, Jackie and Shirley enter the lobby. They rush over to Hank, and Shirley says jokingly, "Who do we have here? Oh my goodness, it's Elvis in a tux. I wonder, where on earth could he be going?"

Hank laughs. "I know it's the hair. What can I tell you? I got the haircut just for the party. I thought it would be a conversation piece."

"It sure will, Hank. You look more like Elvis than Elvis looked like Elvis. You handsome devil you. Well, I think it's time we go."

They grab a cab and are off to the party. Hank compliments Jackie and Shirley on how good they look. He knows he is going to be the envy of the party. The cab ride took fifteen minutes.

The hotel entry is buzzing with limousines and expensive foreign cars. It looks like a night at the Oscars. Jackie pays the fare, and the three friends walk through the front door and into lobby, where the guests are mingling and drinking champagne. Hank is overwhelmed by the opulence of the affair. He leans over to Shirley and announces that he feels a little bit out of place. Shirley tells him not to worry; most of these people, including Jackie and her, feel out of place. With Hank perched between them, the three of them enter the lobby. It looks as if they are showing off their trophy boyfriend. Shirley knows just about everyone in the room, and if she doesn't, Jackie does. A lot of the guests congratulate them on their exceptional work. Hank knows how hard it must have been to expedite a $75 million hotel renovation project in fast-track time. Knowing that Jackie and Shirley selected all of the material finishes, furnishings, appointments, and artwork makes him feel impressed with his new friends. Hank comments, "Your work is just incredible. I have to tell you, I'm totally impressed and so appreciative that you invited me to such an important event. I'm humbled by all of this and inspired by your unpretentious attitudes. It seems to me that you're the main act here."

"Not quite. Wait until you meet the architect. He's as down-to-earth as gravel and a character to boot."

"How was he to work with?"

"He was a gift from heaven," Shirley adds. "He was more than a gift from heaven. He recommended us for the interiors work. We've known each other and worked together for years. His name is David Anderson. As soon as I see him, I will introduce you, and then I'll have you meet the hotel's owner."

Hank lowers his head and raises his eyebrow. Shirley comments, "Don't do that in front of the owner, Hank. He'll ask you to sing an Elvis song."

The threesome walks out to the pool area to mingle with the other guests. The caterers are setting up multiple buffet tables for the evening's festivities. Hank has never seen anything like this in his life. It seems like somebody is spending a whole lot of money.

The entire bottom floor of the hotel tower is opened for viewing. The upper floors have selected rooms, including standard and deluxe rooms and super-deluxe suites. Hank is the perfect guest for Shirley and Jackie, and they knew that immediately. When Hank asks them to describe how they came up with the motif for the hotel, they are happy to oblige and explain how they came to choose all the colors, materials, furnishings, and artwork. Hank was inspired by their responses. The sisters realize that Hank's knowledge of what they did and how they did it is obvious, however, his humble nature makes him all that more engaging.

Looking around the room, Shirley notices a small group of people talking to a tall gray-haired man smiling and shaking hands with all the people around him. It is the architect that Shirley wants to introduce to Hank. As soon as they get close enough for David to recognize them, he immediately raises his arms and waves them over to join him. He embraces and kisses both Shirley and Jackie and announces to the people standing around them, "The two beautiful and extremely talented women standing next to me are the ones responsible for all that you see and touch in this beautiful hotel. They're with Wright and Wright Interiors Inc. out of Los Angeles, California."

With that, the people standing close to David turn to Shirley and Jackie and shake their hands.

"David, you are just too kind."

"I don't think so. I just tell it like it is." David is glancing over at Hank while he comments to Shirley.

"David, I would like you to meet Jackie's and my friend, Henry Hunk."

David looks at Hank and says, "It's so very nice to meet you, Henry. That's some haircut you have."

Hank laughs and shakes David's hand and replies, "Pleased to meet you, David."

"People who know me call me Dave."

"People who know me call me Hank."

Dave looks at Hank with a whimsical smile and says, "Hank Hunk, now that's a fitting name for someone who looks just like Elvis."

Shirley says, "I told you he was a character, Hank."

Hank smiles and congratulates Dave on the exceptionally good design work and immediately goes into an architectural riff about the overall design of the spaces and how excited he is about everything. Dave replies, "You seem to know something about architecture, Hank."

Shirley answers, "Hank is an architect in training."

Dave asks whom Hank was working for, and Shirley replies that he would be working with them on the Americana project. Dave explains that he could use all the help he could get to meet that project's schedule. Shirley comments, "Maybe we can share Hank?"

"In what way do you mean?"

"Professionally, of course."

"I just wanted to make sure."

They all laugh and shake their heads, and Dave takes out a business card and hands it to Hank. Dave suggests that they should all talk real soon. The sisters agree. Shirley mentions that she and Jackie are going to take Hank up to view some of the rooms. Dave jokingly replies, "I am not going to say a word."

"You better not."

Hank, Jackie, and Shirley took the elevator up to the top floor to view the super-deluxe suites. Hank again is genuinely impressed with the suite's furnishings and appointments. He repeatedly compliments the sisters on their fine work. The three friends spend the next hour looking at the other hotel rooms and the public spaces. Jackie announces that she is starving and that they should head out to the poolside and get something to eat.

The buffet tables are adorned with food. Every type of gourmet dish one could imagine is impeccably displayed on the tables. There are six meat carvers located at different points along the pool area. Jackie notices a couple of men talking at the bar and nudges Shirley.

"There's Stephen and Ralph. Let's go say hello."

Shirley grabs Hank by the arm and walks to the bar. Shirley explains that Stephen is the owner developer, and Ralph is a general contractor. As soon as they are close enough to the two men, Stephen smiles and says, "Hey, you two, everyone in the place, including me, loves what you've done."

"Thank you, Steve. We're so glad it all worked out for you."

"And how are you, Ralph?"

"I'm happy it's finished."

"Aren't we all?"

"Who's this dashing young man?"

"Steve, I want you to meet Hank. He's an architect in training and may be helping Dave and me on the Americana project."

"I'm so glad to meet you, Hank. I hope you realize that these two women are going to work you like a rented mule."

Hank smiles. "I didn't know that."

With that, Steve shakes Hank's hand and introduces Ralph, who looked somewhat familiar to Hank, but he couldn't place him yet. They talk joyfully about the success of the hotel's design and the hardships that were encountered during the construction. Hank is very articulate when it came to construction, and Stephen and Ralph picked up on it immediately. Steve announces that he is going to give a little appreciation speech in twenty minutes and that they should all stay to hear what he had to say. Shirley confirms that they wouldn't think of leaving without hearing Steve's speech. Stephen thanks Shirley. A moment later, he is interrupted by someone who whispered in his ear. Stephen excuses himself and heads to the podium next to the pool area. Hank notices a young man up at the podium asking everyone for his or her attention. The crowd quiets down, and the young guy asks if everyone is having a good time. A squeal of delight bellows out from the crowd. He then says, "I want to introduce the man whose vision was to turn this hotel into a first-class experience for all to enjoy. Ladies and gentlemen, Steven Cloud!"

Steve gets up on the podium to a blast of cheers and applause that lasts almost a minute. Steve's mannerisms at the podium are not what Hank expects. Steve seems very down-to-earth, almost shy, in front of all the people. He thanks everyone for coming out to be with him on this very special night and talks about his concept of recreating a hotel that would be user-friendly and exceptionally exciting for its guests. He speaks about how very happy he is that so many people worked so hard to make his dream a reality. He talks about the people who would be working in the hotel and earning money to prosper in Las Vegas. He thanks the banks that stood behind him; he thanks Ralph and his construction company for all their hard work; he thanks the politicians, building officials, and marketing people; and finally he pauses and says, "I want to make it perfectly clear to everyone that if it wasn't for Dave Anderson's drafting ability and my design talents, this could never have happened."

With that, the crowd breaks into a roar of laughter.

Steve responds, "Seriously, folks, Dave and I have known each other for over twenty years. We attended architectural school together. When we graduated, I went to work for a real estate development company, and Dave pursued an architectural career. Our first project together was a small Mexican restaurant in one of the strip malls owned and managed by the company I worked for. Dave's passion for his work left an everlasting impression on me. A few years later, I moved on to form my own company. It all started with a small motel project in Santa Barbara. Dave again showed me his willingness to work with me on shoestring budget. We turned the little motel into a business success. Since then, it's been all uphill for us. He recently introduced me to a couple of women designers who shared his passion and commitment to their work. All the furniture, appointments, finishes, bedspreads, curtains, you name it, Shirley and Jackie Wright picked it out.

They are standing over to my left with the guy who looks like Elvis."

With that, everyone turns to look at Hank, Shirley, and Jackie. Steve adds, "If I didn't say Elvis, you probably wouldn't have known where to look."

He thanks everyone again and leaves the podium in the roar of applause. Shirley and Jackie are so excited by the acknowledgment Steve gave them. It put them on cloud nine. The three friends spend the rest of the evening drinking, eating, and talking to the other guests. The party starts winding down at 11:00 p.m. Hank is beginning to feel the wear and tear of the day. Jackie is also looking very tired, so she excuses herself and takes a cab back to her hotel. Shirley and Hank stay for another half hour longer until Shirley announces that it is time for them to go. Hank is enjoying the evening immensely but is happy to be leaving. He has two very big days ahead of him. They take a cab back to the hotel after they made the rounds of saying good-bye. The cabs are lined up at curbside. As soon as they get in the cab, Shirley asks, "I hope you had a good time, and I hope you weren't offended by all the Elvis remarks."

Hank assures her that he isn't.

"I meant what I said about you helping Jackie and me on the Americana project."

Hank is very excited about her gesture to help them with the project and thanks her sincerely. They arrive at the hotel at 11:30 p.m. Hank insists on picking up the cab fare. Shirley reluctantly allows him to pay. When they arrive on Hank's floor, Shirley gives him a very sincere kiss on the cheek and says, "We have to get together before you leave so we can talk business."

Hank confirms he would call tomorrow afternoon.

Hank gets off the elevator and walks to his room feeling very encouraged by the turn of events with his special new friends. He now feels there is a bright future ahead of him, so much brighter than he could have ever imagined.

Chapter 59

Bobby Shrimp, It's Time to Fish or Cut Bait

THE RENDEZVOUS WITH Kate tonight has Bobby all excited. Things have been going extremely well between the two of them. The more he sees Kate, the more attractive she becomes. His commitment to Lynn also needs to be considered. He likes Lynn a lot; she's a wonderful woman, and she's very easy to get along with. However, he feels a little uncomfortable with Lynn being six years old than him. He could live with that if a solid commitment is in hand, but at this point in time, there's none. He's also bothered by Lynn's apprehension to having a family. Kate, on the other hand, is young, spirited, charismatic, and a joy to be around. Her whimsical and happy-go-lucky attitude is a breath of fresh air. He's getting to a point where he's going to need to fish or cut bait. Knowing that Kate could easily find someone with more to offer than he has is constantly on his mind. The wrong decision could result in him being alone. Bobby worried about that a lot. Up until now, Kate hasn't mentioned a follow-up date after the vacation's over, nor has Bobby. However, he has a reason for not pushing it with Lynn waiting for him back home. He wonders, is the same true for Kate? Could she have someone back in Portsmouth waiting for her? Tonight will be the breaking point. Somehow, Bobby will have to fish around and see if he can get a feeling for where their relationship is going. With all that's going on with Hank and Kate is a definite test of his endurance.

His cell phone rings; it's Terance.

"Hey, Bobby, it's Terance. How's everything going?"

"Everything seems to be going very well at this end. How's thing going with you?"

"I'm doing great. What's up for tomorrow?"

"I think we should meet around 9:00 a.m. tomorrow to rehearse with Hank. We should take some videos of him and see how he looks from different angles and distances. I was thinking of using my cell phone to record the video and then e-mail it to you so that we can view it on your laptop. From there, we can view them repeatedly, edit out the bad stuff, and create what we feel will work best for Hank. If we come to a workable conclusion, we can fine-tune Hank's performance until he gets it down perfectly. It may take some time to perfect it. We'll see how it comes out after the first couple of tries. I would like to try to wrap it up no later than 4:00 p.m. I'm hoping, if everyone's free, we can all get together Friday night for supper and have a little fun to take the pressure of Hank. What do you think?"

"It all sounds good to me. I know I'm free Friday night. I'll call Jeremy and fill him in, and maybe you should call Hank?"

"Good idea. I'll call Hank right now."

Bobby gets Hank's voice message, so he describes the plans for Friday morning and evening and requests that Hank call him back. Immediately after signing off, his phone rings. It's Kate.

"Hi, Kate."

"Hey, there, Bobby, what's up for tonight?"

"I think we should get together around 7:30 p.m. and play it by ear. What do you think?"

"That sounds good to me, except for one thing: can we make it a little earlier, let's say around 6:30 p.m. at my room?"

"At 6:30 p.m. it is. I'll see you then."

As soon as they end the conversation, Bobby begins to wonder why she needed to make it earlier. Could it be their last night together? The last time they were together, Kate had all kinds of wonderful things planned. Why didn't she have anything for tonight? Has Bobby lost his luster? This kind of thinking is bringing out his insecurities, so to avoid trauma, he decides he should pick up something special for Kate tonight. He decides that flowers and a bottle of wine would be appropriate, so he heads down to the concierge for some advice. He arrives at Kate's room at 6:30 p.m. sharp. When Kate opens the door, she is surprised to see Bobby standing there with flowers in one hand and a bottle wine in the other. Bobby smiles and walks in. Kate greets him with "You didn't need to go through all of this for me."

Bobby is somewhat worried by Kate's comment but doesn't dwell on it. So with a big smile, he simply says that she deserves it. Kate seems flattered and overconcerned that Bobby has brought her a gift, which makes Bobby feel a bit vulnerable. To avoid his vulnerability, he gets right into what he thinks they should do that night and suggests a quick supper, and after maybe a casino, or they could try to get into one of the local shows. Kate agrees that the quick supper seems like a good idea, but she feels a bit tired, so the casinos and shows wouldn't work for her. She feels she needs to get back to her room early. Bobby is taken way back by her comment but doesn't push it. So he suggests supper at Canaletto's restaurant at the Venetian Hotel. Kate thinks that is a great idea. They grab a cab and are at the Venetian by 7:00 p.m., where they are seated at a table with a terrific view of Las Vegas Boulevard while listening to a trio playing jazz on the terrace. Kate seems somewhat distracted. It seems she is not her usual happy-go-lucky self, which worries poor Bobby. Things are getting a little awkward. He tries to hold up as best he could good but could see the end was in sight, and to make things worse, Kate is even quieter in the cab on the way back to the hotel. Imagining how she is going to end it is excruciating. When they get to Kate's room, she opens the door without looking back at Bobby. When they walk into the room, she turns to face Bobby; and at that moment, Bobby's stomach swells, expecting the worst. While taking off her high heels, she looks up at Bobby with a half smile and says, "Guess what I have for you?" Bobby couldn't answer quickly enough before Kate walks over to the under-counter refrigerator and pulls out two huge cannoli.

"What you think of these big boys?"

Bobby is confused and doesn't know what to say other than "Where on earth did you get those monsters?"

"At the bakery on East Tropicana Avenue."

"I am so impressed."

Kate replies, "That's not all. I also have this for us."

Kate goes behind the minibar and pulls out a bottle of an anisette and places it with the two cannoli on the coffee table.

"Wow, what a treat."

Kate pours generous glasses of the anisette and sits down next to Bobby on the sofa.

"I hope you don't mind spending the rest of night just chilling out and watching television together. I think I may be coming down with a cold, which is making me not such a great date tonight." A feeling of relief overcomes Bobby. The anisette is also helping to take the edge off his anxieties.

"Kate, this couldn't be better."

"I hope what I'm coming down with isn't catchy. So you may want to keep your distance?"

With that, Bobby puts his arm around Kate and kisses the side of her face. Kate turns to a Bobby and gives him a huge hug with both arms.

"I'm so sorry I'm such a wimp tonight. You probably want to leave as soon as you can?"

"I'm here for as long as you want me."

"And how long is that going to be?"

Somehow, Bobby realizes Kate has turned the tables on him. Now some kind of a commitment regarding their relationship is in Bobbie's hands. Bobby thinks for a second.

"I would like it to be a long, long time, Kate."

"I hope you mean that."

"I sure do."

"Does this mean we will continue to see one another when we get back home?" Bobby realizes Kate has again turned the table on him, and he has to respond with a notion that he is committed to their relationship.

"It sure does."

Kate moves closer to Bobby, and before long, they end up asleep sitting on the sofa. Unfortunately, his cell phone rings; it is Hank. Hank explains that he is sorry to be calling so late, but he got Bobby's voice message and wanted to confirm that everything is a go for him for Friday. Kate is sound asleep and doesn't hear the conversation, and within seconds of ending his conversation, Bobby falls back to sleep. Oddly enough, he dreams he is out on his fishing boat with his brother, Jesse, who is cutting bait.

Chapter 60

The Guys Spend the Day Together Before the Competition

KATE MOVING AROUND the living room awakens Bobby early. Looking at his watch, he realizes the time is now 7:00 a.m. Already dressed, Kate is ready to get on with her day. Being concerned about her condition, Bobby asks about her colds. Her reply is she feels one hundred times better than last night. She mentions that she is going to meet a tax consultant for breakfast at his hotel and asks Bobby to give her a call later on in the afternoon. He is welcome to stay as long as he likes and could help himself to coffee and Danish in the refrigerator. As Kate is leaving, Bobby mentions that he has an appointment at the Mandalay Bay Hotel with his friends at 9:00 a.m. and promises to call her that afternoon. Kate waves good-bye and rushes out of the room. As soon as she leaves, he gets off the sofa and is on his way in fifteen minutes. Unshaven and in need of a shower, all he wants is to get back to his room without being seen, so he takes the stairs down to his floor. He quickly gets himself ready and heads over to the Mandalay Bay Hotel.

Across town, Jeremy is up and about and still in bliss over his wonderful night with Kie. After a quick shower, he gets dressed and is on his way to Terance's hotel. It is now 8:25 a.m. Arriving at the same time as Bobby, they are welcomed by Terance. Coffee, Danish, muffins, and other good breakfast treats are laid out on the bar for his friends. Jeremy remarks, "I'm glad I ate light this morning."

A raspberry Danish and a cup of coffee is his first choice. Bobby follows suit. Terance has the laptop on the coffee table, and the guitar is resting in a guitar stand next to the TV credenza. The three men chat about the rehearsal planned for the morning and how pleased they are with the past days' accomplishments. It is now 9:15 a.m., and Terance asks Bobby if he had reached Hank last night, and Bobby says that he had, and Hank knows the schedule for the day. Terance asks if they should give Hank a call to see if he is on his way. Knowing about Hank's big party last night, Bobby feels that that they should give Hank a couple of minutes before giving him a wake-up call. With that, the three men grab a second cup of coffee and begin discussing the best way to proceed. At 9:28 a.m., Hank is at the door. He apologizes for being late. Bobby notices that Hank does not have the clothes for the day's dry-run rehearsal but doesn't want to say anything at this time because Hank looks a bit ruffled.

Coffee and some breakfast food are offered, and Hank gladly accepts and explains that he had overslept and skipped breakfast. Giving Hank a chance to settle down, they join him with another cup of coffee. The four men sit around for about a half an hour and talk about the rehearsal. Glancing over at the guitar, Hank realizes that he is supposed to bring his clothes for the final dress rehearsal. Jeremy comforts him and tells him not to worry. They could pick up the clothing during lunch break, and there's a lot that they could do before the dress rehearsal. Jeremy asks Hank if he has been practicing his voice control since the last time they were together. Hank is happy to say that he has. Jeremy compliments Hank and adds, "Whatever we can get out of this rehearsal today is what we are going to go with tomorrow night. Do we all agree?"

The other three men agree. Bobby adds that after the rehearsal, they should all go over to the Voodoo Lounge to unwind, and tomorrow they should relax and be ready for the competition with the utmost confidence. Bobby suggests they get started with the rehearsal immediately. Hank picks up the guitar, walks over to the bar stools, sits down, and begins playing a combination of chords that are reminiscent of Elvis's early sound. The more Hank plays, the more excited Jeremy, Bobby, and Terance become. There is something about Hank sitting on the bar stool that catches Bobby's attention. During a pause between riffs, Bobby asks him to move the stool into the middle of the room, which Hank does. Bobby then asks him to sing and play something from Elvis's early years. Hank gets right into "Lawdy, lawdy, lawdy Miss Clawdy. Girl, you sure look good to me." Bobby asks Hank to hold it one second and walks over to him. He asks Hank to get up off the stool and give him the guitar. Bobby sits down on the stool and extends one leg out and places his other foot on the rail of the bar stool. He hands the guitar back to Hank and asks him to try this position, and as he picks up the tempo, he should stand up for a few seconds and then sit back down. Hank obliges and sits down just as Bobby had demonstrated and gets back into "Lawdy Miss Clawdy," and when he picks up the tempo, he raises himself up off the stool and moves forward and back with the guitar. It is amazing; the whole thing looks perfect to Jeremy. So perfect in fact that it reminds him of a documentary that he had seen from Elvis's early years when he was dressed in black leather and was playing onstage impromptu with a couple of other guys. Jeremy asks Terance what they think about it. Terance thinks it is great. Bobby adds that with this approach, they wouldn't need to spend any more time on Hank's choreography. Hank adds that he feels very relaxed and natural sitting and playing on the stool. Terance comments, "Hank, you do look very relaxed, but what's more important, you look like Elvis—*the young Elvis, the one we are trying to resurrect.*"

Jeremy adds, "Bobby, you're a genius."

"I don't know about being a genius, but what I do know is that you really picked up on it, and so will the judges."

Terance comments, "This is a huge hurdle we've overcome in a matter of a few minutes. Now we should help Hank with audience awareness. Hank, when you're performing, remember to look over at the judges, but more importantly, to look at the audience and look them straight in the eye. Elvis was a natural at bonding with the audience. To him, they were his family, just like the kids from Providence that were performing for their families. You need to bond with your audience to show them you're having fun, giving it your all, and they will love you for it."

Hank returns to the stool with the guitar and begins to play, and as he does, he looks at his friends square in the eyes, smiles, and makes it look like he isn't competing but rather just having a lot of fun entertaining them. It looks so natural. Surprisingly, Hank is very good. His charm, his love of people, and his demeanor reverberate from within. Hank goes through a couple more choruses of "Lawdy Miss Clawdy" and then plays and sings a couple of choruses of "Heartbreak Hotel," "Treat Me Right," and "I'm All Shook Up." Each song moves Hank further up the ladder of perfection. Jeremy compliments Hank, "You're doing great. Now what I want you to do is to exaggerate Elvis's voice as if you were trying to bring a comic gesture into your performance. What I mean is, you should go overboard with it and try to make us laugh."

Hank tries to do what Jeremy asks but only reaches a middle-of-the-road performance. Jeremy interrupts Hank, "Hank, I want you try doing this the next time: close your mind to everything around you and make yourself become Elvis and really push the envelope on the voice transformation. Now just sing one line of 'Lawdy Miss Clawdy,' pushing the envelope, and then have Elvis sing that one line."

Hank does it, and his voice improves immensely. He sings the songs over and over again for hours. Hank tries it, and miraculously, he is able to transform himself mentally and physically. And by doing so, his voice sounds exactly like Elvis. The guys are overcome by Hank's performance. It is now 12:45 p.m., and Terance suggests that they should break for lunch, and Hank should go back to his hotel and pick up the clothes. They are all back at the suite by 2:00 p.m., where they all have lunch and Hank changes into his Elvis wardrobe. When he comes out wearing the jacket, trousers, shirt, white stockings, and shoes, he looks perfect. Sitting on the stool with the guitar, Hank begins singing away, while Bobby videos the performance. It is absolute perfection. The electricity in the room is unbelievable. Bobby e-mails the video to Terance, and within a second, Terance picks it up on his laptop. Terance opens the video and plays it on a wide-screen LCD TV. The four overjoyed men sit back in silence and watch in awe. Hank says soberly, "I don't believe that's me."

Jeremy says in complete seriousness, "It's not you, Hank, it's Elvis."

Bobby and Terance agree. Bobby comments, "We're done for the day. Our next stop is the Voodoo Lounge at 6:30 p.m. It's now 4:30 p.m. That gives us two hours to relax a bit and get ready for tonight."

Hank looks humbly at his three friends and says, "I am so excited by all of this. I can't believe what you guys have done for me. There's no way that I can express my thanks to you for putting *so* much faith in me."

Terance replies, "Hank, my young friend, I don't think you know how much you've done for us. We have been waiting for this day for quite a long time."

Hank returns to his hotel room and carefully hangs up his clothes in the closet. As he is emptying his pockets, he notices he has a message from an unknown caller on his cell phone. Viewing the message, he recognizes that it was from the architect, David Anderson, whom he had met the night before. Dave left a message for Hank to call him back and that he had talked to Shirley and Jackie about sharing his time between his office and their office; if he was interested in that, please give him a call back. This is such good news; he immediately calls Kayla to tell her about Mr. Anderson's offer.

Bobby is recalling the good fortunes he experienced this week and wishes he could be sharing this with his special friend Kate. After some deep thought, he decides that now is not a good time to do that. He waits until 5:00 p.m. to call her and let her know what his schedule is for the rest of the week and what flight he would be taking back to Boston. He would also need to call Lynn to let her know when he was coming in. There's going to be a lot of juggling in his future with two women in his life, and time would tell which one of them he was going to be committed to. This is going to be a very uncomfortable position for Bobby to be in.

Jeremy is quick to get on the phone with Kie and to let her know that somehow, someway, they need to get back together again. Now he would need to appraise his living conditions and resolve his relationship with Evelyn. But most importantly, he would need to let Marie know all about Kie and arrange for the three of them to get together. He is very sure of himself and is willing to put the extra effort into making it all work. This is one special trip for Jeremy.

Chapter 61

The Boys' Last Night at the Voodoo Lounge

THE GUYS PLANNED to meet at the Voodoo Lounge at 7:00 p.m., at the Las Vegas Hilton. The competition just so happened to be the night before Elvis's seventy-fifth birthday. Bobby and Terance arrive early at the Voodoo Lounge. The two men sit down at their regular booth and order their drinks. Five minutes later, Jeremy arrives, dressed in his new clothes and looking very successful and happy. Jeremy slides in next to Terance and is immediately approached by the waitress; he orders a light beer. Turning to his two companions, he enthusiastically compliments both of them on their contributions to Hank's successful rehearsal, and they return the compliment to Jeremy. When Jeremy's drink arrives, they propose a toast to Hank Hunk, the new Elvis. Bobby has a manila envelope on the table in front of him, which catches Jeremy's and Terance's attention. Bobby opens the envelope and presents each of them with an eight-by-ten color glossy photo of Hank sitting on a stool with the Gibson Presley Dove strapped around his neck. They stare at the photo without saying a word, and then Jeremy looks up at Bobby and says, "It's him, it's absolutely him. He's Elvis."

Terance remarks, "He's going to bring the place down tomorrow night. All of the competitors will be doing the white emerald-studded jumpsuit attire with the exception of the two kids from Providence College. In the past, there had been some attempts at the young Elvis look, but no one was able to pull it off. The white-jumpsuit look became the Las Vegas trademark prior to Elvis's death. At the Reno competition, all the older competitors did the white jumpsuits, and that's why the kids from Providence had the edge."

"I agree with Terance. Bobby's photo tells it all. It's him, he's Elvis. I have shivers running up and down my spine just looking at the photo."

"I completely agree with you, guys. Elvis will be resurrected, and I can't wait for tomorrow night."

In order to concentrate on Hank, Bobby, Terance, and Jeremy dropped out of the competition. They want to be in the audience when Hank is on the stage in order to experience the moment with the rest of the audience.

Hank arrives at 7:05 p.m. looking very cheerful and confident. Bobby comments, "Hank, my friend, you were unbelievable this afternoon, and I'm so happy about the way everything has turned out for you and for us."

Hank then orders a diet cola with lemon and then glances down at the photo and says, "I can't believe that's me."

Bobby explains that they should meet around 5:00 p.m. to review the lineup for the show. At this point in time, Bobby feels that the best place for Hank should be within the first ten performers. Anytime after that, the audience begins to tune out. Terance adds that he has called the production company manager that afternoon and pitched for Hank to be up in front with the first tier of performers. Terance notes that he explained Hank's act with the manager and that the manager seemed very excited and let him know that he would do everything he could to move Hank up in the lineup. Bobby responds, "Good work, Terance. You seem to always come through."

Jeremy asks Bobby what he has in mind for tonight's activities. His response is that maybe they should take it easy tonight and have a leisurely supper and make it an early night. They all agree and head out to the patio to have supper. They leave the lounge at 9:30 p.m.

Tomorrow is going to be a very big day for Hank, and no one wants him to be stressed out. Terance volunteers to pick up a stool at a furniture store and bring it along with the guitar to the hotel. Jeremy volunteers to help Terance. Bobby suggests, and Hank agrees, that he and Hank should meet at his hotel at 4:30 p.m., and the two of them would meet up with Jeremy and Terance at Terance's hotel at 5:00 p.m. Bobby would make a heads-up call at 3:30 p.m. to all to confirm that everything is on schedule.

Everyone is in very good spirits, particularly Hank, who repeatedly thanks his friends for what they have done for him. Hank insists on giving everyone a ride back to their hotels, which they accept, including Jeremy, who asks to be let off last. Hank obliges. On the drive over to Jeremy's decoy hotel, he explains to Hank that he is actually staying somewhere else. Hank asks why he changed hotels. Jeremy notes that he hadn't. Being confused, he asks his friend what is going on. Jeremy comically explains that he is somewhat embarrassed about his accommodations and that the charade is to spare him from being ridiculed by the group. When they finally arrive at Jeremy's hotel, he looks at Jeremy and, in a wisecracking way, asks Jeremy how much a night. Jeremy answers proudly, "A little north of twenty and change."

"You have to be kidding me?"

"No, I'm not kidding, and it includes breakfast."

The two men sit in the car looking at each other, laughing out of control. Jeremy could still hear Hank laughing to himself as he drives away. Jeremy thinks, what could be a better ending for his friend the night before the competition, laughing his ass off all the way home.

Chapter 62

The Competition, January 9, 2010

JEREMY, TERANCE, HANK, and Bobby all spend a leisurely Saturday morning alone on the day of the competition. Jeremy is very relaxed and self-confident, knowing that his meager means were acknowledged by his good friend Hank without any prejudice. Jeremy is getting things in order for the ride back to Yukon on Sunday and is planning to call Kie midafternoon to make plans to see her before he leaves. The plan for the day is to be at Terance's hotel at 4:00 p.m. to help pick up the stool and guitar and bring them over to the Hilton. Looking back at his two weeks in Las Vegas, he marvels at all the changes that came to fruition in such a very short period of time. The confidence and self-awareness that he gained by being around Terance, Bobby, and Hank have confirmed that resourceful and influential people are the most important assets in one's life. His decision to take a chance, although minor, resulted in his meeting Kie and experiencing the Hoover Dam. These two minor decisions brought about a new outlook on life, which gave him the opportunity to elevate his stature with his special friends. His influence over Hank was also an uplifting experience. Jeremy feels he could never go back to his old ways; he's changed and is ready for more change in his life. At 2:30 p.m., Jeremy calls Kie and informs her that he would be leaving early Sunday morning and would like her to come visit him in Yukon, Oklahoma. Kie is delighted with the invitation and suggests that the first couple of weeks in spring would be perfect.

Terance is on the phone, Saturday morning, with his office manager Gail, letting her know that he would be back in the Coral Gables office on Monday around 10:30 a.m. Terance then calls Terri to let her know his schedule. He also calls his attorney and requests a confirmation on whether he has talked to John's attorneys about the offer and is happy to hear that he did. He notes that there would be some minor changes to the offer, and from his attorney's point of view, it looks like it is ready to be signed. It is now time to go and buy a stool for Hank's performance. He calls Jeremy to inform him that he would be at his hotel by 4:00 p.m. and that the stool and guitar need to be delivered to the Hilton by 5:00 p.m. Jeremy asks Terance if he plans to deliver the guitar and stool to the hotel via taxicab or does he want to go in his car. Terance has no preference, so he offers to pick him up. Terance is surprised to hear that Jeremy has a car. Their plan is to meet at 4:00 p.m. in front of the Mandalay Bay Hotel.

When Jeremy arrives in his light-blue 1972 Ford Falcon, the car and Jeremy get a lot of attention from people meandering around the hotel's grandiose entry. Recognizing Terance standing halfway down the circular drive, he drives up next to him and opens the passenger's side door. Looking inside the Falcon, he notices the army blanket on the front seat, and then he looks up at Jeremy and says, "Wow, this is nice."

Terance laughs, which gets Jeremy laughing.

"I'm an antique car restoration buff."

"I'm glad to hear that, but when is the restoration work going to take place?"

"Presently, I am working with my vintage car restoration consultant."

Terance looks at Jeremy and then the car and shakes his head and says, "I bet."

The two men leave the hotel to pick up the stool. On the way back, Terance makes some overtures to Jeremy about his management experience back home, which Jeremy explains as small-time retail. He is also interested in Jeremy's ability to work with people in a hospitality environment.

Arriving back at the hotel, they are met by a ménage of mocking tourists commenting on Jeremy's car, which Terance or Jeremy couldn't care less about; they are men with a mission. Terance asks Jeremy to give him a call just before he leaves his hotel. He would be waiting in front of the hotel with the stool, guitar, Bobby's DVDs, and his DVDs. Jeremy obliges and is off.

Hank calls Bobby midafternoon to confirm that he would be at Bobby's hotel at 3:30 p.m. or earlier to pick him up and that Jeremy and Terance would be coming to the Hilton in Jeremy's car. Bobby is pleased that Hank seems very concerned about everything going as planned. He could tell from Hank's voice that he is primed and ready to go for tonight's competition.

Bobby calls Kate at noon to see if he could drop by before he leaves for Massachusetts on Sunday. Bobby's flight is at 10:00 a.m., and Kate is flying out at 2:30 p.m. the same day, so the only time they could meet would be early afternoon today or in the early morning on Sunday. Kate wants Bobby to come up anytime to see her before 2:30 p.m., so he does.

When Bobby arrives at Kate's room, it looks like she has been doing a lot of work that morning. Not wanting to take her away from her work, he offers to stay only a minute or so. Kate is very appreciative. Kate and Bobby embrace and say their good-byes. Returning to his room, he calls Lynn on her cell phone. She is happy to hear from him and is awaiting his return home. Feeling guilty about his future plans with Kate and knowing he would have to make a very difficult decision bothers him, but for now, he is going to proceed as if nothing is final. His main concern is Hank's performance tonight.

Hank calls Shirley to let her know that David had called him, and he wants to talk to her when he gets back to LA. Shirley explains that David and she talked about working together, which would include Hank dividing his time up between the two offices. This arrangement is fine with Hank. He lets her know that he would be heading back to LA first thing in the morning and that he would give her a call toward the middle of the week. Shirley wishes Hank a safe trip back, and the two say their good-byes, realizing that this trip to Las Vegas has resulted in more opportunities for him than any other time in his life, and it was all because of Shirley's Elvis wisecrack at check-in.

The guys all arrive within minutes of each other at the Hilton Hotel and Casino. Terance carries the stool backstage and explains to the competition manager that it is going to be part of Henry Hunk's performance. The manager confirms that he would make sure it is in the right place for Henry's performance. When the group is all together, Bobby lets them know that he's booked a room for Hank in the hotel so that he could change into his new wardrobe prior to his performance. He also tells them that Hank would be appearing ninth in the lineup and that the kids from Providence are going on just before him. That sounds good to Hank and Terance, but Jeremy is a bit concerned that Hank is following the two biggest contenders of the night. However, Hank isn't concerned at all.

The four men carry the guitar and clothing up to Hank's room and then return back to the lounge to mingle with the rest of the performers. They run into their old friend Tony, who asks what all the buzz is about Hank's new act. Bobby explains it would be somewhat very different and leaves it at that. Tony wishes Hank the very best and notes that he doesn't understand why Jeremy, Terance, and Bobby would not be performing. Bobby explains that they had put all their eggs in Hank's basket. With that, Tony replies, "Well, then Hank must be really good."

Jeremy replies, "You won't be disappointed."

"I absolutely know I won't."

Terance orders a round of drinks for the guys, and the four men talk about the roster of performers for this year's show and how much Elvis's seventy-fifth birthday adds to the excitement of the event. Tony notes that the theater is sold out, and they had to cut a number of performers from the lineup, which includes him. They all offer Tony their sympathy, which Tony graciously accepts and adds that it's time for him to step aside and let the young and fast have the stage, and who knows, maybe tonight would be the big night. Terance, Jeremy, and Bobby agree that tonight is going to be a big night for everyone. While the guys are talking, they are joined by Ronnie and Ritchie and their parents. The boys seem very excited to be with all of them, especially with Hank. Ritchie mentions that he is eighth in the lineup and that this would be his last show, so he is going to go all out. As he says that, he looks at Hank and rolls his eyes. The atmosphere is very relaxing and friendly, and by 7:00 p.m., the theater begins filling with people. The size of the crowd brings a lot of excitement to the performers. Everyone is getting ready for a big show. Their table is in a perfect location for viewing the performers. Bobby knows he would have to leave the table for a few minutes before Ritchie's performance to make sure all is well with Hank's stool and guitar. The theater is standing room only, and the excitement level is extremely high. When 8:00 p.m. finally arrives, the lights dim over the audience, and the master of ceremonies comes on the stage and greets the audience. He mentions that if the King were still alive, they would be celebrating his seventy-fifth birthday. He also mentions that this year's lineup is going to be something special and alerts the audience that Ritchie and Hank are going to do something that hasn't been done before, so be prepared for a big show. The first performer came out wearing the traditional Presley white jumpsuit and rocked the audience with one of the best imitations of Elvis's Las Vegas act. The next six performers got even more positive responses from the audience with their high-energy performances. At the end of the sixth performance, Bobby rushes up to Hank's room to see if Hank is ready to go. Entering the room, he glances up at Hank and couldn't believe how perfect he looks. They take the elevator down to the ground floor and heads backstage, where Ritchie is waiting in his black leather attire. Ronnie has just finished his performance with a big send-off by the audience. Ritchie looks up at Hank and says, "Man, you look great! You're going to knock them off their feet."

Bobby rejoins his group at the table just in time for the emcee to announce Ritchie. The crowd goes crazy when they see the young Providence college kid in his black leather costume go through his act. His performance is near perfect. Bobby thinks that Ritchie is even better than he was in Reno. Bobby, Terance, and Jeremy reach over and congratulate Ritchie and Ronnie's mother and father and say they are completely overwhelmed with their son's performances. Bobby is very pleased that Ritchie's performance is the same one he did in Reno. This would make Hank's performance that much more unique. Ritchie leaves the stage with a roar of applause. The emcee comes back on the stage while the audience is still cheering for Ritchie. The emcee asks for everyone's attention, and the crowd finally settles down. The emcee announces Henry Hunk to be the next performer and adds that he has seen Henry behind the stage, and the audience is going to be in for something special. The emcee leaves the stage, the curtains closes, and the lights dim down over the audience. When the curtains open, the stage is in complete darkness. Suddenly, a spotlight appears and begins to intensify; and as it does, it illuminates Hank sitting on the stool with his Elvis jacket, flaring shirt, black pants, white stockings, and the Gibson Presley Dove guitar. Hank is looking down at the guitar just the way Bobby had coached him. He raises his head slowly and puts on an Elvis smile like no one has ever seen. The audience is completely stone-cold silent. Hank looks so much like the young Elvis that it makes everyone in the audience spellbound. Hank looks out at the audience, making eye contact with people in the front of the stage, and announces in a perfect Elvis voice, "I'm going to sing you something from one of my earlier songs. It goes something like this." Bobby loves Hank's opening line. He doesn't know where it came from, but he loves it, and so does the audience; they roar with cheers. Bobby knows immediately that when Hank said the words "from one of my earlier songs," that was the hook. Hank begins singing "Lawdy Miss Clawdy" at a level of perfection that puts Bobby, Terance, and Jeremy in a trance.

Jeremy looks up at Hank performing onstage and says quietly, "It's him. It's Elvis. He's come back." Jeremy glances over at Terance's, Bobby's, and Tony's faces and knows that they are experiencing the same moment. Hank's rendition of "Lawdy Miss Clawdy," his clothes, and his use of the stool recall Elvis's early act to such a convincing level that it looks like Elvis Presley is back onstage performing. The audience is spellbound; they couldn't believe what they are seeing. It is a very emotional moment for everyone, even for those standing by on the stage. When Hank finishes, the quiet and subdued audience goes into a state of pandemonium. The cheers are deafening; everyone is cheering, even the other performers in the theater. The cheers and the applause go on for at least two minutes before the emcee could quiet the audience down.

The emcee looks over at Hank sitting on a stool and says, "They weren't kidding when they said we would not be disappointed."

The remaining acts that followed couldn't hold a candle to Ritchie and Hank. The show goes on until 10:00 p.m., when it is time for the judges to make their selection. The emcee comes out and announces that the judges have come to a decision on the runners-up and the winner. The audience goes completely quiet. The emcee calls all sixteen performers onstage. Fourteen of them are wearing white Elvis jumpsuits, Ritchie in his black leather, and Hank in the Elvis Presley sport jacket. The emcee announces, "The second runner-up is the young man from Dallas, Texas, Ronnie Brooks. Please come forward."

The crowd applauds vigorously.

"The first runner-up . . ."—the intensity goes through Bobby, Jeremy, and Terance's bodies like an electric shock—"is Ritchie Evans, from Lexington, Kentucky."

The crowd applauds and cheers for one solid minute until the emcee asks for quiet.

The emcee announces, "And the winner and new King goes to . . ."—Bobby, Jeremy, and Terance immediately start getting emotional—"the young man from Los Angeles, California, Henry Hunk."

With that, the crowd goes wild with cheers, whistles, and applause that last for two minutes. Jeremy, Terance, and Bobby couldn't say a word. Tony wraps his arms around Bobby and says, "Bobby, Hank made my life complete."

Ritchie and Ronnie's mothers and fathers also embrace and congratulate one another. Bobby, Terance, and Jeremy join in the explosion of emotions. The audience wants to hear from Hank, so the emcee asks Hank to say a few words. Hank walks up to the mic and thanks the judges, the emcee, and all the other performers, especially Ritchie and Ronnie. Hank gets very emotional when he looks down at the table where his three friends are sitting and says that none of this could have happened without the total commitment and trust that they had given him. He tells the audience that he came to Las Vegas with hopes of finishing in the top ten, but with the guidance and coaching and, most importantly, the confidence he got from his friends Bobby Shrimp, Jeremy Shrinks, and Terance Best, he's now number one. With that, the emcee closes the show, and Hank rushes down to meet with his friends, who are embracing and congratulating each other for Hank's unbelievable performance. Tony congratulates Bobby and announces that tonight's first-place prize is $25,000. Hank says that he is going to give the money to his friends for all their support and guidance. Terance comically comments that Hank could give his share to Jeremy so he could buy a new car. Bobby laughs and says, "If Jeremy needs a car, I have just the car for him."

Everyone celebrates until 1:00 a.m. Bobby says he has to leave early, so they head back to his hotel. The four men embrace one another for the last time and say their good-byes. Terance says that he is going to be involved in something very special in the next month or two and that he would call each of them to fill them in on it.

"Until then, I wish you all the best."

All the best is certainly in the future for Bobby and Jeremy and particularly for Hank. Now that he is crowned King, he could make more money than he could ever have imagined, if he chooses to.

Hank drives back to LA that morning with the $25,000 check. Bobby and Terance insist that they wouldn't take any money. Hank decides he would give $10,000 to Jeremy. On the way back to LA, he calls Kayla and explains everything to her. She is completely surprised and delighted with the news. Arriving at home, he is greeted by his family and friends, including Kayla and her mother and father. As soon as he gets out of the car, he hears his grandma yell, "It's Elvis. He's back home." With that, everyone starts hugging and kissing their lovable Hank.

With all that is going on in Hank's life, it isn't a surprise that he would be experiencing unexplainable feelings toward himself and the people whom he cared about dearly. He couldn't describe exactly how he feels, but he does know that his life has forever been changed. He couldn't explain it other than to say that he feels like he left home as Hank Hunk and returned as someone else.

Epilogue

The Beginning of a New Life

HANK SETTLES IN with his family in Los Angeles and weighs his options. He receives an e-mail from David Anderson. David wants to set up a meeting with Hank to see how they can begin a working relationship, which will include the two sisters. Hank also receives a phone call from a talent agent who wants to talk to him about going on the road with a group of musicians and singers. With all of this happening at once, Hank is thrust into an interesting dilemma. He is torn between being an architect and being on the road with a group of musicians. He knows he wants to be an architect, but he also wants to be Elvis. The Elvis experience would be very exciting, and the money could be a blessing.

Hank has his meeting with David, Shirley, and Jackie and explains his situation. They are very understanding. He also meets with the talent agent, who introduces him to the manager who manages the group he wants Hank to team up with. The group is also present at the meeting. They all witnessed Hank's performance in Las Vegas, and for that, they treat him like a god. Hank is a bit taken back by the recognition given to him from these seasoned professionals. He explains his dilemma to the agent, the manager, and the musicians, and they too are very understanding. Hank is uncertain what to do, so he calls his friends Bobby, Jeremy, and Terance and asks for their advice. Each of them tells him to follow his heart. Terance, however, offers him additional advice. His advice is, if you can't make up your mind, try doing both. Hank takes his advice and is now working weekdays for David, Shirley, and Jackie and one weekend a month with the group. The $8,000 he earns for two nights of work with the group is income way beyond his wildest dreams. They normally tour the western part of the country and occasionally tour the northeast and southeast states. When they're on the East Coast, Terance, Jeremy, and Bobby attend all the performances. Hank spends a lot of time with them at their homes. He is overwhelmed by Terance's status and wealth, as are Bobby and Jeremy. Hank enjoys taking Kayla along on the tours. As Hank expects, she is 100 percent behind his decision. Hank's mother and father are very proud of their son's accomplishments, and his grandma is totally convinced that he is Elvis. Life is very good for Hank and all the people around him. He and Kayla have plans for that big day.

When Jeremy returns home, he orchestrates a plan that would make major changes in his life. His first priority is to break off his relationship with Evelyn. His second priority is to sell his trailer and rent a small house in a respectable neighborhood. This arrangement becomes necessary because as soon as Jeremy returns from Las Vegas, he receives a telephone call from Terance, who explains his partnership deal with the owners of Graceland in Las Vegas and his plans to develop a second Graceland in Miami, Florida. Terance asks Jeremy if he would like to be a part of the management team. Jeremy, of course, accepts. Working at a first-class restaurant in Miami would be the best thing that could have possibly happened, along with being within minutes of his beloved daughter. The change in jobs and living arrangements would do wonders for him, not to mention the generous salary that Terance offered him.

A month after Jeremy settled in to his new apartment, he invites Kie to visit. He explains his job offer from Terance in Miami. She is very excited about what is going on in his life and wants to know all about his friends. Explaining every detail about his relationship with him, Bobby, and Hank, she immediately understands the attraction that Jeremy has with his friends and what all of them have for Elvis. Jeremy rented a house fully furnished, and that spring, he invites Kie to come for a visit. Kie and Jeremy spend three wonderful weeks together, and in doing so, their relationship blossoms into a full-blown courtship. He invites Kie to come and live with him in Miami as soon as he gets settled, which she joyfully accepts. Jeremy also arranges a conference call with Marie during Kie's visit. The two women talk for a good hour about Jeremy and how happy they are about the changes in his life. His relationships with his three friends and Kie have forever changed his life.

Terance couldn't wait to tell Terri all about the restaurant deal. His secret meetings with his unique friends are also explained and now are a thing of the past since Hank become Elvis. Terance is equally excited about telling Terri how Bobby, Jeremy, and he helped Hank become the next Elvis. She asks a lot of questions about the restaurant but seems more interested about Bobby, Jeremy, and Hank. Oddly enough, it is a wonderful experience for everyone when they all finally get together at Terance's house in Coral Gables.

Terance's home has enough bedrooms to accommodate all of his guests and then some. The night of the show is a moving experience. Hank and his group are unbelievable. The sight of Hank up on the stage with thousands of fans cheering and rushing to the stage to get a picture of the newly crowned King is an emotional experience. After the show, Terance treats everyone to a meal at Joe's Crab House.

Terance and Jeremy talk about Jeremy's role at the restaurant and his plan to bring Terri into the management group. They all get along fabulously together. Hank, however, is the big event. Everywhere they go, people notice him. He is a true celebrity, and he handles his newfound fame with humble appreciation. His rise to stardom doesn't affect his attitude one bit. He explains how easy it is for him to keep things in perspective. One weekend a month, he is Elvis, with all the notoriety; and the rest of the time, he is Hank, the struggling architect living with his mother and father. What could be better? Terance is very impressed with his young friend's attitude. His ultimate experience will be to have Hank put on a show at the restaurant. He's visualized it over and over again in his mind. He sees Hank performing in front of the Graceland with a packed house.

Bobby arrives at home with a lot on his mind. He is caught up in a love triangle that is not going to be easy for him to handle. His relationship with Lynn has always been good for him, and he doesn't want to jeopardize what he has with her. The two weeks he spent with Kate in Las Vegas were the best two weeks he has ever had with a woman. He knows he needs to be with Kate to confirm if they have the same attraction for each other without the mystique of Las Vegas. So one weekend, while Lynn is visiting her sister in New York, Bobby visits Kate at her house in Kittery, Maine. Bobby is very nervous about how it is going to play out for him. One thought is that without the lure of Las Vegas, the magic would be gone for the both of them, but that doesn't happen. Kate is as charming and witty as ever, and her living arrangements are way beyond Bobby's expectations. Kate has a beautiful Cape-style home on the banks of the Passaqaunit River. Bobby and Kate have a wonderful weekend together, and when it is time for Bobby to leave, he tells her all about Lynn. She is happy that he is upfront with her and is compelled to tell him that she also has someone in her life. However, her relationship isn't as serious as his. This is somewhat good news; it gives him time to get his thoughts in order. Bobby and Kate keep in contact for a couple of months, and everything is going along fine until Kate makes an overture about Bobby's commitment to her. Kate makes it known that she wants to have a family, and she wants Bobby to be part of that. Bobby is surprised that Kate puts it all on the line to him. So now he has to make a decision. He knows that Lynn isn't pushing marriage, so now it is time for him to talk to Lynn about his future with her. So he does, and Lynn explains that she isn't ready for that kind of commitment, which is no surprise to Bobby. He doesn't come right out and tells Lynn that there is someone else in his life, so he lets her know that he feels it is time for him to have a commitment. For reasons beyond Bobby's rational thinking, Lynn wants nothing to do with marriage or children, which puts their relationship under severe strain; and soon after Bobby returns home one night, he finds a note on the table explaining Lynn's desire to move out of the house. It goes on to say that she cares very much for him and doesn't want to get in the way with his plans for marriage. It ends with that she would like to remain friends with him and wishes him the best. Bobby is upset with the outcome. He wonders if he may have caused undue sorrow to Lynn, so he calls her on her cell phone to see if she is upset with all that is going on. But to his surprise, he is relieved to hear that she is not at all unhappy with him or with the circumstances of their relationship. They talk for a long time, and Lynn explains her distrust in marriage and her concerns about having children at her age. Bobby is both pleased and disappointed. He is pleased that Lynn was the one to call off the relationship and disappointed that she did it with such ease. He is now wondering about Kate. What if the same thing happens to her?

Lynn moves out, and Bobby goes through a couple of tough months wondering about his future. And then one day, when Bobby receives a phone call from Kate; she explains that he's been on her mind and that she wants to see him. Bobby tells Kate about his breakup with Lynn and that he is feeling somewhat down in the dumps. She comforts him and says that she would be there for him when he is ready. They get together that weekend, and soon after, their romance blossoms, and they make plans to get married.

Kate accompanies Bobby to Miami to see Hank perform. She loves it, and she loves Hank, Jeremy, and Terance. Now she is one of the Hank's groupies, as are Kie, Kayla, Terri, and Marie, and what a group they are—one big happy family drawn together by a young man who goes by the name of Elvis one weekend a month.

Competing for Elvis

The Theme

The central theme of the book derives from the belief that "we do not pass through life" but rather "life passes through us." Our destiny is rewarded by not allowing life to hold us hostage. Our principles and character are the foundations of our journey. As we become more aware of the world around us, we realize that it's the people we welcome into our lives that will provide us with the opportunity to achieve all of the goals and dreams that we set forth for ourselves. Thus, we travel through life with confidence, knowing that good people attract good people; and taking chances, be it relationships or adventures, will ultimately improve the quality of our lives.

The Characters

The characters in *Competing for Elvis* have something unique that draws them to competitions. This story has nothing at all to do with their beloved Elvis but rather with their mission to resurrect his life. Jeremy Shrinks, Bobby Shrimp, Terance Best, and Henry (Hank) Hunk meet secretly in Las Vegas to compete in the Elvis competition. Jeremy is a convenience store clerk living in a trailer park in Yukon, Oklahoma; Bobby owns an auto body shop in Lynn, Massachusetts; Terance is a multimillionaire developer residing in Coral Gables, Florida; and Hank is an unemployed architect living with his mother and father in Los Angeles. Jeremy, who looks nothing like Elvis, has the perfect Elvis voice. Bobby looks and sounds somewhat like Elvis; however, it's his body language that sets him apart from the others. Terance lacks Elvis's looks and voice; however, his presence portrays Elvis's charisma and persona pervasively. Hank's good fortune is he looks exactly like Elvis. Ironically, for Jeremy, Bobby, Terance, and Hank, winning is not why they continuously compete, but rather it's an ends to a means to find Elvis, and their persistence finally pays. This trip to Las Vegas brings about miraculous changes for them. Their relentless vigil to find Elvis bonds them together and allows them to achieve their ultimate mission while "competing for Elvis."